Threads of Compassion

Healing Hands in Lady Zainab's Neighborhood

The story of Ehsān Jāvīdī's unique experience
as the head of a hospital set up to see to the needs of
the families of ISIS members and sympathizers after
the liberation of Al-Bukamal in southeast Syria

Written by
Zainab Erfāniān

Translated by
Blake Archer Williams

Copyright © 2024 by Lantern Publications
All rights reserved. No part of this publication may be reproduced, distributed, or transmitted in any form or by any means, including photocopying, recording, or other electronic or mechanical methods, without the prior written permission of the publisher, except in the case of brief quotations embodied in critical reviews and certain other noncommercial uses permitted by copyright law. For permission requests, write to the publisher, addressed "Attention: - Permissions (Threads of Compassion)" at the email address below.

    Lantern Publications
    info@lanternpublications.com
    www.lanternpublications.com

Ordering Information:
Quantity sales. Special discounts are available on quantity purchases by corporations, associations, and others. For details, contact the distributor at the address below.

Shī'a Books Australia
www.shiabooks.com.au
info@shiabooks.com.au

A catalogue record for this book is available from the National Library of Australia

ISBN- 978-1-922583-59-8

First Edition

Originally published by Shaheed Kazemi Publications (شهید کاظمی) under the title همسایه‌های خانمجان.
ISBN: 978-622-285-035-7

In the Name of God,
the Most Compassionate, the Most Merciful

Prayers of God's Peace and Blessings

In keeping with the Islamic practice of showing respect for the name of God, and sending prayers of God's peace and blessings whenever the name of His blessed Prophet, Lady Fātima, and the Twelve Imams is mentioned, as well as for asking God to hasten the reappearance of the Lord of the Age on the Earthly plane, one or more of the following Arabic symbols have been employed throughout the text. They are repeated for their great rewards.

 Used exclusively after the name of God, meaning "the Sublimely Exalted", or, as a prayer, "[May His name be] Sublimely Exalted".

 Used exclusively after the name of the Prophet, meaning "May the peace and blessings of God be unto him and unto [the purified and inerrant members of] his family"

 Used for any of the Twelve Imams or past prophets of God, meaning "May God's peace be unto him".

 Used for two or more of the Twelve Imams or past prophets of God, meaning "May God's peace be unto them".

 Used for Lady Fātima, and Lady Zainab, meaning "May God's peace be unto her".

 Used for a plurality of the Fourteen Immaculates, meaning "May God's peace be unto them all collectively".

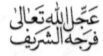 Used for the Lord of the Age (the Twelfth Imam), meaning "May God hasten the advent of his noble person".

1

April 1, 2018

I'm in an ambulance. I'm feeling woozy. I've done well to have been able to bear the pain this long. I try to stay fully awake until we get to the hospital, but it's impossible. Pain snakes through the labyrinth of my being like a venomous viper. My chest is about to explode. I'm breathing hard. Something is searing through my lung, causing me incredible pain.

    I can see Fātima's bruised face and Somayyeh's motionless body. Somayyeh had fainted right at the start. My legs feel heavy, and I can't move them. I can't move a muscle. I struggle to say something, but only a moan makes its way out from the back of my throat. I don't know which bones in my body are broken.

Threads of Compassion

The light of the fluorescent lamps of the hospital corridor passes in front of my eyes like a continuous white stripe. The smell of Savlon and Deconex make me nauseous. I never got used to that aseptic smell, even though I'm a nurse by profession.

Somayyeh is draped across the steering wheel and is wheezing. She can hardly breathe. On the day of our marriage, her father stressed that he was giving her to me in trust. I turn my head towards her. Death does not discriminate between trusts and trustees. It hovers around the car and waves to us. Fātima's head wobbles loosely on her neck. I press my palm down on her chest. It is useless. Her face is turning purple. It feels like I haven't seen the deep brown eyes of my beloved daughter for years. I pray that she will open her eyes again. I lift her slender body up with my hands. It is slack and lifeless. I press down hard on the middle of her chest to revive her, and shout to her to come back to life.

A nurse starts to cut my clothes open with a pair of scissors. The smell of blood hits my nostrils. Would that I had returned here on my own from Mashhad. Would that Somayyeh and the kids were not with me in the car. Muhammad-Husain is not regaining consciousness. My name is in the weekly flight list to Syria for next week; I cannot become a prisoner to this bed.

I call out to Muhammad-Husain, but he doesn't respond or even move. I scream out his name. He needs to get out and take his brothers and sisters out of the car. My scream echoes in my mind. Muhammad-Husain finally opens his eyes. Hāniyeh pulls her body out from under the broken shards of glass.

I feel the sting of the catheter under my skin. Morphine courses through my being. I can't keep up the struggle anymore. My eyelids grow heavy. I want to ask how Somayyeh is doing, but I can't. I wish I could prevent them from separating the kids from me. Fātima will undoubtedly be frightened in my absence. Am I going to miss my flight? I have to call Dr. Karīm. The morphine is convoluting my thoughts. I can hear Hāniyeh crying in the distance. I can't go to her. Dr. Karīm calls. I have to take delivery of the Al-Bukamal Hospital's weekly palate of drugs. I haven't signed the transport papers. The medical team arrived today. I have to remain in the hospital. I get myself to the Imām Airport. The morphine is stronger than the tenacity of my thoughts. I go back and forth between the hospital's corridors. The commotion has not let me sleep for two nights straight. I'm beat. There's an hour left before the flight leaves. My brain is pounding. I'm floating in time.

Counter 76 is abuzz with the ruckus of commando-trousers wearing soldiers. I make my way into their midst. I love them; the way they present themselves, their code of conduct, the scent of the rose oil they smell of. They're all the same. They are chatting with each other and taking selfies together. But my thoughts are anywhere but here. They're with Somayyeh, in Mashhad with Māmān [Mom], and at home with Hāniyeh, whom I might never see again. I think that she's all grown up now, without my being aware of it. Grown up enough for us to leave her brothers and sisters in her charge until Somayyeh returns home from the airport. I wish I hadn't let Somayyeh come all this way out to take me to the airport.

An official comes over and tells us to hand our passports to him without further ado, so we all hand them over without questioning him. Why? I don't know. The guys are still in a jocular mood. One of them says that they won't let us into anywhere but Syria anyway, so the officials should give us back our passports, and we'll promise not to go anywhere else. The veterans and their jokes are iconic, and those for whom this is their first tour of duty – of which there are only a few of us – are quiet like me and don't say much. It seems as if the sensible man knows them. He smiles and takes his leave without another word. I get my boarding pass and follow the others to the prayer room. I yearn to make two cycles of our ritual devotions. Devotions of thanksgiving. Thanksgiving is indeed for something which – may Satan's ears go deaf and not hear this – something which is getting close to being realized after five years. I am standing in the corner of the prayer room now, where I retrieve a list from the depths of my mind. A list of names. One column for those who I must ask to make me *halāl*.¹ Another column for those who have asked me to pray on their behalf [when I have reached Syria and am in the inner sanctum of the Shrine of Lady Zainab ﷺ]. And the third column is a list of those whom I need to make *halāl*. I make a bold X through the third column right there and then. Let everyone be made *halāl*. A heart that is occluded will not be restituted within the Shrine's inner sanctum. So now I'm left with the first two columns. I am not a *hājī*,² but there have been numerous occasions when *hājīs* have called me from the airport to say, 'Ehsān, I thought of you in these last moments [before takeoff]. Ehsān, make me *halāl*.' Calls that begin in excitement and end in tears. But my trip is different. There are no last-minute phone calls, no "make me *halāls*", no "pray for me's", and no sighs and tears. I can't even take a selfie, put some tear-jerker text under it, and post it to social media groups to the effect that, 'Hey, I finally made it [to the warfront] too.' It's not as if I can't do that; I *can*. But they have told us not to. And being the greenhorn that I am, and this being my first tour of duty, I abide. I said, "Sir, yes *sir!*" and left my phone home.

---

[1] [To ask someone's forgiveness for any trespasses that one might have committed against him or her. This is usually done before a long journey or a pilgrimage, or as in this case, before going off to a war front.]

[2] [Someone who has made the Major or Hajj Pilgrimage is thereafter referred to as a *Hājī* as a sign of respect.]

Threads of Compassion

The guy in charge of collecting the passports shows up again, this time with a list of names tucked under his arm. He goes through the names like a roll call in class, places a check against each name, and then starts to return the passports. Why? Again, I haven't a clue. And I probably wouldn't be able to tell you even if I did.

I'm standing at the counter, and anxiety is gnawing at me. I'm worrying about home and the kids and of whatever lies on the other side of the doors of this departure gate. How will Muhammad-Husain do on his exams? What'll happen if Fātima becomes ill when I'm away? What if Muhammad-Hasan frets? What if Hāniyeh misses me? What if Somayyeh's car breaks down in the middle of the highway? What if something comes up that she cannot deal with on her own in a town that is foreign to her? It's been two years since we moved to Tehran, and I still think she has not been able to settle down in this endless city sprawl. What will she do with four kids, whose ages cover the whole gamut? Mashhad would have been better for them. At least there is the shrine there and the homes of relatives. What does Tehran have? Nothing! They're on their own, with no one else to help them. Muhammad-Husain is the man of the house whose upper lip has only just started showing the hint of a moustache.

I worry about them. From this very moment, when they are alone in the house, to the day when I might no longer be around. Muhammad-Husain and Hāniyeh were born a year apart. They were a real handful for Somayyeh until they grew up to be thirteen and fourteen, which is how old they are now. And now Muhammad-Hasan and Fātima are also a year apart. What will Somayyeh do without me? How is she going to be able to deal with a naughty three-year-old boy and a two-year old girl? It will take forever for them to grow up. How long will it be before they can think for themselves that Bābā [Daddy] isn't coming back. How long will it be before they are able to be of help to their mother? A veritable revolution is raging in my heart and mind from all of these thoughts and worries. I wish I had sent them to Mashhad. At least there, they wouldn't be strangers and wouldn't be on their own. I comfort myself with the thought that Somayyeh is different. She wouldn't have agreed to my going away if she couldn't cope. If she couldn't cope, my going away wouldn't have been countersigned; wouldn't have been given her blessing.

I ask myself, 'What did you do, really, in helping Somayyeh raise Muhammad-Husain and Hāniyeh that Somayyeh could not do for Muhammad-Hasan and Fātima on her own?' I might not be able to cope without Somayyeh – God forbid – but Somayyeh will be able to cope without me. Anyway, it's not as if

Threads of Compassion

I'm not coming back. Who says I'm not coming back? It is not as if martyrdom is attained so easily. If only it *were* that easy. Don't tell me I'm fated to come back home empty handed! Am I going to come back home, is that it? Somayyeh has greater equanimity when it comes to the quarrel that is raging in my mind as to whether or not I will be returning home. It seems she's been able to put an end to the quarrel a long time ago. In the car, when we were on the way to the airport, I ask her to consent to the possibility of my martyrdom, and to make me *halāl*. She pauses for a moment. Her heart implodes, but she tries not to show it.

'Ehsān, go for the sake of *jihād*,[3] not for the sake of seeking martyrdom.'

'Give me your blessing, and I will abide.'

She rolls down the window, perhaps in the hope that the wind will come in and blow both of our heartaches away.

'If I hadn't consented,' she says, 'I wouldn't have packed your suitcase.'

---

[3] [The Lesser Jihād, which is armed combat for the sake of God's cause. The Greater Jihād is the struggle within one's soul, against the desires of the lower self and the base emotions.]

Threads of Compassion

One of the guys' phones rings as we stand in line before the counter. I can tell it's his mom he's talking to by the way he talks and what he says.

I miss Māmān [Mother]. The scent of the little flowers of her prayer *chādor*.[4] I wish she was here. The warmth of the tone of her voice and her fussing over me would embrace my soul and wash away all of my anxieties. I wish that she wasn't so dispirited on the last day. If she had given me her blessings and consented to my leaving, I would have called her now and taken refuge in her words of comfort. I feel like a little boy who misses his mommy. I can't bear to leave like this. I borrow the phone of the person behind me in the line. I'm now worried that my mom will break down over the phone. That will remind her that her Ehsān is on his way to Syria and that this grief will crush her heart. I call my father's number instead. It's easier that way; fathers and sons can talk about anything and everything. Our voices break over the phone; both of us have big lumps in our throats. He has exceeded his fatherly duties at this last moment. He tells me he's gone to Imam Riḍā ﷺ's shrine and asked him to make it so that Māmān will give her consent.

---

[4] [A *chādor* is a full body-length cloth that is worn over a woman's head and which comes down to the ankles. It is open in front but is held closed with the hands. It is worn as a consideration for others, and its purpose is to veil the female body so as not to temp those who do not have the wherewithal, so to speak, to satisfy any temptation that might otherwise have arisen.]

He says, 'Go, and don't worry about it. It's a done deal.'

The line inches forward. The official inspects my passport, stamps the exit stamp, and returns it. Someone told me that on one of his pilgrimages to Karbalā, the official played a game and refused to stamp the exit stamp on his passport. Turns out he had a condition for stamping the passports of pilgrims, which was that the pilgrim had to give him a smile. Seeing that everyone smiles big smiles in this line, that guy would've enjoyed being here now.

Anxiety continues to come over me in waves. My turn arrives. The official looks me over, and boom! He stamps my passport. Short and sweet. As if he's stamped it on my heart that I'm a goner from this world. It brings a smile to my face. With this stamping of my passport, all of the bitter anxieties of this world that were domiciled in my heart bid me farewell and leave town. 'God grant me detachment from everything other than You.'[5] Grant me detachment from each and every one of Your creatures so that I can reach You in a perfect union – this is what was written in the idiomatic translation in small print under the original Arabic. But I say, 'God, let me come to you in such a way that I don't even look back to see who or what's behind me!'

The servicemen are making a loud ruckus. They're all gathered at the Gate Two exit gate,

---

[5] The sixth verse from the *al-munājāt ash-sha'bānīya*.

oblivious to this world and the looks that they are receiving, sending blessings of peace (*salawāt*) [unto the Prophet Muhammad and his Purified and Immaculate Progeny] and smiling.

The people at the airport are all staring at us in wonder and amazement, but their stares don't have the slightest effect on how we are feeling or on our sending *salawāts*.

'Excuse me, sir, I took fifteen hundred. Is that enough?'

I look at the young man standing behind Gate 1. Of all these experienced people, he had the bad luck of putting his question to me.

'You took fifteen hundred what, brother?'

'Dollars. What else?'

I look at him and then at Gate 1, which will be opened soon for a flight to Istanbul. Before I can answer, his friend whispers something in his ear. Now it's his turn to look. He looked at me and looked at my fellow travellers and looked at our gate that opened to heaven, but the name of the flight and the destination were not written on the information board.

Gate Two is the most tearful stage of the airport. The soldiers from the *Sepāh*[6] have gone all out

---

[6] [The Guardians of the Revolution, better known as the Revolutionary Guards.]

Threads of Compassion

in seeing us off. They are burning *esfand*,[7] filling the atmosphere with smoke and their tears, and their entreaties for us to pray for them when we get to Lady Zainab's ﷺ Shrine. The inspection anteroom is only lacking a large loudspeaker out of which Āhangarān's[8] 'O Army of the Lord of the Age' could blast down on our heads, even though our hearts are filled with that same kind of atmosphere that his elegies evoke, with or without the loudspeaker.

I turn my eyes to look at the faces. How many of them won't return? How many of them have been selected [for martyrdom]? Have I? On which list is my name written? In the list of those who will return or those who will depart? Now that I've gone to all lengths possible in order to make this trip happen, am I destined to come back? It is not the custom of going to war to expect to return with your life. We fight in defence of our cause to the last drop of our blood. You either become a martyr, or you stay *until* you become a martyr. There is no third option in my mind.

---

[7] [*Peganum harmala*, commonly called wild rue or Syrian rue. Its common English-language name came about because of a resemblance to rue (to which it is not related).]

[8] [The famous singer of elegies and laments for the soldiers on the front lines of the 8-year Iran-Iraq War, known in Iran as the Sacred Defense.]

Threads of Compassion

We're all on the bus now, but no matter how far it goes, it doesn't arrive. We have been exiled to the farthest point of this wide runway. We're happy exiles. We're packed like sardines but happy to chat with our fellow soldiers. It's also Mansūr's first tour, as it is mine, but he has more to say than anyone else. I was heartened to hear the stories of the guys assigned to medical services. I'm excited to finally be going to where I can see these events firsthand. I'm thrilled that I will have my own tales from tomorrow. I feel like threading my way through to the circle of the medical servicemen when the bus comes to a stop with an extended groan. We finally arrive at the airplane that is waiting for us, which is an Airbus 300 that has a beige logo of *Cham Wings Airlines* on its tail. It's tucked into a cozy corner away from the other planes.

    I'm sitting in a window seat. I look at my watch. It was ten at night, Saturday, November 25th 2017. The plane takes off right on time. My face is glued to the window, while the other guys continue to be loud and have fun. The lights have sprinkled a golden dust on the city and are striving to push back the darkness of the night. The higher we go, the darker it gets. I try to find the road that leads back to our home, and I think I might never take this route back home again. Two hours ago, Somayyeh and I were so excited to take this road to the airport. Somayyeh must still be at the airport, waiting to make sure my flight takes off okay.

I think of her look as she stood behind the glass of the transit hall, waving her hand with a smile. I have one eye on the heaven that lies before me and one eye on the woman who is my whole world and whose look is different than usual. I indicate to her that she should go with a wave of my head, but I want her to stay. She too wants to stay and does not move.

Whatever we demurred to say to each other, we now communicate in our glances at each other. Not what we demurred to say over this last week, but what we haven't said over the last seventeen years; from the time I was twenty years old and started to share my life with Somayyeh; from the day she was eighteen years old and became my life partner. Only now that this glass has placed a distance between us that I understand just how dear she is to me. She wants to say, 'I love you,' but she is too bashful. She closes her eyelids, which is her way of saying, 'Go, don't worry about us.' I want to say, 'I love you too,' but I'm too shy as well. I close my eyelids too: 'Don't you worry about me either.' When I open my eyes, Somayyeh is no longer there. It's just me and the glass behind me, and all I can see is strangers looking back at me. She is gone, taking my whole world with her, leaving me behind with heaven before me.

I place my right hand on my chest as a sign of respect and say, '*as-salām alayk, yā aqīlah al-arab! as-salām alayk, yā Zainab!* Peace be unto you, O wise one of the Arabs! Peace be unto you, O Zainab!'

Threads of Compassion

My brothers-in-arms are making jokes and laughing so much that it puts smiles on the faces of the stewardesses, who are amused at how much energy our group has and at the ruckus we are making. It is as if we're on a school bus that's taking us to one of the *Rāhiān-e Nūr* summer camps. My thoughts went back to Javād[9] and the mischief he would get up to. If he had been here, he would have taken over control of the plane!

I miss him so much. I miss the corner of plot 30 in the Behesht-e Rezā cemetery, where he is buried. I feel like sitting beside him there and reading his name a hundred times on the gravestone and asking, 'Javād, have you really gone?' And then recount all of his mischief episodes, laugh at them, and weep at his no longer being here. I feel like sitting beside him there and telling him my name finally made it to one of the flight lists, too. And to ask him to write my name down next to his in the heavens. Javād is everywhere, even here, on this flight. His spirit, his thoughts, and his memory.

---

[9] Shahīd (Martyr) Mahdī Muhammadi Munfarid was born in Mashhad on 16 May 1977 and attained martyrdom in Syria on 3 February 2016.

Threads of Compassion

I've climbed the stairs of the basement of the base slowly, groping in the dark with my hands on the sidewall. There is a bitterness in my throat that I can taste to the bottom of my lungs. Tears fall out of my eyes like a waterfall, burning as they flow out. The others are like me too. My coughing won't let up. When the open-air hits my face, I can finally breathe in some fresh air. My eyes find Javād, who is staring at me and chuckling. I expected him to shed tears anywhere but in a meeting of the Commanders' Council in the presence of twenty commanders of several bases. The meeting is a veritable mess. Everyone is huddled in some corner, trying to catch their breath. I want to grab his collar because of this awkward prank that he has pulled, but I can't because I love him too much. My coughing and laughter merge and become indistinguishable. Nobody says a word to Javād. Javād is who he is, pranks and all. I go toward him. Before I say anything, he takes the initiative.

'I know what I'm doing, bro. Worry about yourself.'

It was this kind of "knowing what he was doing" that landed him in Syria and with an Afghan identity at that. He went to Syria and left us all behind.

It was February of 2014, and I was sitting in the monthly board meeting when one of the guys' phones pinged, indicating that he had received a message. It's a photo of Javād. He's sitting in a Toyota, and has taken a selfie in which he isn't smiling. He has captioned it with the words Shahīd (Martyr) Javād Muhammadi

Munfarid. We all break out laughing loudly. He doesn't stop these antics of his in Syria, either. The phone with the selfie is passed around, and we all talk about our memories and recollections of Javād. We think that this move of his and his latest antics take the cake. We enjoy the fact that he has expended so much effort and creativity in pulling these pranks on everyone. If we hadn't seen it with our own eyes that he had installed a high-gain antenna on the 18-meter-high telecommunication tower of the Mashhad Electricity Authority, we might have believed it. Still, with the pranks and shenanigans that Javād got up to, everything was hidden except his martyrdom. An hour later, one of my friends called. His voice is filled with concern.

'Ehsān, has Javād been martyred??'

I realized that he'd seen the photo. In my heart, I curse Javād for these pranks of his.

'Nah, man. He's not martyred. That's just Javād having a laugh at our expense.'

When I put the phone down, a doubt enters my mind. Could it be that something has happened? I do a search using Javād's name. The blue hyperlinked results are all lined up on the search page. I'm stunned. How far can one go in carrying out a prank?? I call Ali. He starts crying as soon as he hears my voice.

'What's going on, Ali?'

'Javād was martyred.'

I can't believe it.

Threads of Compassion

'No way! If Javād's been martyred, our plans will fall apart.'

I try in vain to escape from the reality.

There were only two martyrs on the night of the operation to liberate Nubl and Az-Zahrā, one of whom was Javād. But that has put everything in turmoil and has wreaked havoc with all our plans. Everyone is shaken by the news of Javād's martyrdom. We just call each other on the phone and cry our hearts out. We're waiting for someone to speak up and say that he talked to Javād, that he is fine, and that this is just another one of his pranks; but no one has been able to get through to Javād. We cry out loud into the microphones of our phones for each other. Can we even have a meeting of the Command Council without Javād being present? Can we even carry out any of the activities of the seminaries and the Basij bases without Javād being a part of them? Is it even possible to pilgrimage to any shrines without Javād? Is *any*thing even possible without Javād?

We struggle for four days in disbelief, hoping for Javād to come and ask how we liked his latest prank. They said that he was shot in the leg, and this was enough to give us a false hope that he might still be alive. We didn't know that they weren't able to transfer him back from the front line and that his life had bled out of him. His last message on the two-way radio was that he had lost a lot of blood and didn't have any strength left. We didn't know that the ISIS forces had advanced to where Javād was, and that they had shot him in the head after a skirmish where he had put up the last of his resistance. We didn't know this was not just another of Javād's pranks.

'We are flying over Karbalā now.' Words to this effect were being spoken on the plane. Some people strain their necks to get a look out of the plane's windows. The veterans don't need to look out the window; they go by their watches and the time it has taken to get there. And they are on the money. We have been airborne for about an hour and are now flying in Iraqi airspace, and should be flying over Karbalā now according to the flight coordinates. I squint my eyes, hoping for a glimpse of the matte golden light being emitted from the *bayn al-haramayn* [from the 378 meters between the two shrines of Imam Husain ﷺ and Abu'l Faḍl]. But all I see is pure darkness; it is as if nothing is going on down there. But up here, my heart has turned upside down, being next to Javād and being over the shrine of the Lord of the Martyrs, Imam Husain ﷺ. My gaze pierces the darkness of the sky above me. What's going on up there?

Javād finally returns after four days, following his coffin, wandering from one ceremony to the next, and from one street to the next, and from one group of mourners to the next. There's no mistaking him; its

Javād alright; being transported on the shoulders of various pall-bearers from the Mahdīyeh to the sanctum of the shrine, and from there to the Behesht-e Rezā cemetery. We follow him through all these twists and turns, but reaching him eludes me. No matter how much I run after him, I cannot reach him. I'm short of breath. It doesn't look like I'm going to reach him. I can hear his voice amid the bustle of the crowd:

'I know what I'm doing, bro. Worry about yourself.'

His mausoleum is exactly in the corner of plot 30 in the Behesht-e Rezā cemetery dedicated to the burial of 'the Defenders of the Shrine' [the martyrs who died defending the shrine of Lady Zaynab in Syria].[10] It's a place that I yearn to visit a lot. Javād, who always ran our meetings, is now resting in a quiet corner. A corner that, for me, is like a corner of the world, away from all of its hustle and bustle: quiet, cozy and peaceful. It is a corner that is full of Javād and his jolly moods, quiet and serene, and without any of his jokes or pranks. I kneel next to him. We have a small account to settle, going back about ten or twelve years; to the days of our youth. I look at his picture. Our

---

[10] [Defenders of the Shrine: this is the name given to the Iranian military forces who are engaged in the Syrian War. The shrine in question refers to the shrine of Her Eminence Lady Zainab, Imam Husain ﷺ's sister, who is buried in Damascus. Lady Zainab survived the massacre of the Plain of Karbalā and lived to tell the tale and spread the word of the massacre, which she did with courage and eloquence.]

meeting has been relegated to the Day of Resurrection. The unsettled status of our small account together gives me the hope that our meeting on that day will be somewhat more prolonged than it otherwise might have been.

We fasten our seat belts and prepare for landing. Damascus was as dark from above as Tehran was bright. The anti-aircraft artillery of the armed forces provides cover for the airport, which translates to the fact that they can strike and pulverize us at any given moment! The guys have switched their voice boxes off, in sync with the lights of the airplane cabin. The only thing that could be heard was the S's of the *salawāt* (the invocation of blessings unto the Prophet and the purified and infallible members of his family), which were being whispered under everyone's breath. I experience the quietest descent and landing of my entire life. Everyone is quiet and tranquil. We are even more focused on the landing than the pilot! I close my eyes. How close I am to the coming to fruition of my dream. Our feet have yet to touch the ground, but the taste of Jihād has already taken over my emotions, making my heart flutter. We hear the squirming sound of the plane's wheels touching the asphalt of the runway, and a few moments later, the pilot welcomes us to Syria. The sound of the boys sending out *salawāt* fills the cabin.

Threads of Compassion

Our boarding the aeroplane at Imam Khomeini Airport could not be characterized as anything within the normal range, nor could our disembarking the aeroplane at the al-Asad military airport. No buses are waiting to carry the passengers to the terminal. As soon as we climb the stairs, we have to duck our heads and run towards the red light of the laser to our right. I wait for the veterans to take the lead so that I can learn from their example. Not a peep could be heard from anyone. The atmosphere is serious and heavy. My turn finally arrives. I climb down the stairs in my best guerilla imitation and run the thirty-meter distance to the red laser in a single breath. A person standing next to the laser guides us towards the terminal's entryway. The lounge could be anything but a lounge in an airport terminal. It is completely military in its appearance. It is small, narrow, dark, and definitely covered by the crosshairs of armed guards. There is no Welcome sign, advertisements for SIM cards for mobile phones, or any duty-free shops where we can smell all the perfumes on offer, or any sweets or anything else. There aren't even a couple of Syrian officials for us to offer them a *salāmun alaykum* with a thick, put-on Arabic accent. We're on our own, with no one else to greet us.

We hand our passports over to the official in a ritual that is different from the arrival rituals that are the norm the world over, and in what was even more different, we are each given a *muhr*,[11] a keffiyeh, a pocket Koran, and a dog tag, complete with its neck-chain. One might have encountered any of these differences somewhere around the world, but the last difference, the dog tag, complete with its neck chain, would not have been found anywhere else. Our blood group and special code are embossed on the tags. I touch the tag, feeling its embossed lettering in the form of a code, which will lead them to my identity, wherever and whenever they find my tag. It will lead them to Ehsān Jāvīdī, health worker, father of four children, 37 years old, and born in 1981. All of this information is somehow made to fit onto the dog-tag; a tag which I yearned to possess for such a long time; a tag which might return without me.

The hall is brimming with the sounds of the boys meeting each other anew. It's as if the fire of war is not waging right next to us. That trivial matter does not stand in the way of reuniting old comrades who have not seen each other in a long time and now have a lot to catch up on. The thought crosses my mind that this much intimacy between the boys is an attribute of being under fire. When you wake up every morning knowing you might not live long enough to see nightfall, you return to your factory settings: kind and

---

[11] [A cake of clay that is used in the ritual devotions for placing the forehead on, in keeping with the Prophet's instruction that the forehead should be placed on the ground when prostrating oneself in the ritual devotions.]

friendly. This is all the more so if you know that your friend might not live long enough to see nightfall.

The voice of a young cleric echoes through the ruckus and reaches my ears. 'Dear brothers, please refrain from going to the Syrians' houses, and from contacting the locals.'

He is standing on a chair among the guys, cautioning us and giving us advice. Most of all, his emphasis is on not going to parties at the locals' houses. I am amused by the scenes that I have seen about this war so far, as well as the strong presence of the Iranians in it, a presence that has been so strong that the locals have opened the doors to their homes to us and invited us in for dinner parties. And this had been taking place to such an extent that we need to be cautioned and warned about accepting such invitations from the Syrian locals.

I look around the hall. Each person is there for a specific purpose. Intelligence, operations, support, artillery, armour, drones, telecommunications, and health. The nurse, in my mind, is acting up. I see the al-Asad military airport as a heart, the heart of Syria. Each one of us is pumped in a specific direction from this central organ to give life and to take death away from the tired and wounded body of this country. There are traces of ISIS everywhere, from al-Hasakah to al-Mayādīn, Deir ez-Zūr, Tadmar (Palmyra), and Aleppo.

They have sent a van to pick up all the medical staff. There are ten of us. Everyone except for Mansūr and I is an experienced veteran. By this point, I even know their names. Mansūr, who is the most important one among us, is still talking and doesn't give anyone else a chance. There are others who are more important yet than him. There is a specialist in Tehran, for example, who is held in very high regard. Like me, he has come to Syria in order to take hold of and shake a corner of the carpet of this war, and maybe by so doing, to take hold of and shake a corner of the carpet of his own heart.

Given the way they deboarded us off the plane, I was expecting artillery shells and rockets to explode right next to us as we stepped out of the airport, and I was expecting to have to crawl on my belly from one fortification to the next. But there's no need for such antics. There is nothing but darkness and silence. We board a van along with Mansūr and the veterans. The guys turn their wristwatches back an hour and a half. I don't wear a watch, nor do I have a mobile phone to occupy myself with.

'Abu Abdu, *mai mawjūd*? Do you have any water?'

The guys want to engage the driver in conversation. The good-natured Syrian driver shakes his head and looks at us through the mirror.

'*Lā mawjūd.* Not available.'

'Abu Abdu, *madfa' mawjūd*? What about a heater?'

'Lā mawjūd.'

Whatever the guys asked, they got the same answer. I tell the passenger sitting next to me with a smile that the driver only has one answer. He translates my words for Abu Abdu, who chuckles bitterly and shakes his head sadly, saying, 'In Syria, whoever asks you for something, you have to say it doesn't exist. There's nothing left in this country.'

I feel sorry for him. I turn to the window to watch the streets of the country in which there is nothing left. Darkness has swallowed everything up. What a dark night has come over Syria. An elegy about Syria invades my soul. The sound of the caravan bell; the sound of people cheering, the voice of a lioness who alone is the refuge of everyone. What kind of events did those people see in Syria that night, and what kind of events are we witnessing in Syria in these times... What horrors befell the family of the Merciful Apostle [Muhammad], so that the Fourth Imam, Imam Zain al-Ābidīn ؑ summarized all of his frustrated emotions in a single sentence, 'God save us from Syria'.

What horrors befell the lady who was the beloved of the Prophet in this place? What kind of pain did those who followed in the footsteps of Muʿāwiya thrust into her heart? I rest my head on the glass. I don't know the route their caravan took [from Karbalā] to Damascus, so I didn't know whether or not we were taking a similar route. But the sky was the same sky; we were under the same sky. I thought that if Lady Zainab ؑ had had the same defenders in those days, things would not have turned out the way they did. I feel at a loss, like those who have arrived late. It is so late that no matter how much you run, you will still not be able to catch up. About 1,376 years too late, or maybe more.

Two kilometres later, a glass building comes into view. It is the building of the administration offices of Damascus Airport, which has an all-glass veneer. The Syrians know it as the Banā adh-Dhahabi (the Golden Building) because of the golden hue of its glass, and we [Iranians] referred to it as *shīshe'ī* ([the] glass [building]).

I gather my things and prepare to step out of the van, but the driver continues on down the road at full-throttle. I didn't know that the health centre had been moved from here. Everyone's head is turned towards the golden glass building, and, like me, one or two others say under their breaths, "*shīshe'ī*". The fact that we won't be working there is a downer; something is lacking in a *jihād* without the *shīshe'ī* building. I look at it as it passes with regret. For me, the *shīshe'ī* building is like a two-edged sword. Before the relocation of the health centre, the guys who made up the medical staff came here from all over and were dispersed throughout Syria from here. The glass façade of this seven-story building hides numerous flavours that I will miss. The flavours of the night-time devotions of the guys and their religious gatherings and mourning ceremonies. The flavours of friends' jokes and those of friends weeping for lost friends. The flavours of waging righteous *jihād*. All of these are flavours that I had spent five years running around town trying to get to be a part of and to 'taste', and now I saw how easily I was passing them by.

The driver continued to drive away, and I turned around in my seat to keep looking at the *shīshe'ī* building as it faded into the distance. Ashrīn, the new location of the health centre, was as far from the airport as the *shīshe'ī* building was close to it. One has to go for eighteen kilometres to get to two warehouses belonging to the Syrian Agricultural College called Ashrīn. It's the name that we have given the medical command centre in Syria. Why? I have no idea. One of the old warehouses is for those who are stationed here to be able to rest. The other warehouse is for people like us, i.e., for new forces who have newly arrived to stay for a night and then make their way on to their final destination. It is not much in terms of its outward appearance; it is just a warehouse. But it is equipped to the teeth. It has six double rooms on each side of a central corridor. At the end of the corridor is a lobby, reception, and VIP room. I don't know Dr. Karīm, who is the general commander of the medical services and the person who set up these facilities; but the way this facility and its rooms have been set up speaks volumes about the fact that he knew what he was doing. The fact that someone can take a warehouse in the heart of a government complex in another country, equip it, and have it serve your forces means that such a person knows his business. I was carrying out a field reconnaissance of the warehouse when someone excitedly announced, 'Doctor Rezā has arrived!'

Threads of Compassion

I really appreciate the fact that the staff here sent a doctor to welcome us, nurses. Dr. Rezā asked how everyone was doing. He took off his sunglasses and hat and ran a hand over his head. He seemed to me to be a wise man who had been waiting for us to arrive for a long time. His Ahwazī accent matched his tall and square-shouldered figure. When his gaze reached me, a smile broke out on his face, and he said, 'You must be Dr. Ehsān; is that right?'

I pull myself together.

'No, I am a nurse, doctor,' I reply.

I have yet to learn that everyone here is a "doctor", even the nurses. Let it be a lesson for you as well. From now on, all of the Iranian "doctors" whom I call by their *first* names are actually nurses. The doctors, whom I call by their *family* names, are *real* doctors. Like Dr. Mohebbī, in whose room I am to spend the night. Whatever I say about his knowledge, experience, expertise, and skill is like Tantanāni halva: you won't know how good it is until you have had some! To leave all of the facilities one has at one's disposal as a doctor in Tehran behind and go into the mouth of the lion just so that you will have made some contribution in life and just so that you will have been able to come to the help of some poor wretch who would have been utterly helpless without you – all of this must be experienced firsthand in order for it to be understood and fully comprehended; it cannot be described with mere words.

Threads of Compassion

Dr. Mohebbī is busy negotiating with Dr. Rezā to arrange it so that he can go to the shrine for the morning prayers. As I listened to their conversation, I suddenly saw that there was a phone in his room. I go towards it excitedly. It is 4:00 a.m. in Iran, and I am sure that Somayyeh has not gone to sleep. I have yet to learn that calling Iran has its customs and rituals. Like buying credits for a SIM card, you have to enter a bunch of numbers, followed by the star and pound signs in various stages, before you can get a dial tone that you can use. And while you are doing all this, the Arab operator blurts out things that you don't understand and which rile you up in frustration. Poor Dr. Mohebbī. I call out to him every two minutes that I have entered the number followed by a star and a pound sign, but nothing has happened, so what now?? How many times do I have to enter the pound sign? What is this Arab lady saying in the middle of all this?! He explains everything to me kindly and with good cheer. I try again, only to hit a wall of frustration again and again; and again, Dr. Mohebbī explains the procedure and what needs to be done, doing so with even more kindness and understanding than the previous time. If he wasn't so kind, he would not have left that prestigious job of his to come to Syria.

Hearing Somayyeh's voice breaks my heart. Her vocal cords are puffy, and she sounds like she has been crying, which is just like what her eyes must look like. I had guessed right; she had not been able to sleep. And I know that she won't be able to sleep after we hang up either. I regret my having called her. It's as if I didn't allow her to be on her own, to allow my absence to sink in; I didn't allow her to be on her own so that she could just sit and cry her heart out. I just wanted to say that I had arrived, so that she could relax and go to sleep; but that didn't work, of course.

I head out of the warehouse early in the morning. My excitement woke me up early. With the amount of fatigue that I had felt, I should have passed out and not woken up until noon. I breathe the crisp and delicate morning air into my lungs and walk through the empty furrows of agricultural fields, which are bereft of life and have no possibility of being planted. It is as if they are just sitting there holding their chins in the palms of their hands, staring at our warehouse, wondering when they will be planted. I think this fertile soil should be brimming with summer plants' bloom. Like the fertile lands of Khair-ābād. The story of Khair-ābād and its *Muharrams* is a whole other book in itself. If the month of *Muharram* comes around and I don't spend its first ten days as a *rawza*[12] reciter in the Mutiwassilīn beh Haḍrat-e Ali-Asghar religious delegation, then I will have a sense of loss following me for the rest of the year. The residents of the small village of Sādāt-Neshīn, which is about two hundred kilometres distance from Mashhad, place a blessing in

---

[12] [A *rawza* is a religious gathering where elegies are recited in honor of the Imams and Lady Fātima ﷺ and Lady Zainab ﷺ and other heroes and heroines of the Ahl al-Bayt.]

the vessel of my life every year after I lead the *rawza* in Khair-ābād. A blessing such as making this trip possible in the midst of the restrictions that have been placed on people going to the Syrian front from Mashhad. It was because of these restrictions that people like Javād and many others left for Syria from Mashhad using Afghan identities. And now that I am here, it has been less than three months since a planeload of the guys from Mashhad were returned at the airport in Damascus. My friend Mehdi was on that flight. It took only 3 minutes after they had disembarked for them to be told to get back on it again. We poked fun at him for a long time, saying that he should be more appreciative of his own worth, as he set a record for being a Defender of the Shrine: a Three-Minute *jihād* is no small feat!

Since 2012, when the fire of the Syrian war started to rage, I have been beseeching Imam Riḍā ﷺ to intercede on my behalf with God, and have been going to and fro, asking, 'What about me?' Sometimes I get so tired of banging on a closed door that I try to convince myself that this is where I actually belong. I try to convince myself that even if I save someone's life on the front line of the resistance as a front-line medic by getting someone's bleeding under control and bandaging their wounds, the effect of my presence in Syria would still not be as great as the service I provide here in Iran. Let me stay here, I reason to myself, in this Health Department, and see to the needs of God's creatures. Let me stay here and provide a medical team for the Rāhiān-e Nūr camps, and not let any pilgrim wander through the hospital without having his problems properly seen to and taken care of. It is a strong and convincing argument, but my heart doesn't care about any of these things. It only wants one thing, which is to go to Syria. When the Muharram of 2017 arrives, I will get myself to Khair-ābād somehow to obtain the benefit I usually get from there, and I will get it this year, too.

Two days after the first ten days of Muharram, my phone rings. It's an old colleague who says,

'Ehsān, do you want to go to Syria?'

I have been waiting in anticipation for five years for someone to ask me this question.

'I need an hour to go home and pack my duffle bag.'

He laughs, saying that there is plenty of time between now and Saturday's flight for me to pack my bags.

I count the days from Monday to Saturday a hundred times on the fingers of my hands. Five days. Five days that go by so slowly that it is as if they are refusing to go by at all. Now I have taken to checking the Nekhesā group's website every minute. I have memorized the names of the neighbourhoods and cities in Syria. I know the Syrian brigades better than the Syrians themselves. I know the names of the cities that are still occupied and the ones that have been liberated already. I know the extent of the progress made against ISIS's front lines, and I know all about all of the militants in Syria and everything that is going on there. I even know the famous number that is used for calling from Syria. I owe all this to the Nekhesā group, which was formed spontaneously by some of the forces within the Revolutionary Guards.

Three days later, my phone rang again. It's that famous number with a bunch of zeros in it, calling from two thousand kilometres away. Rahīm is on the other end of the line. He is the Head of the military hospital in Aleppo. He saw my name in the list and called with glee in his voice, saying that I should come over as they are waiting to slaughter a sheep in my honour. His joke cracks me up. His words are so encouraging. It gives me a resolve to sit in front of Somayyeh and say there's not much time left before my departure.

I am restless for the entirety of the remaining two days that are left before my flight. Me, my mom and dad, Somayyeh, the children, and Ali. I was hoping to travel together with Ali, but it didn't pan out that way. Staying here has made him more impatient than anyone else. When I came to Tehran from Mashhad in 2015, Ali could not bear for us to be apart. He took the hand of his wife and child and came to Tehran too. My friendship with Ali is not about us being childhood playmates, the secrets we shared as teenagers or all the time we spent in each other's company as young adults. It is not about the fact that we are colleagues either. Ali is my soul mate. We shed the same tears. He sheds tears for the same reason I shed tears, and he understands why I shed those tears in the *rawzas* that the two of us hold together in private.

'Dr. Ehsān, please get in.'

Dr. Rezā calls out to me so that I do not get left behind from the group of pilgrims. The guys go towards the van, and I follow them. The auxiliary military forces that come to help Syria cannot stay in Damascus. Regardless of where they have come from or for what particular purpose, they have only one day to go on their pilgrimage to Lady Zainab's shrine, then they have to continue on to the region of their mission. We take our places in the van. First pilgrimage, then *jihād*. The guys have struck up a conversation with Abu Abdu, and it is as if Arabic is their mother tongue. They speak it with accents that are thicker than the accents of the Syrians themselves.

Abu Abdu transported so many Iranians in Syria during the war that his phone was full of Iranian religious elegies and laments so he could act like a kind of disc jockey and play whatever request they had. We wanted to hear Helālī sing, so he started searching to find him on his mobile phone.

I wasn't able to see the city in the dark last night, but now I am able to do so. My eyes are drawn to the streets and alleys whose security had been breached by ISIS, like the Aqraba district, for example. Nothing is left of this neighbourhood. No alleys, no streets or houses, no children running after each other despite the war. Only piles of ruins and the corpses of houses lying on top of each other. My heart trembles

Threads of Compassion

at seeing how close the dark shadow of war and destruction has come to the shrine. It trembles for the men who, I'm certain held the city with their bare hands. All of the images that I had seen of the Syrian war and its devastation go to the wayside; the real picture of the war is what is before me now: a fine layer of dust covers the neighbourhood like a powder of death.

'My mother's prayers have had an effect on me. It has changed the trajectory of my life.'

The sound of Helālī's voice tears the bonds that bind my heart. The light of the *rawza* rises up. Abu Abdu sings along with Helālī under his breath. All of the ruins of this neighbourhood become a heavy grief that fills my heart. My shoulders start to convulse as I start to sob uncontrollably and cry out. There is no longer any sense of self and other, only the road leading to the shrine and all of the pent-up emotions of the past five years, whose dam has finally burst open. Pent-up emotions changed the course of my life and brought me to this neighbourhood. The van carrying the delegation of pilgrims has become mobile. It sings and moves to the beat of Helālī's voice and sprinkles the light of the *rawza* on the city of Damascus.

"The Hall of the Martyrs". I don't know the name of this corridor leading to the shrine, but nothing is more fitting than the name "the Hall of the Martyrs". It's the same hallway that was later filled with paintings of the faces of the martyrs, the last place of which was dedicated to a portrait of Hāj Qāsim [Soleymāni]. My pace has slowed down. I submit myself to the magnetic attraction of the shrine. The portrait of Martyr Mustafā Badriddīn looks at me from the middle of its frame. His image is so impressive that it makes me want to salute him. The look in his eyes is heart-warming, even now that he is no longer alive. Mustafā Badriddīn was one of Hizballah's most intelligent military commander, whose tactics ensured that American and Zionist planners' desire to create instability in West Asia would remain unfulfilled. I turn to the right at the end of the hallway, and see the golden dome of the shrine appear before my eyes. I put my right hand on my chest [as a sign of respect and submission, and say],

      As-Salāmu alayk, yā 'aqīla al-'Arab, yā Zainab

      'Peace be unto you, O wise one of the Arabs, O Zainab.'

On Wednesday, the 22nd of November 2017, a particle suspended in the Earth in Time comes to rest in the sanctum sanctorum [of Lady Zainab's ﷺ shrine]. A particle named Ehsān Jāvīdī. A particle that has forgotten he is 37 years old and has four children. A particle that does not even remember its own identity, no matter how much it thinks. It is appropriate for me to bow deeply, and that is what I do. I feel that it is appropriate for me to place my forehead on the threshold of this court, and so I prostrate myself. The Commander of the Faithful, Imam Ali ﷺ's honor (*nāmūs*[13]) lies here. The *nāmūs* of Abu'l-Ghayra. I lower my head down and move forward. The silence of the courtyard and the hall of the shrine sends a fire through my soul. The loneliness and sense of abandonment of its court and its beauty grips my throat. The recitation of the *Ziārat-Nāma*[14] runs through my soul, setting it ablaze. I recite it and burn.

السَّلامُ عليكِ يا بِنتَ أَميرِالمُؤمنين.
السَّلامُ عليكِ يا بِنتَ سَيِّدِالوَصِيّينَ.

Peace be unto you, O daughter of the Commander of the Faithful.
Peace be unto you, O daughter of the master of God's Wasīīn.[15]

---

[13] [*Nāmūs*: the order, honor, respect and dignity of one's self and one's wards and household.]

[14] [*Ziārat*: The act of making pilgrimage to a pilgrimage site, usually a shrine of a prophet, Imam or *imām-zāda* (the righteous progeny of an Imām). A *Ziārat-Nāma* is a liturgical form of supplication or ritual prayer recited specifically during one's pilgrimage to a sacred shrine or location.]

[15] [*Wasīīn*, singular: *wasī*: one who is the ministerial inheritor, legatee, executor, and successor of a prophet.]

Threads of Compassion

Tears prevent me from being able to see properly. I am no longer on the Earth.

$$\text{السَّلامُ عليكِ يا بِنتَ عَلِيٍّالمُرتَضى.}$$
$$\text{السَّلامُ عليكِ يا بِنتَ فاطِمَةَ الزَّهراءِ.}$$

Peace be unto you, O daughter of Ali al-Murtaḍā.
Peace be unto you, O daughter of Fātima¹ az-Zahrā.

Her mother's arm hurts so much that she cannot even comb Zainab's hair. Her father is so ill that he has no appetite, even for a cup of milk. This lady has suffered so much. I offer my *salāms* to her parents. Woe, for there are tears even in the opening of the *Ziārat-Nāma* of this family.

$$\text{السَّلامُ عليكِ يا عَمَّةَ وَلِيِاللهِ المُكَرَّمِ.}$$
$$\text{السَّلامُ عَليكِ يا أُمَّالمَصائِبِ يا زَينَب.}$$

Peace be unto you, O aunt of God's honourable walī.[16]

---

[16] [*Walī*: the divinely-appointed Just Ruler over the community of Muslims. 1. regent, sovereign, lord and master; 2. patron, guardian, protector, custodian. Plural: *awliā*: those of God's creatures who have spiritual proximity to Him, inclusive of prophets and Imāms and, to a lesser

*peace be unto you, O mother of
difficulties and misfortunes, O Zainab.*

I am drawn to the sepulchre. All of my friends who were martyred made this same journey. Javād is with me now. He is leaning against the wall in a corner of the hall and looking at me. I wish someone would stand in the middle of the court and recite a *rawza*. One of those elegy reciters (*maddāh*) who have been blessed by Abā-Abdullāh.[17] One of those who recite elegies as if a handful of salt had been poured on his palate, so that his recitation is painful and heartfelt. He could then recite an elegy and we would gather around him and our spirits would soar. We would beat our chests so much that we would be out of breath. I wished the shrine did not feel that it was so lonesome and abandoned.

السَّلامُ عليكِ يا مَن نَطَحَت جَبينَها بِمُقَدَّم المحمِل
إذ رَأَت رَأسَ سَيِّدِالشُّهداءِ..

*Peace be unto you, O you who butted her
forehead when she saw the bearer of the*

---

degree, the *ulamā* and *fuqahā*. The guardian-sovereign (*walīy al-amr*); the Just Ruler and Guardian-Sovereign of the affairs of the believers (*walīy al-amr*).]

[17] [Abā-Abdullāh literally means 'Father of [all] God's Bondsmen' and is an honorific (*kunya*) of Imam Husain ﷺ's.]

head of the Master of the Martyrs[18] advance.

I wish someone would move the heads away from the caravan so that she would not see them again. I have become the *rawza* reciter and the one who beats his chest and sheds tears in response to the elegies myself. I am bewildered between Mashhad and Qom, between Karbalā and Damascus. A sister comes all the way to Qom in the hopes of meeting her brother but doesn't make it.[19] The pain of not reaching and not seeing her brother still burns in the hearts of pilgrims to her shrine in Qom. And another sister from the same august family travels all the way to Karbalā for the sake of the love she has for her brother and is taken to Damascus empty-handed and in mourning. "God save us from Syria."

I want to give up the ghost. I want her to buy my soul, just as she bought Javād's. I work my fingers through the steel latticework that guards the sepulchre. Its fragrance is so moving. The moment of union…

The foot of Her Eminence becomes one with the stones around the steel latticework. I can't keep it together anymore. Every corner of the shrine that I

---

[18] [Another reference to Imam Husain, whose head was borne on the top of a spear after it was severed from its body, and taken from Karbalā to the court of the Umayyad caliph Yazīd ibn Muʿāwiya in Damascus.]

[19] [The reference is to Lady Maʿsūma, who travelled from Madina to Qom in order to see her brother, Imam Riḍā.]

look at pours a prayer into my soul. I can't get enough of its walls and portals. I wish my life would end right here. I wish I didn't have to leave this paradise. I wish I could become the earth underneath the feet of her pilgrims. Why can't I just die [in this state of bliss]?

This is what an elegy reciter is all about. When he is present at a shrine, he must either shed tears or have others do so; that is the only way his heart will find peace. I have recited so many elegies and shed so many tears and had others shed tears that everyone has become enervated from shedding so many tears. And I, too, have left my body in some corner and am just staring at the walls. The bullet holes and shrapnel marks on the wall make my heart gloomy. The loneliness of the first days of the war... Whoever took a stand here and defended the shrine did so with his own blood. The days of General Hamedānī. I wish he was here and could see how the Syria which was falling when he first entered the scene has repulsed the armed men who had reached the walls at the back of the presidential palace and how it has come back to life. I wish he was here and could see how his genius in irregular warfare pushed ISIS back. I wish he was here and could see how the local defence forces, which were formed at his suggestion, have now become a branch of the Syrian military. He already knew these things would happen. I wish I could kiss his hand. On behalf of myself, all the Defenders of the Shrine, and all of the people of Syria,

Threads of Compassion

Abu Abdu drives our group towards the Damascus market and the shrine of Lady Ruqayya ﷺ. I am sitting next to Ali, who is one of the war veterans. I don't know where I got the idea that I was going to be sent to Aleppo. Maybe it was because Rahīm had called me from Aleppo. I start up a conversation with Ali. I ask about Aleppo and its medical bases. Ali is highly informed; he answers every question I put to him and much more besides. I yearn to reach Aleppo soon. The sound of explosions reaches us from near and far. The city shakes every ten minutes or so with the shock waves from these explosions. I look around at the people, and see that they don't care about the explosions and go about their own business. War has brought them closer together. They live more communally now. The explosions are meant for the Ghūta, a branch of the Syrian armed forces formed at the instigation of General Husain Hamedānī from the muster calls of the people's volunteer forces. It does not matter how near or far the explosions occur; in war, you have to go on living as long as you are alive. Just like these people.

When we leave the van, I tell myself to remember where I am going. Lady Ruqayya ﷺ was no more than three years old [when she was killed by Yazīd's forces]. A tired and grieving girl who was grieved before being given the chance to understand the meaning of grief. They didn't give the dust of her long journey from Karbalā to Damascus to settle before they refreshed her grief anew. I remind myself that I haven't come here to open up my heart, although this lady is known for untying the knots in people's hearts. I remind myself that I have come here to soothe her little heart. A heart that had been shaken from the galloping of horses and the flames of tents set on fire. A heart that is no more than three years old.

We pass by the Umayyad Mosque toward the Damascus market, with its entrance adorned by brick arches. The entryway opens onto a large yard of cobblestones that shine under the rays of the sun. Everyone is tired. Their faces are sunburnt, and their legs are exhausted. Lady Ruqayya ﷺ is wearier than everyone else. I wish Ali-Akbar was here so that I could hug him. I wish Abbas was here and hadn't been moved to try to get some water. I wish his brother had not been taken ill and was not so weak. I wish the sound of the leather whips had not broken the bonds of his heart. I wish the heat of the sun was not so sweltering. I wish her aunt wasn't so lonesome. The liturgies of the tragedy of Karbalā have set my soul on fire. I wish I were blind and had not seen this market. "God save us from Syria."

We are sitting around a table, waiting for Dr. Karīm, the regional commander for medical services, to join us for lunch. Each person recalls a different story about him. Seeing Dr. Karīm and spending time in his company is considered to be an honour by the soldiers.

Threads of Compassion

I don't know him, but from what I've heard others say about him, he seems to be an older person with a very busy schedule and must either be a specialist doctor or a surgeon. He probably is on the board of some prestigious university, and "Dr. Karīm" is probably his *nom de guerre*. Like all busy administrators, his meeting has run over and he doesn't show up. Dr. Rezā apologizes on his behalf and places the shawarmas in the middle of the table. The guys are disheartened as they had set their hearts on having lunch with their commander. Dr. Rezā takes out a document from his pocket, puts on his glasses, and reads out the names of the guys and their assigned destination, doing so in a kindly manner so as to make up for the fact that Dr. Karīm was not able to join them.

'Dr. Mostafī and Dr. Ahmadī, Palmyra; Dr. Ali, Deir ez-Zūr; Dr. Abu-Rezā, Deir ez-Zūr.'

I was staring at his mouth.

'Hamīd Jān! As always, you have to go to Aleppo, and take Dr. Mehdi with you.'

I strain my neck so that he doesn't forget me.

'Dr. Rahmati and Dr. Dūsti are assigned to Al-Bukamal. And Ali-Rezā and Mansūr go to Al-Mayādīn.'

There are no more names or regions left. From Aleppo, Palmyra, and Deir ez-Zūr to Al-Bukamal and Al- Mayādīn. Everyone was assigned a region except me. My head starts to itch. I was concerned that they might want to send me back. The guys are making jokes, laughing and having a good time with each

Threads of Compassion

other. I envy their carefree demeanour, which is unlike mine.

Dr. Rezā continued, 'The brothers who are going to the east should be ready to fly to Deir ez-Zūr in an hour. And the brothers who are going to Aleppo: your ride is waiting for you in the front of the building. After lunch, *yā Alī*.'

Again, my name is not called. It's as if I don't exist. I want to say something, but Dr. Rezā beats me to it.

'Doctor Jān! Dr. Karīm sends his *salāms* and says that you are to remain in Damascus for the time being. And he said he wanted to have lunch with you today.'

Everyone turned to look at me. I don't know what to say. What does Dr. Karīm want with me? Why didn't they send me off to the front lines?

Dr. Rezā continued, 'Did you hear me, doctor?'

I pull myself together. 'Yes, doctor. Perfectly.'

It's 2 pm. I'm lying on a bed, my mind teeming with my thoughts. I feel hungry and despondent. I'm thinking, 'The shawarma already slipped through my fingers. What if my chance at *jihād* is going to do the same?!' I remember the plane full of volunteers from Mashhad that was sent back; I remembered my friend's "three-minute *jihād*", and thought that I was probably going

Threads of Compassion

to have to go back too. I wish we hadn't laughed so much at the poor guy and hadn't poked so much fun at his "three-minute *jihād*". I'm sure his resentment at all of that has now come back to bite me. All the guys have gone now, and the hall is empty and silent. I wish my name was on the dispatch list like everyone else so I knew where I stood. I'm restless, turning from one side to the other. I live out the memory of the morning pilgrimage in my heart. No one steps on Syrian soil without Lady Zainab's ﷺ permission. I leave this whole journey entirely in her hands. *O thou who has called me, show me the way.*

Dr. Rezā opens the door and says, 'Doctor Karīm is waiting for you.'

I jump up out of bed, run a hand through my hair, and straighten out my clothes. Wearing a pair of army camouflage commando pants is half the *jihād* for me! I stop at the door of Dr. Karīm's room and knock twice.

'Come in!'

I'm stunned. Dr. Karīm is neither old, nor is he a member of any board at a university. Nor is he a surgeon or a specialist doctor. He's my old colleague at the Imam Rezā Training Center in Mashhad! The only thing that I got right was that Dr. Karīm wasn't his real name. What a difference there was between the night shifts of the Imam Husain ﷺ hospital and the work that was involved here in the middle of Damascus, in the crossfire of the armed forces and ISIS! What a small world it is. The Commander-in-Chief of the Syrian

Threads of Compassion

Medical Service Corps, my buddy from the days of my youth. I hugged him, and my tears started to flow again.

Karīm and his driver Muhammad, and I hit the road towards Al-Mayādīn first thing in the morning. Why al-Mayādīn? I have no clue. They probably have my name down for Al-Mayādīn, just like they had the names of the guys who were on Dr. Rezā's list yesterday down for other regions. But had I known yesterday that my mission was going to be in the same area as Karīm's, I wouldn't have been so despondent for my name not being on the list. I am happy that Karīm is with me; but I don't know why I wasn't sent out with the rest of the group. If I had known, I might have changed my mind from the beginning at Ashrīn. Or perhaps I would have taken on airs and said that I had come to Syria to wage *jihād*, not for these kinds of things. Whatever the case, I followed Karīm willingly, but not knowing exactly what was happening. I look Karīm over. He is wearing a khaki uniform that seems to have been made to order for him. With the two-way radio in his hand and the sunglasses and the chest pockets on his shirt, he looks like a different person. A true commander. Especially since the sun has given him a deep tan. We have a lot to talk about; enough to fill the twenty years of our friendship. He talks about his children. His daughter is now full-grown and has become a lady like Hāniyeh. He fills me in about what's going on in the region and about the days he has spent here and the people he has seen. He asks after Ali. I tell him that he was supposed to come, but it was not in the cards. When we talk about Ali, it reminds us of our trip to Karbalā.

In 2008, we were stuck behind the Khosravī border on our way to Karbalā, because the Iraqi authorities would not allow our caravan to pass. We had taken four buses, and they were lined up, waiting for permission to pass and proceed on to Karbalā. But now they were saying the road was closed. So I take a load off and sit on the ground right there behind the border. I pull a keffiyeh over my face and start to recite the Āshūrā *ziārat*.[20] Karīm, Ali, and our womenfolk are also with me. With every *salām* of the Āshūrā *ziārut*, emotions flutter in my chest like the wings of a dove. We have met him half-way; the rest is up to him, whether or not to get us there. If we had known that they were going to close the border to us, we would have started to wail while we were on the way to the border and would have washed the road with our tears from the time we started on our pilgrimage. A few more people have joined us and are wailing and lamenting like us for having been left behind a closed border. We have been driven from our homeland, as the expression goes, and denied access to Heaven. I

---

[20] [*Ziārat*: 1. The act of making pilgrimage to a pilgrimage site, usually a shrine of a prophet, Imam, or *imam-zāda* (the progeny of an Imam); 2. A liturgical form of supplication or ritual prayer recited specifically during one's pilgrimage to a sacred shrine or location. The Āshūrā *Ziārat* is a leading case in point.]

complain [to Imam Husain ﷺ]: we miss you; we have come so far, don't break our hearts and allow us to be returned without being allowed to come and see you.

We are all waiting on one solitary signature. The master's signature to allow us entry. I read one line, then Karīm reads a line, and then Ali, and then back to me again. We come to the place in the *ziārat* where promises are made:

يا اَباعَبْدِاللهِ اِنّى سِلْمٌ لِمَنْ سالَمَكُمْ وَ حَرْبٌ لِمَنْ حارَبَكُمْ اِلى يَوْمِ الْقِيامَة.

> *O Abā-Abdullāh [O Imam Husain ﷺ], I am at peace with those who are at peace with you, and at war with those who are at war with you until the Day of Resurrection.*

We call the master again and renew our promises with him. We do this again and again. It is not a petty matter. I am at peace with those who are at peace with you, and at war with those who have drawn a sword against you until the Day of Resurrection. It is no small matter; but I reread the ziārat.

Suddenly, there is a flurry in the caravan. I get up to go see what's going on. They say that the authorities have given their permission and that our convoy can cross the border. What a trip. Karīm and I take turns recollecting various events that took place on that trip. We place the memories side by side, like sweet morsels of Arabic baklava, in an imaginary serving dish, and delight in their sweet nectar. Our adventures on that trip were so sweet that Karīm's driver has also become eager to hear them. We used to go around from shrine to shrine, from morning till night. We'd spend an hour in one of the courtyards of Imam Husain ﷺ's shrine, then go and hang out in one of the courtyards of Abu'l-Faḍl's shrine. And we'd take our afternoon nap right there in one of those courtyards after we made our noon prayers. We didn't want to take time away from the shrines by returning to the hotel. Now, ten years later, in the November of 2017, the master has brought us together here. Right at the same point where we call the master and renew our promises with him. The point that ensured our passage on to Karbalā, and the point where the master believed our promise that we would be *at peace with those who are at peace with you and at war with those who have drawn a sword against you until the Day of Resurrection.*

Oh, how I miss Ali and all of his kindnesses. Would that he was here with us so that we could continue to place the pieces of this sweet puzzle together. Not as a figment of our imaginations, but in Syria itself, where they drew a sword on the sister of the Imam who was dearer to him than life itself. Where they drew a sword on anyone whose heart beat for the Imam's ideals and objectives and sense of morality. How Ali's presence is missed. Would that Ali was here so that we could fulfill the promise we made that day behind the Khosravī border, so that the Lord [of the

Martyrs] could see how faithful we have been to the covenant we made on that Āshūrā pilgrimage. Would that Ali was here so that we could take turns reading from the Āshūrā *ziārat*:

$$وَ لَعَنَاللَّهُ آلَ زِيَادٍ وَ آلَ مَرْوانَ$$

And may God curse the House of Ziyād and the House of Marwān.

The driver drives at speed. At sunrise, the city is still asleep. I have 800 kilometers in which to see Syria and the traces of ISIS and to recite,

$$وَ لَعَنَاللَّهُ أُمَّةً اَسْرَجَتْ وَ اَلْجَمَتْ وَ تَنَقَّبَتْ لِقِتالِكَ$$

And may God curse those who have gathered together and harnessed their forces to fight you.

The more we travel, the more I realize how little I knew about this place. The feeling I get on the road from Damascus to Palmyra could not have been obtained by watching any movie, any news report, or by seeing any pictures. Before reaching Homs, the road is spotted with stalls serving coffee and refreshments. Discoloured plastic chairs are waiting in the sun to welcome professional hookah smokers and even more serious coffee drinkers. Karīm gets off and returns after a while with three cups of espresso and a few packets of Bin Hasīb instant coffee. The car is filled with the aroma of the world's largest business, second only to oil. Coffee roasted to the taste of the Arabs. The first sip runs a shiver of acrid bitterness through me. Bitter like the silent ruins of Homs and Al-Furqlus.

A little further down the road, the colourful gables of abandoned houses can be seen through the foliage of the trees. It is a region brimming with a wealth of natural resources, such as a phosphate mine and numerous oil wells. Never mind the oil whose refinery was supposed to have re-opened one of these days. It was looted, like the oil wells themselves. And never mind the phosphate mine either, which was so sought after as its product is essential for agricultural fertilizer. But what about the Kamāya, which should by rights belong to these people. Kamāya is a root vegetable that is potato-shaped but as soft as a mushroom. If you dig the crevices of the soil a day after it rains, you will come across Kamāya, a soft and delicious golden root vegetable.

It seems to me that all of this wealth should be a source of income for the government and for the local population, and things should not be so stagnant. The road leading to the village should now be full of happy people and tourists brandishing cameras, taking snapshots and spending loads of money for a small plate of Kamāya, and reveling in the region and the good nature of its people. But there is no such thing, thanks to the war.

Threads of Compassion

I am heartbroken by the utter ignorance that has brought a country to the ruin of war. Before Syria burned in the fire of ISIS, it burned in the fire of ignorance. A country whose people never thought they would see war is now a prisoner of war. And the most destructive type of war at that: [a foreign-imposed, funded, and even manned regional proxy war, disguised as] a civil war and a clan war.

In the far distance, seven or eight chocolate-coloured mountain ranges reach up into the sky. Jabal al-Tharda girds Palmyra like a fortification that makes for a spectacular scene when you enter the city that will stay in your mind forever. Up to two kilometres from the city, one cannot see anything but this mountain range. The approach to the city is made by way of a winding road that climbs an incline, and before you know it, in the blink of an eye, the chocolate-coloured mountain range is behind you, and Palmyra is spread under your feet like a precious old carpet; a carpet whose most prominent medallion is Palmyra, right there before you, wounded and tired.

If we divide the map of Syria into four parts with two perpendicular lines, Palmyra is located right where these two lines intersect, at Syria's most central and strategic point; which is why it has been the subject of many battles throughout the entire duration of the war between ISIS mercenaries and the forces of the government. There is no need for me to write about the extent of its destruction. The city is so war-damaged that even now, a few months after its liberation, people are loathe to return to their homes there. More painful than the empty houses of its people is the historical castle of Palmyra. A castle usually refers to a safe fortification, sometimes build on a height. When I look at its old columns, I am reminded of our own Persepolis; but there is no trace of any fortifications or towers left of the castle. It is nothing but a ruin wherein the wind blows dust hither and dither. I feel like sitting at the foot of some of these pillars that are still left standing and having them compare the atrocities committed by ISIS at these very columns with the tales of how various good and evil governments have acted over the centuries. The Arabs named Palmyra the Pearl of the Desert, but nothing is left of this burnt pearl. Everything that was there was either destroyed by ISIS or stolen by them. According to one analysis, what they did here was to create fear among the people under their dominion, and according to another analysis, they ravaged Palmyra to sell its antiquities in order to finance the war.

Dr. Karīm shows me around the Bassel hospital, which is the main hospital of Palmyra or Tadmir city, and is named after Bassel al-Asad, Bashar al-Asad's brother. It is a five-story hospital whose doors and windows have been removed. When Palmyra was first recaptured by ISIS, they realized that this hospital was under the control of the Iranian forces. That's why they destroyed everything within it, so that it would serve as an example of not allowing Iranians under the roofs of other buildings. In 2017, when the city was recaptured by us again, a field hospital was built by the order of Dr. Karīm within fifty meters of Bassel Hospital. The field hospital was a two-story building that was originally supposed to be just a relief outpost. But when it was equipped with an operating room, it became a proper hospital.

When I enter through the hospital door, I find myself standing in the middle of the operating room. It makes me laugh. It's like entering a house and finding that you have entered the bedroom. It's funny because I still haven't learned that this is the way hospitals are built in war zones. During conditions of war, there is no time to take the injured parties to some corner of even a building as small as this one. The injured must be taken directly into the operating room and be operated on immediately, or else some of them will not survive their injuries. This 5-meter square operating room has turned this relief outpost into a hospital. I might not know much yet, but I do know that equipping this relief outpost with an operating room and turning it into a hospital right under the nose of ISIS requires a gargantuan commitment of will, like that of Dr. Karīm's. A surgery platform, an anesthesia machine, an electrocautery machine, a suction machine, and a solid diesel-powered electrical generator – being able to bring each one of these here during wartime conditions is a feat that is the equivalent of the re-conquest of Palmyra. Being able to being them all is nothing short of miraculous.

Threads of Compassion

The smell of blood pervades the whole city and makes me nauseous. Medical personnel such as myself are used to the smell of blood, but not this smell of blood. Blood that has been shed unjustly doesn't just have a distinct odour; it also burns. The blood of the people of Palmyra who were executed *en masse* in the streets and squares of this city. The blood of the people who were beheaded in front of their loved ones. The blood of the soldiers who freed Palmyra one street at a time, so that the heart of Syria could be secured and ISIS would be cut off from the highway connecting it with the east and southeast of the country.

I say street-to-street and person-to-person fighting because Palmyra was the jewel in the crown of ISIS's conquests. Not because of Palmyra and its antiques, nor because of its oil and gas fields, and not because of its centrality and strategic importance. But because of the at-Tanf US base and the 55-kilometre perimeter that the United States created around it. This at-Tanf base is the junction that connects Jordan, Iraq and Syria to each other. More specifically, it is the border crossing from Syria into Jordan, Iraq, Saudi Arabia and Yemen. The at-Tanf base has a military airport with a 55-kilometer radius no-fly zone. Now what is the use of this no-fly zone? I will tell you. Firstly, it creates a safe area for the training of terrorist forces. Secondly, it ensures the security of the skies of the Zionist forces which are occupying Palestine and prevents any attack by the forces of the Axis of Resistance from this point. Thirdly, it acts to cut off

Syria from Iraq [militarily and from Jordan, Saudi Arabia, and Yemen commercially]. And fourthly, it functions as a vortex for sucking mercenary forces from Sudan and pumping them into Iraq and Syria. If I were to continue to count [the benefits of the at-Tanf base for the enemy], there would be no end to it. But common sense will tell you that this 55-kilometer perimeter that the United States created has enough value for the US for it to come from half way around the world to a hot desert and build a military airport and to enforce a no-fly zone, and claim that this is their turf [in violation of all international laws and against the will of the UN-recognized government of Syria]. Let me put it this way. If we hadn't stopped the wheels that Saudi Arabia had put into motion, their proxies would have marched onto Damascus and what should on no account happen *would* have happened. If America hadn't occupied this strategic crossing like an incubus on steroids, their mercenaries would have been wiped out and wrapped up a hundred times over by now and what should have happened *would* have happened.

But let us go back to Palmyra and its windowless houses that are leaning up against each other for support because they have become so tired of taking bullets and shrapnel. Houses whose keys, I'm sure, are still being kept in their owners' pockets like prized possessions. Houses that no longer have the strength to continue to be houses.

Threads of Compassion

Up until Palmyra, the traces of war could only be seen on the ground, but after Palmyra, they could be seen in the sky as well. Fighter jets are circling above us and making their presence felt. The sounds of explosions in the distance and nearby accost my eardrums. We proceed on a road in the middle of the desert. Suddenly, the driver hits the gas and the car jerks forward. I'm still wondering what's going on when Karīm ducks his head and tells me to do the same. I am doubled over on my knees and praying in earnest. Karīm explains that the road is within reach of Kornets. From where we are, which is Al-Sukhna, to Kabājab and Al-Shawla is about 120 km. What is a Kornet? It's a Russian man-portable anti-tank guided missile (ATGM) that seeks and is guided by the human body's temperature, so it does not require accurate targeting. All you have to do is to press the button and the missile will seek you out using infrared homing technology until it finds you and pulverizes you.

We covered 120 kilometres in an hour and a half; now we have stopped and are looking at our surroundings through the car's windows. The closer we get to our destination, the more we see signs of the war that is raging. The villages that we pass on the way are empty like Homs, or even more abandoned than that. There are checkpoints every ten kilometres. *Hājaz*, the call them. Barriers that cause long lines of cars waiting to pass. We are waiting in one such line. It will take half an hour for the guards to inspect the trunk of every car, to walk by each car with a handheld

X-ray machine, and to check everyone's papers. I'm running the calculations in my head to see how many more hours we have to go with all of these checkpoints that we have to go through when a driver in front of us gets out and gestures for us to get out of the queue. The driver next to us has noticed us too. He too, gestures for us to get out of the queue. It's as if they're informing each other one by one. Everyone wants the same thing now, and they are gesturing for us to get out of the queue and to go forward. We get out of the queue and make our way towards the checkpoint. The drivers raise their hands to us as a sign of respect.

Karīm explains, 'They recognized our car. They allow us to pass because we are Iranian.' They don't say 'Iranian', they say 'friends' (*isdiqā*'). Here, 'Iranian' means friend, and in their book, 'friends' does not stand in inspection lines. A crystal-clear expression of love, Arab style. Emotions well up in my throat. The seeds of this love are the lives of the Defenders of the Shrine whose bodies are buried here. Seeds that have been irrigated with the shed blood of the martyrs, turning 'Iranian' into 'friend'. We pass the checkpoint. Palmyra and its ruined castle are behind us now, and Deir ez-Zūr and Al-Mayādīn are before us. We have close to another 500 kilometres ahead of us that we must traverse in the heart of the desert to reach Al-Mayādīn. Whenever I have a long drive ahead of me in the heart of a desert and through mountains, I think of

Ahmad,[21] and this time it's no different. Maybe because he was martyred as a result of a road accident. Ahmad and I become bosom buddies in 1996, when we are both in tenth grade. We used to hang out with the *hay'ats*,[22] going from the Bayt al-Zahrā *hay'at* to the Bayt ar-Rezā *hay'at*, then to the Āsheqān-e Abā-Abdollāh *hay'at*, then off to the shrine [of Imam Riḍā ﷺ], and reciting *tawāshīh* psalms and the Āshūrā Ziārat. I don't know when we found time to study. We went everywhere together and did everything together. Even our illnesses were together. We both got 'asthma' together. Not real asthma, but persistent dry coughs that were similar to asthma. We both felt like visiting the shrine together. We recited *ziārāt* together. We used to hang out in the different courtyards of the shrine, coughing our lungs out together. Our coughing was chronic. What if it didn't go away and we could no longer recite *tawāshīh* psalms? Reciting *tawāshīh* psalms, *rawzas*, and the Quran were our whole world. Now we can't even take in a full, deep breath, let alone being able to recite any of these.

We lie down on our backs in the courtyard of the Gowharshād Mosque [which is within the Imam Riḍā ﷺ shrine complex] in order to rest and catch our

---

[21] Shahid Ahmad Dāvarī was born on March 3rd 1981 in Mashhad and was martyred in a traffic accident during his mission.
[22] [Groups formed within mosque congregations for performing religiously oriented public services.]

Threads of Compassion

breaths. It's cold, so we pull half of a six square meter carpet over us to keep warm, and thus swallow the dust of the feet of countless pilgrims deep into our throats. What a wonderful sky, what a wonderful sleep, what a wonderful house, and what a wonderful owner the house has! We don't understand the significance of the place where we are sleeping, but we enjoy ourselves nevertheless. It is not something that Imam Riḍā ﷺ is not fully aware of, nor should it be something that is hidden from you either: we *still* do not understand, but we enjoy ourselves nevertheless.

At the morning *adhān* or call to prayer, an old man kneels down over us. He is one of the custodians of the shrine. He adjusts his green hat on his head and pulls back our carpet covering. Before we have had a chance to open our eyes, our coughing fits begin. It's like Ahmad and I are competing with each other to see who coughs the most. The old man offers us two fruit juices, packaged in individual portions. We get up from the middle of the prayer line, which is where we had fallen asleep and where people had started to line up for the morning prayer, and go to the middle of the courtyard to perform our ritual ablutions. The fruit juice hits the spot. After the morning prayers, I look at Ahmad to see if he has noticed too, which he has. He pushes his chest out and takes in a deep breath. There is no sign of our coughs anymore.

Threads of Compassion

Chapter One Photos

Shahīd (Martyr) Javād Muhammadī. This is the picture that I saw after he had just been martyred, and I laughed at it because I thought it was just another one of his pranks.

Threads of Compassion

A part of Lot 30 of the Behesht-e Rezā Cemetery. A corner of the cemetery that for me is a corner of the world; next to Javād and his neighbors.

Shīshī (The Glass Building). A place that I had dreamed of becoming intimately familiar with.

Threads of Compassion

Inner view of one of the 'Ashrīn warehouses. The rooms to either side of the corridor are the troops' quarters.

The portal of the 400 km long road that leads to the front lines which I had dreamed of fighting in.

Threads of Compassion

Palmyra, the Burnt Pearl of the Desert, tired and wounded.

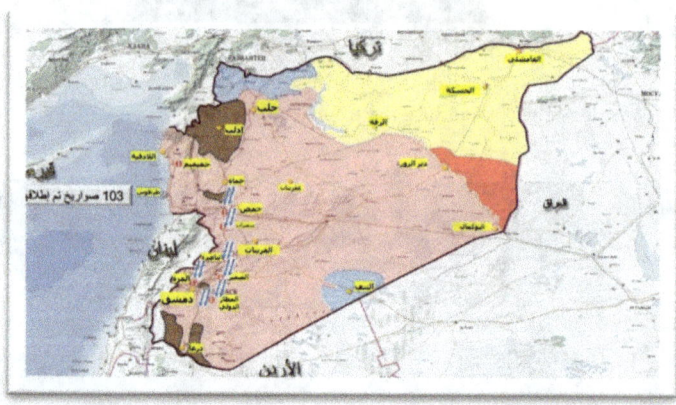

A map of Syria in which the 55 km no-fly zone of the US-occupied at-Tanf crossing is shown in blue.

Threads of Compassion

This is Dr. Rezā, who called out everyone's name on the muster list except mine. This is how he was dressed the first time I saw him, which left a very positive impression on me.

Threads of Compassion

2

The smell of Savlon and Deconex makes me feel nauseous again. I look around for Somayyeh and the kids. I'm alone, and feeling anxious that something might happen to the kids. My IV drip continues its constant drips. I am wearing the blue uniform of the hospital. I shouldn't be here. I have a thousand things to take care of in Syria. I want to get up, but there is some force that has pinned my body to the bed. I strain my neck and see that my leg is bandaged. The pain starts gnawing at my soul. It's as if it was waiting for me to become conscious. I close my eyes.

Threads of Compassion

"Welcome to the City of Al-Bukamal". This sentence can be seen on the eastern gate of the third capital of ISIS. Al-Bukamal, their capital of seven years. A city that once flourished but is now nothing more than a burnt city. Columns of smoke can be seen here and there, twisting up into the sky from the city's heart. The sound of explosions can be heard one after another. Al-Bukamal sits on the border of Iraq's Al-Qā'im province, which is chock full of scattered villages that have given their support to ISIS, either willingly or by force of arms. Now they have placed the white flags of surrender on their houses, saying, 'We surrender; we are not with ISIS; we are with you.' After it was surrounded, this is this city where Hāj Qāsim [General Soleimāni] ordered that all the women and children should be allowed to come out of the city safely before the troops enter it. It's the latest governmental headquarters that has been lost to ISIS. It has only been about a week since the city's liberation, and the city is still full of traces of ISIS. The first of these is the subterranean level below the city. I have not seen it personally, but I am told that it is a veritable city in itself, consisting of a series of subterranean spaces interconnected with tunnels. Tunnels link various facilities that range from warehouses and underground hospitals to prisons and bunkers, above all of which there are people's houses, the congregational mosque, the town square, schools, and everything else that can be found in a city. There is also a layer of thick polyethylene sheeting covering the alleys and streets that have been placed there to prevent our drones from being able to monitor and record their movements.

My imagination comes alive between the shaded alleys under the layer of polyethylene sheeting covering them. It runs through the city like a dream, fluid and free. It goes back to the year 2011, give or take; the year when members of ISIS used to buy houses and land here and dig tunnels under them for eventualities that were to happen in years that were to come in the not-too-distant future. My imagination took me to the workshops where suicide cars were outfitted with steel sheeting welded all over them and where they were packed with explosives. Then, these cars would be boarded by those who most eagerly sought martyrdom, but not without first sending *salāms* and *salawāt*. The car is driven to a place such as a military headquarters, a warehouse full of weapons, medicine, or food, or even a busy street. By pressing a button, the suicide bomber engulfs the lives and livelihoods of a number of innocent bystanders in shrapnel ejected by the shockwave and in the flames that follow the explosion. For what purpose? So that his horrid existence will reach a paradise, an entry to which he can continue to dream about in his eternal sojourn in Hell.

There is a volcano hidden in the heart of this city, full of words, tears, and blood. Following the fancy of my imagination, I have moved away from Karīm and his driver Muhammad, moving to sewing shops where

Threads of Compassion

the orange uniforms are sewn that are for the special purposes of the execution of ISIS's enemies, to the black military clothing that they wear. It then moves on to ISIS's dark prisons, which are full of moans and the smell of wounds and pus, and where blood is everywhere. I then move on to the congregational mosque of the city, which has become a school for training ISIS loyalists. How do they do this, you ask? By injecting the brains of children with the alphabet of the beliefs of their so-called "Islamic caliphate". For seven years, they raised predatory animals in this city who put people to death by cutting off their heads with a blade. Individual executions in the town square and mass executions next to a water well outside the city. My imagination takes me next to Hamdān village, to a two-story building called Mahal as-Sabāyā. I just translate its name and move on, which is what I recommend you do as well. Mahal means shop or place of business in Arabic, a place for buying and selling. And *sabāyā* is the plural of *sabia*, which means maiden. So "Mahal as-Sabāyā" is a centre for the buying and selling of maidens. How much do the maidens sell for, you ask? Three euros. The price of a young girl in this region, who is not even 20 or even 18 years old, due to the low threshold set for being able to marry them. Hopefully, you will be able to pass by and leave this village and this disgusting building behind. Hopefully, you will be able to pass by the fear that wells up in the eyes of these wretched slaves every time the door opens and closes and their wish for death that is uttered a thousand times a day from their mouths.

Kermānshāh, Hamedān, Khūzestān, Īlām. I shudder to think which of these cities would have been chosen to become the next three-story city modelled after Al-Bukamal, if we had not stepped on their throats here in the middle of Syria? Where would their tailor shop have been? Where would their suicide workshop have been? I chain my imagination to a stout column and do not allow it to go any farther. Enough is enough.

Why did ISIS struggle so hard to keep this province under their dominion for seven years? Why did they dig so many tunnels to enable them to go back and forth to Iraq? Why did Al-Bukamal become their capital? Why was it so important? I'll tell you.

Al-Bukamal is a bottleneck. Its importance is on account of its being located in the path that connects the branches of the Resistance (meaning Lebanon, Syria and Iraq) to their trunk, which is Iran. Its artery is Beirut, Damascus, Baghdad, and Tehran. The Tehran-Baghdad section of the artery was 'asphalted', as it were, after Saddam's fall. The rest of the artery, from Baghdad to Lebanon, will soon be paved with the capture of Al-Bukamal. Do you remember the 55-kilometre perimeter and no-fly zone at at-Tanf? The perimeter that is only a feint blue line on the map whose sacrosanctity our beloved American cousins insisted that Iran respect? There was supposed to have been another 55-kilometre perimeter and no-fly zone created at Al-Bukamal. Just as furtively and effortlessly as it takes to draw a beautiful blue line on a map. A line that represents barbed wire, a minefield, an airport, a construction ban, and a no-fly zone on the ground, and whose colour is the colour of blood. Why? For it to prevent the forces of the resistance from being able to connect with each other. For it to become a private backyard for our blue-eyed cousins in the region. A backyard that will have all sorts of conduits and raceways and everything else under the sun connected to it, and will later become a full-blown military base, later still to become their undisputed freehold property. As patches of desirable real estate, Syria, Iraq, Lebanon, and the Middle East more generally were gradually falling into this kind of status. And later? I don't know. My knowledge extends only to what I have already written down. May God accept what little I have to offer.

If you want to know more, all you have to do is a Google search about the US military base at at-Tanf. And if you can't be bothered, then this amount of information is enough to get you started. How? I'll tell you again.

We have heard many stories from know-it-alls who say that the war in Syria is a war between two countries [which has nothing to do with Iran] and that the presence of the Defenders of the Shrine there is nothing but a form of adventurism [on Iran's part]. And an adventure with high salaries for the participants to boot. Well, that is not the case. Syria is a turning point. Besides preventing US military bases being installed at the choke points of the arteries of the axis of resistance, the fact is that Syria helped Iran a lot during the Iran-Iraq war, and was in fact the only country that helped Iran to bypass the sanctions that had been imposed on us as a result of the world war[23] that had been launched against us.

Now, while Dr. Karīm and his driver Muhammad and I are heading to where we need to be from the back alleys of Al-Bukamal, send a *salawāt* in honour of the Defenders of the Shrine, without whom Uncle Sam would have installed yet another of their military bases here. Send a *salawāt* in honour of the Defenders whose names you have not heard and will probably never hear but who washed away with their blood everything that was on the map and on the ground, like the 55-kilometre perimeter, the blue line, the barbed wire, the minefield, and every other US imperialist ambition.

---

[23] [The Soviet Union as well as the Western block took the side of Saddam Husain, who was the aggressor in the war, against Iran.]

Threads of Compassion

It is almost dusk when we finally arrive. Our destination is a half-built building outside the city, on some high ground that overlooks Al-Bukamal. There's a white banner over its entrance that identifies it as a field hospital. It is located in the southernmost point of Al-Bukamal.

Being the optimist that I am, I think this is where I will be based. Five kilometres from the front line, give or take. I get out of the car. A doctor comes out to welcome us. He is wearing military-style boots, and the Kalashnikov machine gun that he is holding in his hand says it all: We are on the front line of the war. He is none other than Dr. Ahmad, whom we talked about in the car: an anesthesiologist and the commander of the army's medical services corps in the Al-Bukamal region. He asks me how I'm doing and welcomes me. I appreciate his medical services corps appearance. Our arrival seems to have had a positive effect as the sound of the artillery shells seems to be receding a little farther away. I suddenly feel fear rising in my heart. I fear for my life; for this sweet life. I am so scared that even though the explosions are 4 kilometers away, I'm still concerned that one will hit me. I'm really and truly scared.

I'm looking at the large dirt yard of the field hospital, which used to be the house of one of the fugitive leaders of ISIS. He is not present to see the lengths the Iranian fighters go to in order to establish the congregational prayers. They spread a carpet in the courtyard and call out the call to prayer, handing out the cakes of baked clay[24], which are then passed from hand to hand. I walk to the entrance of the two-story building of the hospital. There has been heavy fighting in the area this afternoon. Moaning sounds are let out by the wounded from inside the building. They are the sounds of pain returning after the injured return to consciousness. In my opinion, these moans are not let out due to pain here and in this region. These moans are symptoms of being away from heaven, and being turned back from its gate. Three new wounded soldiers are brought in. I go near the ambulances. I can smell blood and the scent of medical alcohol. The young man lying on the stretcher is writhing in pain. Without the need for any further examination, it is clear that his leg should be amputated from above his ankle. It's the last moments that his foot will continue to be with him. I have seen a lot of wounds, blood, and surgeries, but everything is different on the field of battle. I have become engaged in the pain and injury of this young man. We are all like a big family here.

After the prayers, Dr. Ahmad and Dr. Karīm want to stop by some medical posts on the front line. When I hear that they want to go to the front line, I insist that they take me with them. They are surprised

---

[24] [These are used by the Shī'a to place their foreheads on when in the position of prostration in prayer, in accordance with the instruction of the Prophet and the Imams that one's forehead should always touch the ground (and nothing else) when in the position of prostration.]

that I am not tired after having travelled for such a long distance. I don't know how tired I am; all I know is that the closer I get to the front line, the closer I get to my dream of participating in a *jihād*.

As soon as the prayers are finished, I run to the car and take a seat so I don't get left behind. I am excited at the prospect of finally being able to be on the front line. I want to grab a rifle and dive behind the embankments of the front line. I want to smell the soil of the embankment and the gunpowder, and hear bullets buzz past my ears, and say *Allāhu akbar!* as I lob grenades towards the enemy. The driver suddenly puts his foot on the gas, and my dream reaches its peak. We start going up and down on this bumpy and narrow dirt road. Dr. Ahmad and Dr. Karīm duck their heads and tell me to do the same. We are in the range of the Kornet-guided missiles again. The cost of buying large quantities of Kornet-guided missiles is even higher than covering Al-Bukamal's streets and alleys with that polyethylene sheeting. I can't believe that all these costs can be covered by the sale of historical artifacts to the West. After all, how many Palmyras does Syria have, and how many of its historical artifacts have survived ISIS's barbarism for them to be able to cover these heavy expenses. I cover my head with my hands. The driver is going full throttle now. The engine howls and the car is moving forward at speed.

As the sun sets and darkness falls, the roads become narrower and more entangled. The closeness of the sound of bullets passing by and the sound of shrapnel tells me that we are one step away from the line; but we can't find the way to reach it. Houses and their shadows are now indistinguishable from each other. A soldier could emerge from the darkness at any moment and block our path. The driver slows the car down, and we proceed cautiously through the winding dark alleyways. Dr. Ahmad checks with the guys back at our station to see where we should be heading. He chats with them casually, laughing occasionally, completely oblivious to the fact that we are entirely lost. We reach the end of the alley, which we discover has been blocked with a few barrels and some scrap iron. Taking the wrong path and getting lost has been the cause of many people being taken captive by ISIS. I'm getting very anxious now. We have to go back the way we came. Dr. Ahmad still laughs:

'Ahmad! Ahmad! Sayyid Abbās!'

'Go ahead, Hāji'

'We still haven't been able to find your position.'

Anxiety washes over my heart in waves with every burst of static of the two-way radio.

'Hāji, did you go past Ya'qūb and the car mechanic's shop?'

'Yeah.'

'Take the paved road to the left until it's no longer paved and you reach the blue-eye.'

The driver is bent over the steering wheel, trying to make his way through the darkness. Dr. Ahmad is still talking to Sayyid Abbās on the other way of the two-way radio, and shows the way to the driver with the antenna of his radio. We finally find the outpost after much trial and error and confusion. It is a large house that belongs to one of the locals of the village of Sukayrīya. Its front yard is large enough to accommodate ambulances entering it in order to evacuate the injured. Five ambulances are parked in the yard, which means that we are close to an active front line. The hotter the front line, the greater the number of ambulances that are assigned to each battalion. There are black patches of spilt diesel scattered throughout the yard. I go forward. The acrid smell of blood fills my nostrils. The black patches turn out to be blood stains that have blackened the soil.

The crossfire has intensified. I can hear the sound of 120 mm mortars whistling past my ears. I find out later that the reason for the artillery fire is that we are right next to the materiel warehouse. The ground shakes constantly with the force of explosions. I have struck up a conversation with Ali, who oversees the outpost. We go up to the roof. The reek of a large garland of garlic hanging in the stairwell fills my nostrils. Garlic is a staple of Syrian cuisine, at least in this area. The guys have not touched it. They haven't even moved it because of its odor. We are only trustees when we have no choice but to enter people's houses. We take nothing, and don't even move anything unless we have to, even this large garland of reeking garlic. I am thrilled to witness how the frequency of the guys' radios are tuned in to that of their commander's. I say commander, but he is more like a father to them. I'm talking about Hāj Qāsim [General Soleimāni]. He spent a night right here in this city, in the house of an absentee resident who was a Dāesh (ISIS) supporter.

General Soleimāni was a commander concerning whom Abu Bakr al-Baghdadi stated that if he was captured by ISIS, they would burn him like they burned the Jordanian pilot. Before leaving the house, General Soleimāni wrote the owner of the house a note addressing him as 'brother', and asking him to forgive him for his having occupied his house without his permission. He prayed for him and asked him to pray for the general as well. He wrote down the phone number of his home in Iran so that the owner of the house could get in touch with him so that General Soleimāni would not be in his debt. We, who were the foot soldiers of this commander, would not move a smelly garland of garlic out of our way when using someone else's house during conditions of war, and we would also use the water we needed to make our ritual ablutions sparingly; and many other considerations of the sort...

Fatigue is written all over Ali's face, but he does not allow that to interfere with the work that has to be done. In war, you only sit down to catch your breath when there is nothing left to do; and that situation never arises, of course. The work is over when the war is over, so sleep and rest must be relegated to after one's martyrdom.

Threads of Compassion

Ali told us that there were nearly 40 wounded this afternoon. Caring for forty "packs"[25] and cleaning up after them is a tiring business. Now I understand the reason for the large blood stains that had darkened the soil of the yard. I am eager to work at this outpost. Not because of the large number of wounded soldiers that needed to be cared for but because of its proximity to the front line. Here, one is in the heart of the *jihād,* and martyrdom greets you every morning and waves his hand at you.

The sky is lit in the distance with the light of explosions. My mind picks up its abacus again and starts to calculate ISIS's income and that of the combatants. I review the information that I garnered by reading articles about their financial resources. These included the sale of women and girls as slaves, which came into their possession after they captured various cities and towns, as well as taking hostages and exchanging these hostages for money, as well as the looting of banks in cities such as Mosul. I don't remember the exact figures, but I do remember that after looting the banks of Mosul, ISIS became the wealthiest terrorist group in the world. But even granting that, it still wouldn't be able to splurge on buying weapons like they have. There will naturally be

---

[25] The name given to the unit of caring for a casualty of war, from controlling his bleeding to dressing his wounds and preparing him to be released from the care of the medical ward.

a limit on how much money they have and how much they will be able to spend, as their wealth is limited and is not a bottomless pit. I work my abacus again. This time, I look at Syria's mineral resources and fossil fuel reserves and control of its essential oil and gas fields such as the ones in Deir ez-Zūr. ISIS sells barrels of crude oil to dealers for $12, who send the oil to Europe and America through controlled networks. But why do they sell $20/ barrel oil at $12/ barrel? The question is still stuck in my mind like a thorn: Where does the money for so many weapons come from?

I want to continue to stay on the roof. I take in a deep breath. The smell of dirt and gunpowder. The cold smell of the night. Except for the medical station and a few other houses, the rest of the buildings are single stories. Sakayrīya is like a flat plate, every corner of which can be seen from the rooftop of the medical station. Some night vision binoculars would be really handy now. We could sleep right here on the rooftop and use the night vision binoculars to monitor 360 degrees around us, including the Dāesh front line, which is 200 meters ahead.

An hour later, we are sitting around the dinner table, waiting to be served Indomie, a front-line specialty and royal feast that had been promised us since we arrived at the post. I'm so hungry it's as if I had walked every one of these 800 kilometres. We all chat and have a good time waiting for dinner to be served; Ali and I, and Dr. Ahmad and Dr. Karīm, and a few other young men like Ali, whom I have just gotten to know, but who I have become so familiar with, as if I have known them for years. None of us give a second thought to the explosions and the shrapnel that flies over our heads. None of us are concerned about the battle of life and death that is taking place within a couple of hundred yards of us. We are just excited about the delicious dinner that we are going to be served. I look at a piece of paper on which something is written and which is pasted on the mirror in the room. It reads *'Alā hubbak, Ali.* I am trying to figure out how it would translate into Persian, when Ali comes to my aid.

'It says, 'For the sake of my love for you, Ali.'

Before I ask if the owner of the house is Shī'a, he indicates another piece of paper on the wall with the movement of his eyes. It is a line of poetry that reads,

اذا حدك ما بقيت و على كتفك ما غفيت
يعني انا ما عشت بعمري و ع الدنيا ما جيت

*If I'm not beside you and I don't get to sleep in your arms,
it's as if I haven't lived at all and wasn't even born.*

I don't bother to do an exact translation; all I know is that it has a subtle romantic meaning. And at the bottom of the sheet, 'Ali' is written in small lettering. So it dawns on me that the scroll is addressed to the owner of the house, and that the words are written in his wife's handwriting, and that we are sitting in their bedroom. Needless to say, the boys have not touched these notes either.

The psychologist in me thinks what a clever woman the woman of this house must be and what a clever way she has employed to put words on paper to move the heart of her husband. I am thinking these thoughts when the Indomie is placed in front of me. It is a plate full of yellow noodles, not unlike our own Ramen noodles, spiced in the style of the Arabs. And the taste... wow! I have yet to learn that a royal dinner in a war zone doesn't get any better than this.

My patience has been on duty since the early morning. Dr. Karīm, Ahmad and I are heading towards al-Harī village, and I'm wondering why we didn't stay at the Sakayrīya outpost. I was thinking to myself, 'If we weren't going to stay there, why did we go all the way out there? Why don't we settle down somewhere? Anywhere. Why is my posting not clear like everyone else's? Why haven't I been told which group I should go to?' My heart is chomping at the bit to pick up a gun and start my *jihād*, but I'm left wondering what will happen next within a few steps of the front line.

Dr. Ahmad points to the far distance, somewhere in the heart of the desert. The seventy-kilometer-long front line starts from the border of Iraq and extends to al-Mayādīn. It is a front line that is chock full of abandoned villages. Al-Harī is a village at the beginning of the front line; it is a village on the eastern side of Al-Bukamal and on the banks of the Euphrates. It's a village of people who have been afflicted by the war.

The Euphrates divides Al-Bukamal into two parts of about 30% and 70% each. The part that falls north of the Euphrates makes up 30% of the city and is under ISIS control. The part that falls south of the Euphrates makes up the other 70% and is in our hands. The village of Al-Harī is in the southernmost part of Al Bukamal. It is a village full of women on the outskirts of the Euphrates. It is as if the waters of the Euphrates have washed them all away from where they were and brought them to Al-Harī, where women can be seen who used to live in Deir ez-Zūr, Al-Mayādīn, Sālihīya, and Al-Bukamal. These are the women of the areas that have been liberated from the blades of ISIS; they are the wives of men whose loyalty is to ISIS. Each of the camps has been identified, screened, separated, and transferred to Al-Harī, which is the last point before the Iraqi border. Their men are busy fighting us, and we are busy transporting their women and children to safety. Are you surprised? I was surprised, too. Not here, of course, but a little later when I realized what we are doing here in Al-Harī. In addition to this immigrant population, we also have the tribal population of Al-Bukamal, who you can be certain are

100% Dāesh without the need for any screening or investigation.

I have not seen any scene in any other city like the scene of our arrival in Al-Harī. There was a huge crowd of women and children waiting for a car to pass by the road so that they could ask for food and water. There was maybe one old man for every hundred women. The driver knew that he had to drive slowly. The women showed the bellies of their babies, saying things like,

'I swear to God, he's hungry.'

They are wearing shirts in the style of the Arabs, whose colors have faded. Their faces are deeply sunburnt in the dry and cold air of this desert region. Most of their faces are covered with the shawls that they have wrapped around their heads. We can only see their eyes and hear their voices; looks and voices that betray a deep female fatigue.

Dr. Ahmad distributes the water and bread he had placed in the car among them; but a crowd of this size was not going to be ameliorated by a few bottles of mineral water and a few pieces of bread. Even if their hunger was sated, what about all the skin and digestive diseases that they obviously suffered from?

I lower my window. These are people who used to live under the dominion of the ISIS government and who are now begging for a morsel of food that will keep them from dying. These are people who used to cooperate with the ISIS government when the region was under their dominion. There is no limit to the places where ignorance will lead human beings. Their ignorance is such that it is not possible to tarry among this crowd. Dr. Ahmad says that these are walking human bombs. He's right. Seven months is enough time to train someone who is loyal and who is willing to sacrifice him- or herself, let alone seven years. ISIS has spent so much time in this city and has worked so hard on brainwashing these people that even now that they have seen the patent hypocrisy of its government, it is not unlikely for some of them to seek to open a path to heaven by wearing suicide belts and exploding them in our midst.

I am carried away by my free imagination once more. It looks at the situation from another angle, taking me along for the ride to a parallel universe where this time, the guys who are here in Syria are in their homes [back in Iran]. I'm talking about the Defenders of the Shrine. Rather than coming out here to fight, they follow the news from their homes like armchair strategists, committed to the theory that the war in Syria is an internal affair and has nothing to do with anyone else, let alone with Iran. The news reports a war in which the *takfiris* take over Syria and Iraq one village and town and province at a time, and continue in this fashion until they reach Iran. Our cities are conquered, and they raise their flags and write on our walls, 'We're here to stay'. They separate the men from the women and children, and lead them to the main square of the city where they cut their heads off in front of their families, after which all that will remain is ISIS and the river of blood that they have shed, and the women and children of the men they have massacred. You know what will happen next, and I know it too, so I won't say it. Not because we both already know, but because of the bitter taste that dries up the words in one's mouth and does not allow one to put them to paper.

Now, we have conquered the region here from Al-Mayādīn to Al-Bukamal. Nor have we cut off anyone's head. It is just us and the women and children of the men who are fighting us. What do we do?

We go from region to region and load these people on buses and bring them to Al-Harī. And what I mean by "these people" are those who have been proven in our investigations to be members of Dāesh. Those who, when asked where their father or husband is, say, 'With Dāesh'. A hundred to a hundred and fifty of these women are brought to this area every day. They arrive with a big bundle tied around their waist. There is invariably an infant or toddler tied on top of the bundle, and inside it is the rest of their belongings. We gather them here from the conquered areas from al-Mayādīn to the Iraqi border in order to make it easier for us to monitor the other half of ISIS's forces. But why Al-Harī? Because it is like a closed container. A container between Al-Bukamal and Al-Qā'im in Iraq. The Al-Bukamal road towards the east and Al-Mayādīn is in our hands and is thus blocked to them. To the west and Iraq's Al-Qā'im, it is in the hands of Iraq and is even more blocked to them. To the north is the Euphrates River, disputed territory but within our firing range, and in which we will fire upon anything that moves. And to the south, the desert stretches as far as the eye can see. These geographical realities have turned Al-Harī into a closed container. Now what would ISIS do if it were in our place? What would it do with this closed container outside of which no voices could be heard anywhere? The most that their sense of justice could muster would be a mass grave in the desert. And that does not even take into consideration the bitter events that would inevitably occur before their captives would reach their mass grave. Now, what have *we* done with this container? We have clothed, housed, fed, and provided clean water for them.

    I place both sides of the war in the plates of a scale. On one plate is their ignorance, which is heavier than their weapons and facilities. There are hungry women and children who take bread from our hands while we do not know whether or not they are wearing a belt that is set to explode under their long shirts, which they wear in the Arab style. And on the other plate is our side, by which I mean Hāj Qāsim [Soleimāni] and his way of thinking. A way of thinking that says women and children should be able to leave the city safely. A way of thinking that is expressed in his letter to the owner of the house, who was a member of ISIS in which he spent a night. A way of thinking that provides shelter for ISIS families. By 'us' I mean soldiers who do not touch a garland of garlic or the papers on the walls of people's houses. That is, people like Dr. Ahmad, whose heart aches for the future of the children of this land. Someone who brought a few bottles of water and some bread so that he could do what little was in his power for the women and children of people who were doing their best to kill him. By 'us' I mean the soldiers of the Haydariyūn, Zainabiūn and Fātimiūn.

I look at the women who have fallen on hard times who have gathered around our car. The bulging belly of one of them catches my attention. She's pregnant. I am concerned that she might receive an unintended blow to her stomach in the crowd. I want to give her a piece of bread when I see the woman next to her, who is also pregnant. I look around. There is another one behind them that is in the same condition. I am flabbergasted. They are all pregnant! I tell Dr. Ahmad about what I have observed, and he shakes his head sadly and says,

'And those of them who are not pregnant probably already have a toddler in tow.'

Dr. Ahmad talks about the statistics of deaths during childbirth of this region. He says that even if the mother and the baby survive the childbirth, their lives will definitely be in danger later, given this level of poverty, hunger, and the terrible health conditions that go along with it. I don't know what to say. As a nurse, my heart goes out to any mother who has to give birth

Threads of Compassion

to her baby under these conditions, but as someone who came here to fight, I don't understand what these statistics have to do with us? I feel sorry for these women and children, but I don't feel as sorry for them as I do for the parents of a girl whose daughter's raw heart was eaten by the husbands of these women.[26]

I start at hearing a loud sound and when one of the tires of our car hits something. I notice a few young boys who are standing in the dirt with dejected spirits, just like their ball that has just burst under the tire of our car. Karīm hits the dashboard to signal the driver to stop the car. Muhammad hesitates. He expresses his concern in Arabic that it is dangerous to stop here. Karīm overrules him wordlessly and quickly with a gentle look. The children hesitate to come forward, but they take courage after seeing the smile on Karīm's face and slowly circle around him. He jokes and laughs with them, strokes their heads, and gives them two thousand Syrian liras to make up for the damage caused to their ball by the car. They can't believe it. All that money for an old plastic ball? Karīm asks them if they are satisfied a couple of times, in order to put his mind at ease. I'm delighted to witness this kindness and to see the children laughing. And I'm delighted and

---

[26] This horrible incident occurred in the summer of 2013 after the fall of Mosul in the Diyala province of Iraq. Hāj Qāsim [Soleimāni] makes mention of it as one of the crimes of ISIS in his speech at the 40th anniversary of the martyrdom of Sha'bān Nasīrī in 2016.

proud to be under the command of the commander who has trained these kinds of soldiers.

When the inspection of this troubled region is over, I hope I will finally join the other fighters. I am ready to be sent anywhere but here. I secretly ask Lady Zainab ﷺ to intercede on my behalf and to have me sent to one of the places which those who have become the Defenders of her Shrine have been sent to. I have already seen this place and have spent a lifetime in hospitals and don't need any more of that. I'm after guns and bullets and flying shards of shrapnel!

We arrive at a large house in the center of Al-Harī. There are hungry women and children there too. There are many of them behind the iron door of the house, and there are some inside the house too. They are gathered in a disorderly and crowded queue. It turns out to be a queue for water and for medicine.

'We opened a small clinic here two days ago to prevent the spread of new diseases. But we don't have the necessary resources or manpower. We just have a little medicine, which we have taken from our own quotas.'

My eyes widen in surprise. I thought that what we did here was only to provide housing, water, and food. I had no idea that we also provided them with medicine. Whatever I might not know about this war, I *do* know the meaning of "taking them from our own quotas". Medical quotas were being spent on ISIS families. What kind of medicine? Acetaminophen, which can be found in every home's first aid kit, but is

Threads of Compassion

as valuable as gold in a war zone. And then to turn around and share one's own medicine, of which there is always a shortage, with the families of cannibals who show us their claws and teeth on the opposite side of the front line?? I can't think of anything to say to Dr. Ahmad. I think there must be some principles in this war that I am unaware of. There must be some expediency or reason for what they are doing. Maybe we are buying the freedom of some people by giving medicine to our enemies' families. Maybe we have more medicine that I thought we did. Maybe...

What do I care anyway? I head off to take a walk around the house or 'clinic' to cool off.

There is a small, warm room on the first floor. The Syrian doctor and nurse don't even have time to scratch their heads. They sweat, see to the needs of the next patient, then sweat some more. The medicine is so scarce that the pills are dispensed one at a time to the patients. I don't know what good a single antibiotic pill will do, when its dosage must be consumed for the full period that is indicated. I feel sorry... for the doctors and nurses, for the patients, and for ourselves, for depriving ourselves of much needed medicine. I roll up my sleeves to help. There is no time to get to know each other. We only tell each other what our names are. I make my way confidently to the medicine cabinet. The beauty of medical science is its language, which is the same everywhere in the world. That is, before I went to Syria, of course. In Syria, I realized that the language of medicine is also different. For example, acetaminophen, which is called acetaminophen everywhere in the world, has a completely different name in Syria. Here, they call it Citamol. Sterile gauze is also known by another name here: *shāsh muʿaqqam*. I have yet to learn that this is the Alice in Wonderland of pharmacology. Amazing made-in-Syria stuff such as ceftriaxone 1500,[27] dexamethasone syrup, and diazepam syrup are available in tablet form everywhere else in the world but are available here as syrups.

Given this, I had no choice but to resort to the international language of pointing and sign language. It is the best way to help people whose needs never wane even for a brief moment. The people here constantly call us, have innumerable questions, and continually ask for medicine. No matter how hard we work, we cannot get ahead of the work that has to be done. A little girl enters the room with burns from her elbows down to her fingers. No one sees to her; everyone is too busy already. Boiling water has scalded the skin of her hand. The child is in tremendous pain. The pain of the burn cuts to the marrow of her bones, yet, instead of crying out loud, she just lets out moans. I hold her hand under cold water to reduce the inflammation of the underlying tissue. I disinfect the open blisters and start dressing them. One of the

---

[27] A strong, broad-spectrum antibiotic that is available in Iran up to 1000 mg doses and whose injection is allowed only in hospitals. I saw 1500 mg doses of this medicine in Syria.

Threads of Compassion

guards comes over to us for the third time. This time he scolds the little girl, saying,

'Lower your face!'

He wants her to lower her veil. I am shocked at his insistence. I have yet to learn that when you are dealing with members of ISIS and their families, you can never know whether the person standing one step away from you is ill and in need of medical attention, or is a suicide bomber. Is the person a woman or a man? You have to rend their veil to be certain.

I suddenly come to my senses and realize that I have been dispensing medicine to the families of members of ISIS in tandem with the Syrian doctor and nurses for the past two hours, and that Dr. Ahmad and Dr. Karīm must be waiting for me. I say a quick goodbye and leave. It is close to sunset. The crowd inside and behind the doors of the clinic has thinned somewhat. People know that the working hours of the clinic end when it gets dark. I look for Dr. Ahmad and Dr. Karīm, but they are nowhere to be found. Someone tells me,

'Your friend gave this for me to give to you. He said to call him whenever you need him.'

Abūta introduces himself and hands me the two-way radio.

'My friend?'

'Sure. You know, Doctor Karīm.'

Abūta is one of the veterans of the region. He is a very kindly man; kind and friendly. He has a master's degree in psychology. I tell him that he is one of those kinds of doctors who are kind. He laughs and says that I haven't met Hasan yet, one of the kind and good-natured people among the Fātemiyūn corps. He says that it has been more than thirteen months since Hasan has been back to Afghanistan. He himself is leaving for Iran in a week and envy's Hasan's being able to stay for so long. I have yet to learn that leaving here is even harder than getting here. Abūta, who is on his fourth tour of duty, understands this. He has not seen his little sons for seventy days but is more concerned about Hasan. He says Hasan is concerned about the situation of Afghanistan's borders; that he is afraid to leave and not be able to come back to serve Khānūm Jān (Lady Zainab).

The title Khānūm Jān [28] is so fitting and so sweet when spoken with the strong [Afghani] accent of the Fātemiyūn[29] corps. In my opinion, it is the most suitable Persian translation of [the title] *aqīla al-arab* (wise one of the Arabs): a wise and noble lady who manages all matters on her own. A strong lady who is full of loving kindness. The lady on whom all hopes are pinned for the removal of the shadow of war and for saving this country from destruction. Khānūm Jān.

Abūta looks for Hasan in the courtyard so that he can point him out to me, but he is not there. Abūta envies Hasan, and I envy them both. Their duty here is

---

[28] [This honorific which is used for Lady Zainab literally means 'dear lady' or 'beloved lady'.]

[29] The corps of volunteer fighters from Afghanistan.

clear; but what about me? I have been in Syria for three days and it is still not clear what I am to do here. That must be what my job is: to envy others.

Dr. Karīm and Ahmad enter the clinic. I go towards them so that we can leave, but they turn away from my direction. I'm taken aback. It's as if they don't want me to participate in their discussion. Every now and then, their eyes turn towards me. They examine me a little, then continue talking to each other. I feel certain that my tour of duty is in some kind of trouble. A deep sadness nestles in my heart. I think to myself, 'Do you mean to say that I have been waiting for all these years to come here, and that I have come so far, only to return now that I am one step away from the front line? Time stands still. My head feels too heavy for my body. I am very concerned about what will happen next. There is no possibility of any "next" for me at all. How can I even contemplate returning to Iran? Everyone I know knows how much I tried to be sent to Syria during these last five years. So then I should go back and say what? And after just three days? I feel like a schoolboy who has done something wrong and is waiting outside the office of the principal to see if he will be expelled or will be allowed to stay. My heart is beating fast.

Their meeting finally comes to an end. I prepare myself to hear the worst news of my life. Dr. Karīm starts the preamble.

'Ehsān! They have ordered us to build a hospital for the people in this area as soon as possible.'

Threads of Compassion

What he means by "the people in this area" are the walking bombs that could go off at any minute with the pressing of a button whose wires are attached to the explosives they wear around their torsos. What he means is the families of the members of ISIS. Although I don't really care one way or another and am waiting for them to clarify what *my* assignment is, I ask,

'For *these* people?'

'Yeah. For *these* people.'

I have nothing to say. And if I did have anything to say about it, it would have nothing to do with me, so I say,

'God bless you. May your reward be with Lady Zainab ﷺ.'

Dr. Ahmad continues the discussion.

'We must close this clinic and replace it with a maternity hospital.'

Surprised isn't really the word anymore that would describe my state of mind. I am officially freaking out. It seems accommodations, food, potable water, and medicine were not enough. Now we're going to build them a *maternity* ward??

'A *maternity* hospital?! Four kilometres from the ISIS front line for ISIS women???"

Dr. Ahmad gives Dr. Karīm a meaningful look.

'The situation of pregnant women in the area is critical. We are taking casualties every night.'

I want to say, well, if the 'situation is critical', what in Hell does it matter to *us*?? At least it doesn't

Threads of Compassion

matter to *me*. And then I think, For the love of God, just tell me if I'm going to stay or be sent back.

Before I can say anything, Dr. Karīm puts me out of my misery.

'Ehsān, setting up and administering this hospital will be your responsibility.'

All the words I had prepared to say shrivel up, along with myself. My dreams and prayers for the past five years for coming to Syria rush through my mind like a flood. The last time I begged Lady Zainab ﷺ to give me permission to wage *jihād* was the evening of the day before yesterday in her shrine. I want to step on the gas and go straight back to Lady Zainab's ﷺ shrine and stand in front of her dome and lodge my complaint: 'Setting up and administering a *hospital?* Is that your idea of waging *jihād?* And an obstetrics and gynecology hospital at that??'

Dr. Karīm and Ahmad have said what they had to say. Here in the heart of Syria, four kilometres from the ISIS front line, and one step away from my dream, they tell me to lay down my rifle and open a hospital. My brain refuses to issue any command. I am left only with my heart, which yearns for *jihād*. I remember my first meeting with Dr. Ahmad, which was just yesterday. A doctor who wore army boots and an army uniform. I remember the tired women on the side of the Al-Harī road. Women who were carrying another life inside their bodies. A small and innocent pulse that beats with the purpose of stepping into this world. I think of the women and children who are the victims

Threads of Compassion

of ignorance; of women who live within walking distance of Khānūm Jān ﷺ, of mothers who are worried about their children. I think of the fact that Imam Husain ﷺ was concerned for the welfare of the ranks of his enemy's army until the last moment of the battle and until his dying breath. Not all of them were his enemies. Even if they themselves had enmity towards him, at a minimum, their children were not his enemies. Khānūm Jān ﷺ is none other than that brother's sister. How could I have expected her not to be concerned about the condition of these mothers? Khānūm Jān ﷺ is the daughter of a mother who was always concerned for her neighbours, and who always kept them in her prayers, irrespective of how mindless they might be of neighbors' rights. So, how is it possible for the daughter of such a mother not to be concerned about her neighbours?

I had come to defend the sacrosanctity of Khānūm Jān ﷺ. These neighbours are residents of the neighbourhood of a shrine whose sanctity I had spent the last five years trying to reach and defend. What that defence consists of is not something that is up to me. Nor is it a matter in the hands of Dr. Karīm or Dr. Ahmad. It's in Khānūm Jān's ﷺ own hands. She tests each person in a specific way, and I now saw that she had chosen to test me by testing my loyalty and perhaps my patience.

I take a look around the clinic. ISIS women are still moving about: the tired and disappointed neighbours of Khānūm Jān ﷺ. Maybe she has brought me all the way here so that I can make her neighbors feel better. Seeing the faces of some of these mothers and the children who are following them, I keep the words I had wanted to express to Karīm to myself. I cannot shirk this responsibility. A couple comes to mind.

تقدیر عاشقان چو به دستان دلبر است
باشد که میل یار کجا می‌برد مرا

Seeing as the fate of the lover is in the hands of the beloved,
Wherever my beloved's desire takes me, that is where I will go.

I turn to Dr. Karīm and Dr. Ahmad and say, 'I am at the service of Khānum Jān's ﷻ neighbours.'

Threads of Compassion

Chapter Two Photos

What remains of the ruins of the city of Al-Bukamal. What can be seen behind me in the lower image and in the image above are parts of the thick polyethylene sheeting that ISIS used to cover the streets in order to mask their movements from detection by our drones.

Threads of Compassion

Abūta. My likable and kind friend was a nurse in Al-Bukamal.>

Hasan, a soldier in the Fatemiyūn volunteer Corps, whose ten-month-old daughter was in Herāt while he stayed for an extended 13-month tour of duty in Syria. >

Threads of Compassion

The small clinic whose yard is full of people waiting to be examined by our doctors and to have the medicines that they need dispensed.

Threads of Compassion

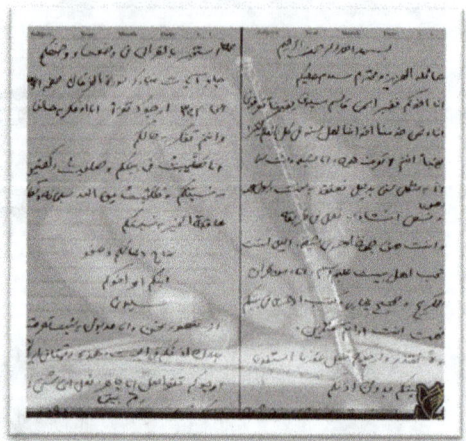

General Qāsim Suleimāni's handwritten note that he left for the owner of the house he stayed in, who was an ISIS member.

Indomie noodles! The memorable royal food of the front line.

3

My mother calls out to me. She's in tears. I open my eyes. Her face is wet with tears. My father takes my hand in his and kisses my head. The morphine is still coursing through my body and making me feel numb. I ask about Somayyeh. I'm told She's alive, as are our children. I wish I could go see them. Tears roll down my cheeks. I pray to Khānūm Jān ﷺ under my breath so that she can help me bear the situation I'm in. I miss Fātima. I wish that at least Somayyeh was by my side. I feel such a need to hear her voice and to have it course through my soul and calm me down.

Threads of Compassion

We have become like tenants who have little money and high expectations. We are fussy about where to live, and the places where we would like to live, we can't afford. Every house we choose has some defect that prevents it from being converted into a hospital. After sunset, we put on our shawls and hats to go and inspect the latest house that one of the trustworthy locals has suggested. It used to be the house of one of the leaders of ISIS, who has been killed in battle. It has high walls and trees that act as security barriers. It's similar to a house of terror. The silence and the moonlight have cast a shadow on the house. The lock of its entry door has not been turned since its owner was killed two years ago. The house's owner is not here now to see who is now opening the door that his guards used to open and close for him with all the dignity and respect he used to command. The door opens with a loud creak. First, the guys from the bomb squad go in to check the situation and neutralise any threat. I enter and take a look around the half-acre front yard. There is a two-story house built of stone in the middle of the lot. There is a driveway that leads right up to the large front porch, which tells me that the house used to be very busy and that the drivers of the commanders used to drive them right up to the porch rather than let them out in the street at the entry door to the front yard. It seemed to me that all these facilities and rituals were a bit too much for one of the low-ranking leaders of ISIS, whose name many of its members probably didn't even know. The bomb squad give us permission to enter the building. The flashlight lights a circle of light in front of my feet. The entrance hall is so big that a 3x4 meter carpet wouldn't fill it. A large wooden door opens into the living room from the entrance hall, and a smaller door leads from the guest hall to the inner spaces of the house that are reserved for family members. The smaller door might have led to a meeting room to which the outer circle would not have been invited. We enter the living room through the large wooden double doors. The living room opens onto the kitchen, two bedrooms, and a den whose walls have been lined with pillows and mattresses in the Arab style. The first bedroom is the primary bedroom and has a door that leads to the yard. A huge bed with one-meter-high leg posts occupies most of the space of the room. Its rough carvings are closer to carvings that are made in ivory, such as dragons and animals with horns and the like, than to delicate curves and flowers and nightingales. There is a terrible, repulsive vibe to the room which makes me turn around and exit the room immediately. I climb up the wide stone stairway which is located in the middle of the hall. There are two bedroom suites and a large balcony with stone railings on the second floor. The guys I'm with call each other in loud and excited voices to show each other their discoveries. One of them had come across another huge bed, and another had seen a new set of pots and pans in the kitchen. And someone had discovered a set of strobe lights that emitted green, red, and yellow lighting from the ceiling, betraying the kinds of nights that this cold and deserted building had accommodated in the dark. But for me, it was a large building full of rooms that was greatly suited for being converted into a hospital.

The first thing we did on the morning of the next day was to transform the house of horror into a hospital. No matter how much we work, there is still work and more work to be done. A lot of my time is occupied looking for beds, mobile partitions, medicine, medical equipment, electricity generators, and everything else you can think of that a hospital needs. We are under a lot of time pressure because we know that the babies that are on the way will not wait for us to equip the hospital but will come into the world in their own time and whenever they feel like it.

Everything is in fast-forward mode. We have no time to sleep or to eat. Each person has taken responsibility for a particular aspect of the project and is pursuing it relentlessly until the work is done. Abūta, Hasan and Ābid, the soldiers from the Fatemiyūn corps, are the most diligent and productive. Ābid knows the area and its various outstations like the back of his hand. One must be in possession of two maps during any war: a map of the region and a map of the people involved. Ābid has both. And he places all of his knowledge in the palm of my hand.

I split my time between the hospital and the clinic, the same clinic where I learned that the language of medicine in Syria is different from the language of medicine everywhere else in the world. We are going to start this hospital regardless. Until the hospital opens, the medical team is stationed at the clinic and sees to the needs of the people there. The team consists of Maryam and Karīma and Ismāʿīl and Doctor Ali. Other than Ali, the rest are nurses. I met Ismāʿīl and Ali on the first day I came to Al-Harī. They were the ones I helped for two hours, sweating in that hot room. I did not see Maryam or Karīma that day. Dr. Karīm has said a lot of good things about them. They are a couple of young ladies who complement each other nicely. They are very young, both being under twenty-five years of age. One is short and the other one is tall. One is quiet and calm, and the other one is talkative and lively. One is jolly and the other one is serious; but both are kind. According to what Karīm has said, they have come 650 kilometres from Mashfi al-Jāmiʿī, Aleppo's medical school, to work with the Axis of Resistance. Where? In Al-Bukamal, which is full of ISIS members and sympathizers. In the morning, they wrap their shawls around their heads in the Arabic style and come to the clinic and will stay there and work as long as there are people there who need to be seen to. And then, after all of the patients have left, they stay and restock the shelves with medicine with the same cheery demeanour that they had when they started their day in the morning.

My first task is to change their living quarters; that room they are in, with its cold, blue walls and the bad smell of sewage rising up behind the building, is no place to live. Nobody should live there, even for an hour, let alone anyone who will be part of the critical personnel of the hospital. Before nightfall, Abūta finds a one-story house for them that has three rooms. It doesn't have much in terms of natural light, but it is better than that smelly blue room. We decided that Abūta and I would sleep in one of the rooms, Maryam and Karīma would take another of the rooms, and Ali and Ismāʿīl would take the third. Things wouldn't have gotten rolling so soon if it wasn't for Abūta. We are the same age, but it feels like he is a few years older than me. I think God kept him here so he would look out for Dr. Ehsān, because he is so skilful and has so much experience in dealing with the locals as well as with the regional officials.

I head for our new home from the hospital at the end of the night, exhausted. Abūta hasn't arrived yet. My feet are killing me. I lie down on my side in our room, folding my arm under my head. My imagination is working overtime, and thoughts rush into my mind by the dozen. I think of my children and how they must be asleep already. They have to get up first thing in the morning for school. But Somayyeh must be awake. She has washed the dishes, put Fātima to bed, and prepared the kids' lunches. She has so much work to do; I wish I could stop by and help her out and return right away. I wish this house had a phone.

Abūta is in the kitchen now, making dinner-preparation noises. I get up to go and help him. I tell him I feel like having Indomie (instant noodles). He laughs and says,

'What do you think this is, a five-star hotel? Indomie is served once a week here!'

'So what are we going to eat for the rest of the week?!'

'Potatoes!'

I understand and say no more. Abūta takes out an Indomie packet from his backpack and hands it to me. I turn on a burner of the gas stove with a big smile on my face. Before I have even had the chance to add the oil and spices, Maryam tightens her headscarf around her ears and runs into the kitchen, saying enthusiastically,

'Dr. Ehsān! It smells like you're cooking up some Indomie!'

The smell of Indomie has wafted to her nose. I gift the noodles and its broth to the girls. My stomach needs to be satisfied with potatoes tonight, even if it has become drunk with the smell of Indomie. If Maryam, Karīma and Ismā'īl are quick-tempered, Dr. Ali is the opposite. On the other hand, if he sees someone with a camera in his hands, he reacts as if someone has drawn a sword on him. He leaves the room immediately. I have yet to learn that people are afraid of cooperating with or being seen in the company of the Axis of Resistance. Not afraid for themselves so much as for their families, whom ISIS can hurt if they found out. Ali is no different. He is afraid that a photo of his presence with the Iranian crowd and in the company of the Axis of Resistance will fall into the wrong hands and that his whole family will be slaughtered in Idlib. This is the main reason for the limited availability of human resources. The fear of ISIS is still greater in people's hearts than is the strength of the Axis of Resistance. That fear is so strong that even if, like Ali, they get the equivalent of ten months' salary for ten days on the front lines, they still would not come here. The fear is so strong that they have no choice but to send Ismāʿīl, who is a 3rd semester student, to the front line here instead of a fully-qualified nurse.

After dinner, the bitter aroma of coffee fills the room. That same Bin Hasīb coffee that Dr Karīm bought for the medical team on the way over. Karīma pours a cup for each of us so that the coffee will wash the potatoes down. We are all completely exhausted and head to our rooms to get some sleep.

After the morning prayer, I can barely open my eyes from the fatigue left over from yesterday's work. I still have half an hour before I have to go to the hospital. I pull the blanket over my head. I had just fallen asleep when someone shakes me by my shoulder. It is Abūta. When I open my eyes, he calls his friend Mahmoud excitedly.

'Mahmoud, come over! He's alive!'

I sit up. It must be late for them to have woken me.

'Doctor, we thought you were so scared you'd had a stroke in your sleep.'

Mahmoud chuckles and says, 'Were you pretending to be asleep, or were you so scared that you froze up?'

I don't understand what they're talking about. I stretch a little then ask,

'What time is it?'

It occurs to Mahmoud that I really was asleep. He says, 'Doctor, the fighter jet flew over, dropped its load and blew everything to kingdom come. Are you telling me that you really slept through all that??'

'What fighter jet?'

They laugh at how deeply I must have slept.

'Are you seriously telling us that you didn't hear the Russian fighter jet come and plow the Euphrates with its bombs and machineguns and leave?'

I finally realised that we were under the machine gun fire of a Russian fighter jet. I get up to go and wash my face. Mahmoud and Abūta are laughing loudly. They're talking about the loud sounds made by the fighter jet and the thoughts they had had about me. I have nothing to say in my own defence. I see that I have become the brunt of their jokes which are about the benefits of a good night's sleep.

At noon, our landlord arrives. He's a 70-year-old man, but he's energetic and lively. He enters the courtyard with 15 women of various ages and a baby girl. He has a frown on his face and orders us to vacate his house with a calmness that is typical of the Syrians. The womenfolk of his family have gathered around the courtyard and are sitting on the edge of the porch.

Threads of Compassion

There is nothing else that we can say. We gather our belongings and leave for the hospital. It's their house, and they have the right to it. They had left their home in the middle of the conflict, and now they have come back to it; that's all.

We hadn't fully settled in at the hospital yet when the voice of a blond-haired man echoed in the hospital's waiting room. It sounds like someone has gotten into an argument. I rush down the stairs. Karīm is trying to reason with him and calm him down. He repeats whatever the man says, and whatever Karīm says makes the blond-haired man speak louder. I'm not sure what to do. On one hand, I'm concerned that they will send me back to Iran, on the other hand, I'm really a nobody and shouldn't be interfering. I leave it to Karīm to resolve an issue that I don't know anything about. Karīm stresses his 20-year friendship with me, but the man is unmoved.

'Your 100-year-old friend doesn't cut it, doctor. Have you given any thought to the reputation of the Islamic Republic?'

That makes the hair of my body stand on end. What's going on here? Dr Karīm swears an oath in defence of my character. The man is not appeased and doesn't lower his voice.

'Doctor! It's not as if they're going to take the Iranian to their houses! All the Syrian women are going to come to *him*. All of the *unmarried* women!'

My ears have turned red. Karīm defends my character again and tries to appease the man.

Threads of Compassion

Their words kept running through my mind all day, making me feel all empty inside. I walk in the courtyard of the hospital, processing their words. I can't get up the courage to ask Karīm what the argument was about. I turn towards Khānūm Jān's ﻋﻠﻴﻬﺎ‌السلام shrine and make a prayer: *O you who have called me here, show me the way.*

Maryam and Karīma call me from the balcony, telling me that dinner is ready. They have gone all out in preparing the dinner spread. They are always kind and cheerful. They have made an appetizing arrangement of slices of potatoes, eggs, cucumbers, tomatoes, and pickles. They have served them on a platter with some yogurt. The local yogurt is served in a bowl where it has been shaped into small ruffles with the edge of a spoon, between which olive oil has been poured, topped with *za'tar*, which is a blend of powdered aromatic herbs. This team will return to Aleppo in the morning. That's why they have laid a dinner spread and invited us to join them. To be able to sit and have a homemade meal after all that work is a real treat. Maryam and Karīma try to put a brave face on their departure, but they are full of sad emotions and their eyes are wet with the tears that well up in them. If truth be told, I am too overcome with emotion and have no appetite. We recollect some of the memories that we shared and some of our own memories. They talk about Aleppo and its sights, and I talk about Arba'īn and its delicious falafels with confidence in my Arabic and with an accent that is even thicker than theirs.

We are standing in the middle of the courtyard of the maternity hospital. It is a well-equipped hospital, which includes an emergency room, examination rooms, a pharmacy, hospitalization wards, and EEG and ultrasound machines. The interior portion of the house and its meeting room have been turned into the emergency room and pharmacy. There is no more sign of that abandoned house of horrors. A hall that was surrounded by mattresses and pillows has been turned into the maternity ward of the hospital. The bedroom facing the courtyard has been assigned to the Fatemiyūn corps. The room near the kitchen is now my room, and rooms on the second floor are where the hospital staff rest. All this we were able to accomplish in 48 hours. The equipping of this hospital in the space of just two days is not something that could be accomplished by any team other than the one made up of Abūta, Ābid, and Hasan, who left the world and all its pleasures behind at Syria's borders.

After we make our morning prayers, each of us relaxes in our own quarters, satisfied with the hard work that we have done that has exhausted our bodies. Sleep comes over me. My mind is full of the hustle and bustle of the hospital. An ambulance arrives; a bed is being prepared in the emergency ward, as the hospital ward is full. I am waiting in the hospital courtyard to receive a consignment of medicine. Sleep blurs my thoughts. We are waiting in anticipation of the birth of our first baby. I hear the sound of a baby crying, the sound of a new life. A gentle warmth courses under my eyelids. I hear the sound of the PA system of the Imam Husain ﷺ Hospital of Mashhad calling my name. I hear the sound of a baby crying again. They call my name again. My mouth has taken on the flavour of sleep. I turn onto my side. I hear my name being called again. It's Dr. Ahmad's voice, on the two-way radio. I jump to attention.

'Ehsān Jān, are you ready?'

My voice is still sleepy. 'For what?'

'Your guests have arrived.'

My eyes open in curiosity. 'Which guests??'

'I doubt you know midwifery. The Aleppo medical team is close by now.'

His joke makes me laugh. After having set up the hospital, we had expected to do nothing but hang out for a week or so until we found volunteer doctors and nurses. But now, with not even a day having gone by, they have sent us a medical team from the Aleppo hospital. There is no doubt in my mind that Maryam and Karīma's work here, and the compliments they must have given us, are responsible for the fact that we have volunteers coming so quickly from Aleppo.

A white van enters the courtyard. I go forward to greet them. Some passengers get out and stretch

Threads of Compassion

their limbs. They had encountered skirmishes along the way, so it took them seventeen hours to traverse a journey that would otherwise have taken no more than seven. Everyone greets everyone else, and I take care to welcome the ladies first.

Amal Idrīs steps forward with a certain firmness and seriousness of purpose. She represents the midwives and nurses of their company. She is the head of the emergency department of Mashfī al-Jāmi'ī in Aleppo. One can tell from the way she carries herself that she is a professional and a serious administrator, but that she is also very kind-hearted, like the rest of the people of Aleppo.

Then there are Khadījah, Umm Munīr, and Umm Ahmad, who are midwives, and Umm Majd, who is a nurse. To be honest, I was concerned about not being able to distinguish between the "Umms" at first, but I eventually cottoned on to which name goes with which face. Khadīja is different from the rest in that she is young, talkative, and lively.

Now, the turn comes for the menfolk. There is Dr. Muhammad, who is a urologist. More interesting than his specialization are the jeans and jacket he is wearing in a war zone. I appreciate his commitment to being well-dressed, regardless of the circumstances he finds himself in. Then there is Ali, who is a nurse and taller than everyone else. Before I can say something in my terrible Arabic, we start to hear the sound of gunshots, explosions, and flying shrapnel. The smell of gunpowder wafts into the crisp morning air and settles into our lungs. Ali takes in a deep breath and says,

'Ah... the scent of Aleppo.'

What lyricism is hidden in this single utterance. A lyricism about one's hometown, full of memories from one's childhood. The war is over for Aleppo, but the smell of gunpowder brings back all of its memories for Ali, who lived through the war as it ravaged his hometown. He has sweet but, at the same time, bitter memories, which I would like him to tell me all about. Memories of bullet-ridden walls. Ali's poetic utterance makes me feel better, filling me with love for my own hometown and homeland, which is more than two thousand kilometres away. I take in a deep breath, taking in a lungful of the scent of soil and gunpowder.

The maternity ward is relatively quiet, but the emergency and pharmacy rooms are hectic. The health situation is dire, worse than our situation with our lack of medicine. I'm in the hospital courtyard when a mother enters with her child. When she reaches me, she says,

'Smoke (*dūd*)'

I quickly look around to see where the fire is that is emitting this smoke. I don't realize that the word for worms in Arabic is *dūd,* and that most of the children here have worms; a long and grotesque worm called *ascaris lumbricoides.* I searched high and low for a single mebendazole tablet, the *dūd*-killer medication which is harder to come by than gold in the region.

Karīm sends us some mebendazole from Damascus. A thousand tablets for a whole city. I give one tablet each to the patients in the emergency room. One tablet should be enough, meaning a thousand people will be cured. But it is not enough. They will come back complaining of worms. I can't sit still: this town is not big enough for me and for the worms. The worms have to go. The children are sick and skinny enough without having to deal with worms having free rein in their innards and intestines. Every Tuesday, a flight arrives from Tehran to Damascus, bringing pallets of medicine and taking back the bodies of the martyrs. I ordered mebendazole, which is Iranian-made and in large quantities. A week later, I have all the mebendazole I need, and the week after that, there is no more complaints about worms. The Iranian mebendazole medicine has eradicated the Ascaris; it is a drug in which I now have great confidence, based on my own field experience.

I wish it were possible to separate the affairs of the children from those of the war. I wish it were possible for them to go after playing their games and for them to be able to live and act like children should, for them not to suffer the psychological wounds that are inflicted by war. But alas, it is not to be. Is it not possible to tell a child to play here but not there when the whole city is unsafe. It's no use to explain to children that ISIS plant mines behind them whenever they evacuate any city that they are driven out of; mines whose mouths are agape for fresh meat, and

Threads of Compassion

which, like the members of ISIS themselves, do not distinguish between children and adults. Children will roam the streets and back alleys, fearless and unaware of the danger that threatens them, until eventually, one day, the sound of an explosion under their feet will show them the ugly face of war, like the image of a boy lying on a stretcher in the emergency ward with a leg whose heel has been destroyed by a mine or by the delayed explosion of an artillery mortar. The flesh of the heel has been separated and is suspended by a thin layer of skin. I won't let him see his ugly wound. I kiss his pale face and help him to recline. The crushed tissues of the flesh require stitches, but we don't have absorbable sutures. I sew the inner tissues with non-absorbable nylon thread and close the wound with some difficulty. The fact that we have anesthetics at all is a blessing in itself. I leave the two ends of the nylon thread out so that we don't have a problem later with pulling out the stitches. The boy writhes in pain, turning his head to the left and then back again to the right of his pillow. My heart goes out to him. He should be busy doing his homework now, not here with me in a hospital. I think about how many people like him there must be around us. Children who have experienced the horrors of war and who have been robbed of their childhood as a result of it. I help him get up. We were able to save his leg for him, and it will remain for him like a line that befell his soul, a scar that will stay with him for the rest of his life as a reminder of this war. I can't conceive of any role for children in the war, and it is this reluctance that does not allow me to stitch and bandage their wounds carelessly. All of the sorrows of this hospital are bearable for me, except for the sorrow of seeing children being hurt. A child must be able to live out his or her childhood.

Not a single healthy child remains in the city. Every morning, mothers appear in the hospital's courtyard holding the hands of their children. It is as if we're running a school and will put them down as being tardy if they arrive late. They line up, asking for medicine for their children's colds and flu and sinus and chest infections. Those of us who go to sleep at night in properly built houses and a couple of blankets over us wake up with itchy throats every morning; so it is not surprising that these children who sleep in dilapidated houses and tents should not be faring as well as us. At times, it seems my heart almost bursts from the sorrow of the grief that they are suffering. Their looks are at once feverish and lethargic. Whatever war destroys, it cannot destroy the world of the childhood that children are in. But for them, the effects of sickness and hunger are worse than the effects of war.

As we don't have all of the medicine that is needed, we dispense syrup to several people. The more I go around looking for medicine, the less results I get.

Threads of Compassion

It's not that nobody wants to cooperate. No; everyone does everything in their power to get the needed medicine. But there is no medicine to be found in the region for anyone to give us. We are the only hospital within a hundred-kilometer radius of Al-Bukamal. There is also the Moshfi al-Maidāni, a military hospital for wounded soldiers. We are the people's only hope, and we don't have any medicine to give them. I look at the line of sick children and at their mothers, then look at the medicine shelves that are almost completely empty. We only have enough medicine for today. It is a very depressing situation. I leave the building so as not to be embarrassed by the expectant looks people give me. I can't think of anyone else I can call; there's no one left who doesn't already know that our hospital is badly in need of basic medicines. I think about what it would take to travel to Damascus and back, and to procure medicine from there; but how and with which money will I be able to do that? If there were any medicine to be had, Dr. Karīm would have sent it already. Then I thought about going to Iran and bringing medicine back with me. But all I would be able to accomplish would be to bring back a maximum of five suitcases or so, whereas what we need is a trailer load of medicine to cure this region's fever for the medicines they need. I look at the Iranian flag that is waving on the roof. We have shed much blood for this flag to be able to fly there. I am feeling emotionally distraught. Khānūm Jān's ﷺ neighbors hold their children's hands and come to the hospital every

Threads of Compassion

morning hoping that this flag will still be flying. So then, what am I supposed to do, tell them that they are mistaken and that we are out of medicine? Am I supposed to apologize to them and tell them to go back to their homes? Even if I can somehow appease these mothers, how am I supposed to appease the martyrs who have sacrificed their lives for the sake of Khānūm Jān ﷺ? All these mothers want is medicine, not blood, which is the hard part. The martyrs have already given their lives and accomplished the hard part. Should Iran's flag be flying above this building only to have people be turned back, disappointed? I let out a great wail, with my eyes sown to the flag waving in the cold breeze. I call on Javād to show me a way out of my bind. I remember Haj Ahmad Mutiwassilīn who wanted to plant this flag in the ground at the end of the horizon. I raise the palms of my hands to the flag and the martyrs that are gathered around it. My hands are empty, and empty hands cannot accomplish anything. I show them the courtyard of the hospital, which is deserted at sunset. If we don't have the medicine we need, it will always be this deserted and will slowly be abandoned.

The cold and silence of the night surrounds the building in a tight embrace. There is no sign of the medical team's noises from their quarters upstairs. Like me, they are despondent at not having the medicine they need and at having to turn back their patients without having given them the medications they need. I'm heavy-hearted with grief and my eyes are welling up with tears that are waiting for an excuse to brim over.

I lie down in my room.

'Dr. Ehsān! Dr. Ehsān!' Imād yells in the corridor.

I say, 'This is supposed to be a hospital. Why are you yelling?'

He laughs and says, 'If you had heard the news, you would be shouting too.'

I look at him and wait for him to speak.

'I won't tell you until you give me a prize!'

I answer impatiently, 'I don't even have the patience to give you a sucker-punch or a kick in the butt, let alone a prize!'

I turn to go back to my grief and despondency.

Imād says sulkily, 'Don't be angry, I found a warehouse full of medicine for you!'

I jump up, as if he had given me an electric shock.

'What did you say?'

'A warehouse full of medicine left behind by ISIS!'

I forget all of my fatigue. I get myself to the car before Imād so that we can go to this warehouse. I pray all the way to the warehouse that it has medicine for children as well. Or that we will at least find important medicines among what there is and will not return empty handed. My thoughts are on the Iranian flag that is affixed on top of the hospital building as we wind our way around the dark alleys and deserted

Threads of Compassion

neighborhoods on the banks of the Euphrates. I think of the martyrs who gave their blood for the values that this flag symbolizes. Imād brings the car to a stop; we have to walk the rest of the way. I take in a deep breath, taking in the smell of the river being brought by the cold wind. The sound of gunfire and the flying shrapnel of the front line can be heard. Our presence here at this time of night is highly dangerous, but I couldn't bear to wait until the morning. We turn into an alley. Imād is a hundred meters ahead of me.

'Is it here?'

We're standing in front of a half-open door. I can see a dark staircase that leads down to the basement. I can't see in front of my feet as we enter the dwelling. I go down the stairs, holding on to the walls. There is a vial of some sort on one of the stairs; I pick it up and carefully place in my pocket, excitedly and respectfully. A warehouse that has vials on its stairs promises to have a lot more besides within its inner sanctum. When we reach the middle of the narrow and dark corridor leading to the warehouse, we are assured that there is no opening for light to escape to the outside, and so we turn on the flashlight with ease of mind. I shine the light of the flashlight all around myself. There is a world of medicine all around us; medicines which we were desperately in need of and whose absence was a continual cause of my shame before Khānūm Jān's neighbours. The arc of the flashlight only reaches about two or three meters in front of us, so all the secrets this warehouse holds in store for us are still not certain to us. But it is already apparent that it is a paradise in which all blessings can be found. All I have to do is to stretch my hand out and pick at its fruits. On the way, I prayed that it would have enough medicine to last us at least for a week. But now I see that there is enough medicine here to last us several months; medicines which we sought in the heavens but ultimately found to have been hidden underground. I'm so happy I want to hug the cartons of pills and ampoules and children's medications and nutritional supplements that I see all around us. They are stacked in the order of what they are indicated for, and look back at me with loving kindness, and it is as if they are asking me,

'Doctor! Which one of us do you want to take first?'

For now, I take a few cartons of children's medicines and emergency medications and leave it for the next visit for us to come to this heavenly basement in order to receive its full measure of grace. More important than these drugs is the notebook that Imād has found in the warehouse. The notebook is half-burnt, but it is clear that it contains the full names and details and exact addresses of the list of the ISIS collaborators in this region, which spans from Iraq's al-Qā'im to Deir ez-Zūr, a territory which ISIS had named the Euphrates Province. A few of its pages are even more interesting to us. They contain the names of Iranian nationals together with their addresses and phone numbers in Iran. Our jaws drop in shock. It's not just one or two names. There are twenty pages of Iranian names! I want to spit on the names of these traitors and their treachery. Imād carefully flips the pages of the half-burnt notebook. Why is it here in this medicine warehouse? Why hasn't it been completely burned? Why should these twenty pages of the middle of the notebook be completely intact?? Is giving up the names of their agents that have outlived their usefulness the easiest way to get rid of them, or is there some other sinister plan afoot? Why should such a notebook become available to us in the first place? Why should it be left in a place where it would be found by people such as Imād and myself?

We head out of the warehouse. On the way back, my mind starts running its calculus again. Where did all those drugs come from? Has ISIS actually paid for these drugs that have been arranged in accordance with the order of what they are indicated for and stored in the warehouse? That I cannot believe. Just as I can't believe that they would actually pay to purchase all of the weapons and materiel that is at their disposal. They don't even have the money to pay for all of their weapons and materiel, even if they *did* want to spend their money in that way. How is it possible to buy so many weapons and medicines continuously if one does not have a continuous source of income that is equal to the task? In my opinion, the sale of antiquities, slaves, oil at sub-market prices, and a thousand other shenanigans is just a cover for what is really going on. ISIS does not pay for their medicine and weapons and war materiel. Even if it does make some contribution towards these purchases, there is no way that they can pay for all of it. What they receive is very stylish and modern – the latest models in everything. It is obvious that it is sent to them free of charge. From where? From the same nasty pit where their leaders were trained. From what budget? Probably from the budgets of the intelligence services of nation states whose line items remain forever shrouded under the cover of official secrets acts. I think about how many of these warehouses there could be hidden in the heart of this country and how many of these warehouses are packed full of weapons instead of medicine.

    The hospital has come to life. The ambulances have been set in motion to go and get the medicines from the ISIS warehouse. We dispense medicine generously to the people and are happy to be able to do so. We have put a stop to the dispensing of individual tablets and splitting bottles of syrup between multiple patients. We are so medicine rich that we have set up a tent in a corner of the hospital's courtyard to store the overflow of medicines that would not fit on the shelves inside the hospital. Although we still don't have specialized radiology equipment and drugs for childbirth, but nevertheless, the drugs that we found have been coursing through the veins of the hospital like a blood infused with a life-giving elixir. People have sensed it too: they come to the hospital with greater hope and return satisfied rather than disappointed. Their happiness gives me joy as well.

These are the same people who would not allow us to touch their children's heads when we first started working here and were afraid of any Iranian approaching them. They were justified in their own way, I suppose. They had been told for seven years [of ISIS's occupation of their lands] that if the Iranians were to ever come here, they would be run over by our tanks. Now the Iranians were here, but we had come without any tanks. I ask all of them a single question:

'How was the situation of healthcare during ISIS's rule? How would you grade them in terms of their provision of medicine and medical treatment?'

The same answer was always repeated: 'By God, ISIS did not give us a single pill.'

I glance at the Iranian flag and then look at Khānūm Jān's neighbours, in whose faces traces of illness or hunger cannot be seen. Were they not under the rule of ISIS? Were the people of Al-Bukamal not Members of ISIS and its staunch sympathizers? Hadn't they proven their loyalty to ISIS during these seven years? Aren't their men *still* fighting for ISIS?? So for whom did they stash away so much medicine? How much medicine did their leaders and their families need for them to deprive these people of access to the medicine they had? For how many more years did they intend to continue this war and this catastrophe?

Threads of Compassion

Chapter Three Photos

The 'House of Horrors' that we turned into a maternity hospital. The size of its courtyard and the lengths of the queues that formed for medicine and examinations can be seen here.

Karīma (right) and Maryam (left), were two young nurses who trusted Dr. Karim and the Resistance Front and volunteered to serve in the region during the first days of the project to provide medical and maternity services to the people of Al-Bukamal. Karīma and Maryam were the two young nurses who returned to Aleppo and told of their experiences, which in turn acted as advertisements for the safety of the region and the services that were being provided by the Iranians, and this opened the way for the next teams of medical staff to come to the war front.

The person in the middle and standing next to me in scrubs is Ali, our kind resident nurse. Dr. Mohammad is the first from the left. The ladies, from the right, are Umm Ahmad, Umm Majd, and Mrs. Amal Idrīs.

Threads of Compassion

The tents that we erected in the courtyard of the hospital to house the overflow stock of the medicine we discovered in one of ISIS's abandoned warehouses that was chock full of all sorts of drugs that I hadn't even dreamed of.

Threads of Compassion

Medicinal shelving before and after the discovery of the abandoned ISIS underground medicine warehouse.

Threads of Compassion

Dr. Ahmed next to the father of all of us, [General Qāsim Suleimāni]. Dr. Ahmed is the doctor I first saw wearing a helmet and army boots. General Suleimāni and Dr. Ahmed are seen here in an area of Al-Bukamal on the day when General Suleimāni announced that the demise of ISIS was at hand. On the day this picture was taken, General Suleimāni passed the bowl of fruit among the guys personally and refused to let anyone help him, saying, 'I had vowed to serve the Defenders of the Shrine personally on the occasion of such a day.' Alas, I was not in the area that day but arrived a week after that. What a pity that I arrived so late.

Threads of Compassion

The Iranian flag flying high on the roof of the hospital and above everything else.

One of the huge beds in the 'House of Horrors' whose sight I didn't want to see, and on which no one wanted to sleep.

4

Mom's stopped crying, but she's still distraught. I finally see my kids, who are surrounding my bed now. Somayyeh holds Fātima up to me so that I can kiss her. I go to raise myself off the bed, but a sharp pain stabs me in the chest and forces me back down. I don't want my children to see my pain, so I force a smile on my face. Somayyeh's face betrays her anxiety. Everyone has recovered already except me. Their recuperation is incomplete, but they have at least been discharged from the hospital and have come to visit me today. I have been trapped in this bed for three weeks. My body's here in this hospital, but my heart is in Syria and the hospital there.

Threads of Compassion

The aroma of cooking has taken over the whole building. When a woman is in charge of the kitchen, the aromas that it emits are different. As long as we were on our own, we used to eat whatever they brought us from the food quotas that were given to the soldiers fighting on the front line. Whatever it was, it was better than starving. When the women had settled into their tasks at the hospital, they did not go for the front-line food quotas, especially since our hospital had a kitchen that was semi-equipped. Now, instead of the ready-to-eat food portions, we get dry goods from the army's support facilities, and the ladies see to their duties in the emergency ward as well as seeing to the cooking. They cook delicious Arabic food that I could never have dreamed of being served. The fare consists of dishes such as *labnīya* and *ma'mūnīya*, to hummus and falafel.

The aroma of flavoured rice and pieces of meat that have been soaked in buttermilk has whetted my appetite. We have Aleppo-style *labnīya* for lunch today. It reminds me of the Syrian proverb, "Syria and its rivers and streams, and Aleppo and its cuisine". We are all waiting with a great anticipation that has built up over several weeks to eat this meat dish, when the sound of an explosion makes us all start.

A small house, one of whose walls is contiguous with one of the walls of the hospital, has taken a hit by an artillery mortar. We were the target, but the mortar landed in our neighbour's home. A few minutes later, a young woman holding a baby in her

Threads of Compassion

arms enters the hospital. She is one of the residents of the house that was hit by the mortar, and is wailing because her child's hand was burned by the explosion. Her two-year-old boy doesn't stop screaming even for a moment. He's really scared. I wash the wound. Thank God the damage to the tissue is not too extensive.

Somayyeh runs towards Muhammad-Hasan agitatedly. The sound of a child's screams and Somayyeh's wailing fills the room. I lift the iron from Muhammad-Hasan's hand, lifting the skin of his hand along with it.

The mother of the Syrian boy cannot bear to look at the wound, but she has to stay in the room with us so that her son will feel safe.

I have taken Muhammad-Hasan to the hospital. The nurse is washing the wound, and Somayyeh cannot bear to look at it.

I ask the child's mother for his name. I'm told its 'Hamd'. I call out his name so that he might calm down for a moment or two. We do not have any Comfeel dressing, so I have to apply some honey instead to keep the wound moist under its dressing.

I'm holding Muhammad-Hasan in my arms. He is enervated, his eyes are puffed up from crying, and his nose is red. He is sobbing. I kiss his hand and place his head on my shoulder to encourage him to sleep.

When I have finished dressing the baby's wound, he stops screaming. I tell his mother that she needs to bring him in every day so that his dressing can be changed. The child's nose is running, and his face is wet with tears. I kiss his head and hand him over to his mother. She raises her hands in prayer, 'May God keep you for your family.'

Hearing her prayer reminded me of my family and how much I miss them. I miss hearing the sounds the kids make. Fātima climbing up on my shoulders, Muhammad-Hasan getting up to his usual mischiefs, Hāniyeh's affections, seeing how tall Muhammad-Husain has grown, and the scent of the dishes Somayyeh prepares and her laughter.

A white Toyota screeches to a halt in the hospital courtyard, waking me from my daydream. Only Iranians can enter the courtyard by car. I go forward to greet them. They are the telecommunications technicians who have come to set up a phone line. Nothing could be better than that.

Before their setting up a phone line for us, if I wanted to call Tehran, I had to travel for ten kilometers to the field hospital, which I didn't have the time for; nor was it as easy to get there as just getting up and going whenever one felt like it.

I keep hovering around the technicians as if they would work faster if I was hovering over them. But I can't get myself to do anything else while they are here working on this most important of tasks. Everything that I have to say to my family back home line up like a train of words in my mind; from the events of the first days when I arrived here in the area, up until today, when I treated and dressed Hamd's hand. I register the first sentence that I want to say to

Threads of Compassion

Somayyeh in my mind, then cross it out. I can come up with something better. What can I say to fill her heart with joy? I register some other sentence, then cross that out too, repeating it under my breath. Finally, I settle on what I think is the most beautiful sentence to start the conversation with. I have reverted back to being the sensitive dreamer of the days when we were just engaged to be married.

The technicians place a phone in front of me and say, 'You only have two minutes to speak, and all conversations are monitored for security purposes.'

All of the words I had in mind leave my mind like air rushing out of a punctured balloon, starting with that first sentence I had concocted. I revert back to being Dr. Ehsān again, the head of the hospital. I pick up the phone and dial. The dial tone changes to a series of long, lifeless beeps.

'Alo? Salām!'

Hearing Muhammad-Hasan's voice makes me queasy. My mind flies the two-thousand-kilometer distance instantaneously. He asks excitedly, 'Why don't you come home, Daddy?'

Hearing the word 'Daddy' makes the rest of the kids animated, and I can hear their excitement over the phone. They now know it's me that is on the other end of the line. They pass the phone to each other one at a time. All of them have the same question for me: 'Why don't you come home, Daddy?'

Finally, Somayyeh's turn arrives. Her voice trembles like my hands. I'm wondering what I can say that would be pleasing to God and Somayyeh both, as well as to the guys from Intelligence who are listening in on the conversation.

'Whenever you get tired, remember the hardships that Lady Zainab went through.'

This statement has a whole booklet full of meaning, and she probably understands the hidden meaning behind its ostensible meaning.

'Don't worry about me and the children. Give my *salāms* to Lady Zainab.'

Before I know it, a dial tone suddenly appears on the line, crossing out any other words that were patiently waiting in line to be given voice to.

After Imād's discovery of the underground medicine cache, I have officially turned into a veritable mole after working hours, spending all my time searching the basements of all of the abandoned houses of this three-storied city; basements out of which no one emerges empty handed. As my colleagues say, after work, I disappear underground. The discovery of the medicine cache has had a great effect on me. I'm becoming an expert mole: I no longer search the basements of buildings that are on the main streets. The prizes are to be found in the basements of houses that are located on narrow streets and back alleys. Whatever I happen to find, I tell Imād about first, because I have to make sure that the place is not booby-trapped, and also that the medicines are not personal property. They can still be confiscated, even if they are a personal stash because with all the strict rules that

ISIS has, and the high number of their beheadings of the doctors and nurses of this area, an ordinary citizen could only have a sizable stash of drugs if he was closely cooperating with the leaders of ISIS. I come up with some good finds in my reconnaissance tours, from a wheelchair to loads of Relief, the Arabs' favourite painkiller. The medicine shelves of the Emergency ward have now been completely stocked. Analgesics and antibiotics are stocked on one shelf, and specialized drugs fill the other shelves. In one corner, we now have 32 brand new wheelchairs. We generously send our surpluses to others regions, such as the Mushfi al-Maidāni Hospital, to the Deir ez-Zūr and al-Mayādīn hospitals, and to Doctor Karīm. We do not leave anyone behind in our munificence. We are as munificent in the distribution of ISIS's medicine as they are stingy.

The emergency room is overflowing with patients. Mothers come and go with their children. Dr. Muhammad examines them and writes prescriptions for them. As always, he is full of verve and kindness, and dressed in jeans and without a doctor's robe. Ali fetches their medicines for them, and Umm Majd registers their names in the registry. The midwives are also present in the emergency room and help out. I'm talking about Umm Ahmad, Umm Munīr and Khadījah. It's better for them than sitting idle in the maternity ward. At least here in the emergency room, they can make a contribution to the work at hand. The main mission of this hospital takes place in its maternity ward, in addition to which we will be providing other medical services. But the maternity ward is closed now. I'm left wondering where all of those pregnant women are that I saw on the road the first day I got here. They are willing to accept the risks of giving birth at home, rather than coming to us. We only find out that they have given birth when they come to the hospital with their babies in hand to get medicine for themselves or for their babies or to get supplies for the needs of their babies. I am standing in front of the door of the maternity ward. My heart goes out to the babies whose health is put in danger by their mothers who refuse to come to the hospital for their childbirth, and for ourselves, who converted the abandoned house into a hospital against great odds in 48 hours in order to be of service to these pregnant mothers. But we don't even have a single caller who is in need of the services of the maternity clinic. I feel depressed.

    The sadness I feel due to these people and because of my distance from Fātima crushes my heart. I take out my black shirt from my backpack. I make my ritual ablutions, smell it, and put it on with a *bismillāh*. I like the black shirt that was given to me by my mother better than my *jihād* clothing and the six-pocketed commando pants. I hear Haj Mahmoud's words running through my mind: "My mother is [Lady] Fātima". He sings about mothers and the grief of these mothers melts my heart. I sing along with Haj Mahmoud: "One woman, and so many shameless enemies. Her *chādor* has been covered by the tread-prints of these shameless enemies".

My thoughts fly all the way to Madinah, taking me with them. I have not yet gone on the Hajj Pilgrimage, but I know the Baqī' Cemetery well. It is the least-lighted and least shaded part of the city. It is dark and silent. I think of a hemistich from a *rawza*. "The blows keep coming, back-to-back, with Fātima tired and wounded and near death." Every year at this time of year, I used to get a stipend from the Fātemīeh *hay'at* (religious group) and the Mādar *hay'at*. And this year, I am next to her daughter. How similar they are to each other, this mother and daughter.

"The blows don't give her a chance to catch her breath." I feel like listening to a *rawza*. I feel like smelling the rose-water scent of the *hay'at*. I feel like sitting in a corner, beating my chest with my hands in sync with the *rawza* and wailing to my heart's content. Wailing at my own condition, at the condition of these people, and at the condition of their children, oppressed despite their innocence. Haj Mahmoud does not let up. He keeps on singing: "Her *chādor* and her head covering has become soaked in blood". I fall asleep with a heavy sadness over my heart. The sorrow of exile (*ghurba*).[30]

---

[30] [*Ghurba*: A feeling of existential homesickness, alienation, estrangement, forlornness, and loneliness, and of separation and being cut off from the source of one's being (God), and

Threads of Compassion

After the morning prayers, I am startled by the sound of someone kicking and pounding at the door of the building.

'Who is the owner of this house? Hurry up, people. A woman is dying!'

I run out in a state of near panic to see what's going on. The person making the ruckus is named Sa'īd, who is a young Iranian whom I had not seen before.

'What on earth is going on?'

'I've brought a pregnant woman whose water has broken and who is about to give birth.'

He said it with such glee, as if he had brought a complete set of radiology equipment with him! I look around excitedly and ask, 'Where is she??'

'If she isn't dead already, you'll find her in the back of the car.'

I raise my voice and just as Sa'īd had paged me, I paged the midwives:

'Umm Munīr, Umm Ahmad, Khadījah. Hurry! A child is being born!'

I don't give my voice a chance to reach the second floor, and again yell louder than before, '*Yallā!* Hurry up!!'

Sa'īd had come across the expectant woman together with her mother and husband three kilometres from the hospital, next to Al-Bukamal's

---

the pining for existential affinity and reunion with that source.]

Clock Square. This is the square where ISIS used to carry out its public executions. She had fallen down in the middle of the street due to her pain. The thought crosses my mind that this square is seeing signs of life rather than death after a seven-year hiatus in which the only thing the square saw was the cutting off of heads and the flowing of rivulets of blood. The midwives come over and take the expectant woman to the delivery room.

The woman's mother says, 'They are not from around here. They've been displaced by the war. Her labour pains started in the middle of the night, and they went from house to house looking for someone who knew something about childbirth who could help her give birth to her child, but they couldn't find anyone. Her condition got worse on the way.'

The old woman pulls me aside and says, 'My son, I swear to God, we have no money. If it is possible, I'll work for you in lieu of paying the hospital bill.'

I am shocked, as we do not charge for any of our services.

I say, 'Dear mother! Our services here are free of charge; and your daughter will be treated as if she were our own sister.'

The old woman sobs convulsively, bringing a stop to what I was saying. I look at her, still in shock at what she thought about our hospital.

'By God, ISIS used to charge us 150,000 Syrian liras for each child birth.'

Threads of Compassion

Now I finally understand why no one came to us for their childbirths. I am overwhelmed by all kinds of emotions. I feel anger for the injustice of a government that held the land and the very lives of a people hostage and did not provide a minimum of services and facilities, even for giving birth to children who were going to be raised as ISIS loyalists in every sense.

With the sound of the baby's crying finally being emitted, all heads turn towards the maternity ward. It is the first birth of the Al-Bukamal Gynecology and Obstetrics Hospital! Khadīja has wrapped the dark-complected girl whose birth inaugurated the maternity ward in a blanket and has brought her over, I take her in my arms and sense the subtle warmth of her tiny body. I run my hands over her black velvety hair. Her father wants me to pronounce the call to prayer (the *adhān*) in her ear. It gives me a big lump in my throat, and by the time I pronounce the first *allāhu akbar*, my voice breaks and I have to pause before I can complete the *adhān*. The child is calm and is in a deep sleep. I can't get enough of looking at her face. I make a prayer, asking God to give her all that is good in this world and in the world to come. By the time I reach the testament of faith in the *adhān*, my voice breaks again and I start weeping. The child's father and grandmother also start weeping. We are all heartbroken by this war. We shed tears in gratitude for this blessing from God; a blessing who is fast asleep as I hold her in my arms. We weep and pray for the war to come to an end. We shed tears for the life of this heavenly angel to end well. The father wants me to choose his daughter's name. I miss the Fatemīya *rawzas*. What name can be more beautiful than the name of my mother?

I kiss Fātima below her throat and place her gently in her father's arms. I think of my daughter Fātima. If she was here, she would be clinging at my leg, asking me to let her hold the newborn infant.

The maternity ward has really come into its own now. Mothers now come to us, we examine them, and record an approximate time of delivery for them in their file. We have about ten births per day. The sound of babies crying is all over the hospital, a sound that is very pleasing to me. We have divided the dates we have received from the Jihād al-Bannā[31] humanitarian relief group into 100-gram packets and hand them to mothers who have just given birth, to help them in their convalescence. All of this resulted from the benefit that baby Fātimah's birth brought about, the news of whose birth spread among the people in the hospital.

---

[31] Jihād al-Bannā is an Iranian humanitarian relief group that started its work in the region with the support given to it by the Syrian government and the Red Cross. Their activities range from building bread bakeries to various other civic services.

Threads of Compassion

But this is the good side of the story. The other side of the story has made us all dejected, and has left a bitter taste in our mouths, rather than the sweetness that would ordinarily accompany the birth of a baby; the bad part is the shortage of dried milk and diapers. The nutrition and dietary intake of the mothers is such that they do not have enough to eat to be able to produce milk. And the few dates that we give them are just enough to keep them alive, and are insufficient to do anything more than that bare minimum. The mother and her child are both hungry. And they are forced to use the plastic bags that the food is distributed in for the baby's diapers, which of course causes rashes on the delicate skin of the newborn.

All of my attention has been focused on trying to obtain these two items, what the Arabs call *hafūżāt wa halīb:* diapers and milk. I can't bear to see the rashes on the legs of the babies, let alone hearing that one of them has died due to malnutrition. I love them like my own children and can't bear to see them suffer. I search high and low for these two items. Husain is one of the guys who works for Jihād al-Bannā, and is very conscientious, leaving no stone unturned in his efforts to help the newborns. Every day he makes inquiries on the radio, calls by phone, and even goes to Deir ez-Zūr, doing so with a singularity of purpose, as if it were his own children who were starving. He has not gone home to see his own boys for two months, preferring to stay here so that he might resolve this major problem that confronts some of God's creatures. He shows me many pictures of his twin boys, but he does not give voice to his longing to see them and be with them. We are all the same: we feel ashamed at not being able to do better by Khānūm Jān ﷺ.

Between Husain and I, we have done everything possible to resolve the situation, but to no avail. What else can we do? The news arrives in our exhaustion and dejection that the Red Cross convoy is on its way with supplies. For a week, our eyes were fixed on the road, but no convoy arrived. It is a day's journey from Damascus to Al-Bukamal, not a week. I feel too ashamed to look in the eyes of mothers whose babies are dying of starvation. The golden days of weighing the newborns and recording their weights in the register are passing us by, and there is nothing that we have been able to do to improve their lot. I have lost hope; in my own abilities to do anything, in Husain's, and in the arrival of the Red Cross convoy which would have gotten here by now even if they were walking here. The mothers begging for powdered milk reminds me of a lady named Rubāb, who suffered tremendously while her newborn struggled to hold on to life, opening and closing its mouth in the hope of being fed some milk, which was not forthcoming. Woe unto us, for what we did to the heart of this woman. Woe unto us, for what we do to the hearts of these mothers. Woe unto us, for my being so empty handed. Woe unto us, for the bird of my imagination, and all of the places it takes me. Woe unto us...

Threads of Compassion

On the first day that I went to pilgrimage to Lady Ruqayya ﷺ's shrine, I said to myself that this lady is no more than three years old; and that I should therefore take my pain elsewhere, and be here in order to help cure the wounds of her feet and her heart, and to help revive her from her fatigue. But now I take my complaints to her. If it was my own pain that I was seeking her help for, I would be ashamed to ask her. But what I ask her to intercede on behalf of is the condition of the newborns. I lock the door of the room and kneel in the direction of her shrine and recite the supplication:

السلام على صاحبة الخطاب العجيب لصاحب الخد التريب ابيك اباعبداللهالحسين عليهالسلام.

Salutations to the owner of a strange sermon, for one whose cheeks are covered with dust for the sake of Abā Abdullāh al-Husain.

What an incredible *zīārat-nāmah* this Mafja'a *zīārat-nāmeh* is. I call from a distance to a lady whom I have called from an even greater distance in the past, and who even then has answered my call.

السلام، حين ناديت يا ابتاه من ايتمني على صغر سني؟

Salutations to you for the time when you called out, 'Father! Who was the one responsible for making me an orphan at such a young age?'

I am lost and bewildered in the ruins of Syria. Would that one of the guards would have been more chivalrous. Would that they had prevented what happened to this girl from occurring.

السلام على جوارحك الذابلة من السير الحثيث.

Salutations to you for the parts of your body that were wounded and shriveled up from the harshness of the journey that brought you here in such haste.

My heart aches for her exhausted body that suffered so many hardships. The wounds and hunger of the newborns of Al-Bukamal are nothing compared to these words; but I cannot stand to see them suffer. I have brought my inability to a baby girl who also suffered greatly, in the hope that some opening might occur.

السلام على من ابكت النساء مصيبتها لهول ما رأوه منها و لعظم ما جرى عليها حينما جيء برأس ابيها اليها. فقال الامام زين العابدين عليه السلام: ارفعوها فلقد فارقت روحها الدنيا.

Salutations to the body that is separated from your departed soul. Salutations to the one for whom women wept because of the horror of what she had witnessed, and the great solemnity of what she experienced when they brought her father's head into her presence [in the caliph Yazīd's court in Damascus]. When Imam Zain al Ābidīn said, 'Raise her up, as her soul has left her body'.

There is such a great commotion in the ruins of this land on account of her lifeless body. I strike my head with both my hands. What is going on in her aunt's heart? Who should her brother try to placate; who should he try to comfort and pacify?

My patience is at an end. I cannot go on. These few lines have been enough to take my breath away. These few lines should be enough to untangle the knot in which the fate of these anxious mothers has been bound.

Loud static is emitted from the two-way radio. Husain is on the other end. He said agitatedly,

'Get yourself to the *jihād* warehouse, Doctor!'

I walk towards the warehouse at the same speed that Husain spoke on the two-way. The train of the Red Cross convoy's trailers is threading its way through a throng of people. The crowd is drawn to the convoy like iron filings are drawn to a magnet. The red crosses on the cartons seem to be waiving their hands to me, as if to say, 'See, Doctor, we finally arrived!'

Husain says that a complete trailer is earmarked for the hospital. I feel like hugging and kissing our trailer. I will no longer be ashamed of facing mothers who show me the wounds on their child's feet. Nor will any more babies die of malnutrition. I am so overcome with emotion that a lump has formed in my throat. Husain is even happier than I am. The contents of the trailers of this convoy will definitely make the children and their mothers feel better. I will no longer feel ashamed at not being able to do anything to help, and the Iranian flag will fly high as always.

I feel the sharp sound of gunfire and the trembling of exploding shrapnel in my eardrums. I smell the bitter odour of gunpowder. I had waited several years to smell this odour and to hear this sound. I had waited several years for *jihād*. The pocket holding the magazine feels heavy on my waist. I take cover behind a broken wall of an abandoned house. The earth lets out a soft crunch under my boots. I wish I had some grenades left. The sound of the explosions gets closer. The gunfire of a '23' (a semi-heavy 23 mm machine gun) coming from behind me makes my eardrums tremble. I walk behind the wall and see that their tanks are quite close. The hospital is under siege. The heavy body of the tank shivers to a stop. Its gun is pointed towards me. I smell the odour of the earth and of gunpowder and hear the sounds of explosions.

Threads of Compassion

I wake up from my dream. My body is sweating profusely. All of the world's sorrows flood into my heart. It is just me now, left with my room, my white nursing gown, and the unfinished dream that I was having in my after-morning prayer nap. A dream that I was four kilometres away from; but which I could not reach. My friends tease me, saying that I am not a Defender of the Shrine (*haram*), but that I am a Defender of the Harem (*haram-sarā*). I laugh, but it's not hidden from Lady Zainab, so let it not be hidden from you either: many a time have I envied the guys who fight on the front lines.

I hear a knock at the door. The door opens and Rasūl sticks his head in. It takes me a while to figure out if I'm still asleep or if I'm awake. I jump up excitedly and give him a big hug to make up for the three years in which I hadn't seen him. It's him alright, with his hair turning to grey. He is now quite a man, having become the commander of the Fatemiyūn corps in eastern Syria. He'd heard from the soldiers that I was stationed at the hospital and came over to see me. A morning that starts with a visit from Rasūl is sweet; a morning full of memories of reciting Tawāshīh psalms together, and our group exercises in the courtyards of Imam Riḍā's shrine; a morning full of memories from twenty years back; a morning full of memories of Ahmad. We recollect our memories of Ahmad and the kind of person he was for a while. We both agree that it felt like he was destined for martyrdom even then. If only he was here with us, we say, so that we could line up, the three of us together, and sing revolutionary anthems together. If he was here, we say, we would horse around so much that we would eventually collapse from having laughed so hard. After we have breakfast, Rasūl is in a hurry to leave, but I won't let him, saying,

'I won't let you go until you recite some verses of the Quran for me.'

He hesitates, then says, 'Then call my driver Dawūd and have him join us too.'

I send Ābid to get Dawūd.

Rasūl chuckles, poking fun at what I do. 'Do you have to give me an injection, or will I be able to do the recitation without a shot?'

I smile and say, 'It'll work without a shot too. But if you want one, we've got plenty.'

'Then go and get one and give me an injection, then I'll recite the Quran.'

I thought that I was the only one who remembered that Tawāshīh group's memories, but Rasūl had outdone me. The story behind this injection goes back to the days of the Sha'bānīyah, when we were constantly going to events that were held in celebration [of the birth of the Twelfth Imam] and were busy performing hymns and singing Tawāshīh psalms. Rasūl had a cold, and his lungs were giving him a hard time, so before each performance, I would give Rasūl a shot of Dexa[methasone] to give him a boost. Ābid and Rasūl's driver enter the room in the middle of the story. They are having a good time and have their arms around each other's shoulder. It turns out that they too are good friends who are seeing each other again after a long time. Rasūl is no longer concerned about his driver getting his breakfast and turns towards the Qibla (the direction of prayer, facing Mecca). He places a hand up to his ear and his voice fills the room. I yearn for being at the shrine of Imam Riḍā ﷺ. I stroll around its courtyards, my imagination riding on Rasūl's voice, and associating it with the sound of the long trumpets (*naqqārehā*) that are sounded at the shrine. The sound of all the pilgrims around the sepulcher rings in my ears, as does the sound of the running water in the small pools spotted around the Āzādī Courtyard. The silence of the courtyard of the Goharshād Mosque. The taste of the water of the Ismāʿīltalā Saqqā-Khāneh. The sound of the pigeons flapping their wings. All of these sounds are contained in Rasūl's voice. I want time to stop, right here in Al-Bukamal, in the women's hospital, among the ruined houses of the people, so that I can hear Rasūl's voice reciting the Quran and cry to my heart's content. He has reached the last verse of Surah Baqarah.

لَا يُكَلِّفُ اللَّهُ نَفْسًا إِلَّا وُسْعَهَا

> [2:286] *God does not burden any human being with more than he is well able to bear...*

The weight of the burden of my obligations weighs down heavily on me, and I wail out in pain.

$$\text{رَبَّنَا لَا تُؤَاخِذْنَا إِن نَّسِينَا أَوْ أَخْطَأْنَا}$$

[2:286] O our Sustainer! Take us not to task if we forget or unwittingly do wrong!

I am afraid that the mistakes that I have made will prevent me from attaining to felicity in the hereafter.

$$\text{رَبَّنَا وَلَا تَحْمِلْ عَلَيْنَا إِصْرًا كَمَا حَمَلْتَهُ عَلَى الَّذِينَ مِن قَبْلِنَا}$$

[2:286] "O our Sustainer! Lay not upon us a burden such as Thou didst lay upon those who lived before us!

I fear the weight of the burden being placed on my shoulders whose weight I will not be able to bear.

$$\text{رَبَّنَا وَلَا تُحَمِّلْنَا مَا لَا طَاقَةَ لَنَا بِهِ ۖ وَاعْفُ عَنَّا وَاغْفِرْ لَنَا وَارْحَمْنَا ۚ أَنتَ مَوْلَانَا فَانصُرْنَا عَلَى الْقَوْمِ الْكَافِرِينَ ﴿٢٨٦﴾}$$

[2:286] O our Sustainer! Make us not bear burdens which we have no strength to bear! "And efface Thou our sins, and grant us forgiveness, and bestow Thy mercy upon us! Thou art our Lord

Threads of Compassion

Supreme: succor us, then, against people who deny the truth!"

I bow down low in prostration. I pray on the right of the blood that has been shed in this path that I can manage and overcome the heavy responsibility of serving the neighbours of Khānūm Jān ﷺ. I pray that our flag will always fly high.

I had left the door of the room open so that anyone could come in if they needed me for anything. When I got up from my position of prostration, I saw that there was a shadow behind the door. I opened the door. The corridor was full of people. The medical team and the people who came to the hospital in the morning were looking at me anxiously. I waited for them to say something. Dr. Muhammad raised the question that was on all of their minds.

'Aren't you Shi'a?'

I think to myself, 'This whole throng of people has come here this early in the morning to ask me this question??'

'Yes, I am.'

'But... the Shī'a don't read the Quran... *do* they??'

I am filled with emotions of bewilderment and resentment at those who have spread such malicious rumours, and I send God's curse on those who started this kind of fire between Shī'a and Sunni Muslims. I send God's curse on those who have brought a situation about in which people still ask, after Imam Ali

ﷺ was martyred in the prayer niche of the mosque, whether Ali ever prayed. May God curse all transgressors and doers of evil.

Rasūl laid the foundation stone of the ritual of the recitation of the Quran in the morning, after which he left. Every day before starting work, the soldiers from the Fatemiyūn corps and I would sit in a circle and read a few pages of the Quran. The maternity ward had become so popular that it was now open 24-hours a day. Frequently, members of the families of those who had come to the hospital to give birth joined our circle. When the Quranic recitation ended, they would ask the same question: 'Do the Shī'a read the Quran too?'

I wish Abūta hadn't gone on leave and was here to translate the thousands of sentences that came to my mind in response to this question. I smile, hiding the sadness that this question generates inside me.

Ja'far has fallen asleep in a corner of my room. He is one of the members of the support staff, a young and diligent worker. This is how working in a *jihādī* way is: at night, you fall asleep in the corner of some room. One night, you fall asleep at home, one night at the office, one night behind the wheel of your car, and one night at the maternity ward.

In the morning, after the prayers, he insists that I do a little *rawḍa-khānī*, which is a ritual in which elegiac poetry or laments about the tragedy of Karbalā and other tragedies that have befallen Islam are recited. He is feeling sad. No matter how much effort you put in as one of the support staff, at least one person will still be unhappy. This is the case even if you go back and forth for a distance of 130 kilometres three times in a single day to see to the needs of the people you are supporting, and in order to support the needs of ten aid stations and four hospitals. Despite this, Ja'far never gets angry, nor does he ever say anything about his frustrations. Today, however, sadness weighs heavily on his heart. I sit facing the Qiblah and start my recitation of the lament of the tragic events of Karbalā.

After this *rawḍa-khānī* has brought out both our tears and lightened our hearts, I bring it to a close, shortly after which there is a knock at the door. I tidy myself up a little and open the door. It is Umm Majd and Dr. Muhammad, who enter the room with their faces wet with tears. Umm Majd prostrates herself in the direction of the Qibla and starts wailing. Ja'far and I are stunned. Dr. Muhammad asks with tears in his eyes, 'Doctor, what were you reciting?'

They had come down to make their breakfast coffee and had heard my recital.

Surprised to see them so over-wrought by emotion, I ask, 'Do you understand Persian?'

'No; but what you recited moves our hearts.'

My tears start to fall again. What can I say to them? What can I say I was reciting? Should I tell them about my lord and master [Imam Husain ﷺ] or about his mother? Should I tell them about how her heart has been so broken as a result of what is taking place here? Should I tell them about my own heart, which is burning with the heat of the elegies I recited? Which one of the misfortunes that befell my master should I remove the veil from? I decide to tell them about his sister [Lady Zainab ﷺ], under whose protective shade we are all working. I decided to tell them about a three-year-old who died from grief that was too much for her to bear. I tell them about the throat that had become the place where this mother and daughter would kiss frequently. I tell them about Rubāb and about her mother. Woe to those who break the hearts of mothers. I say these things and Muhammad wails. I am as much surprised at their wailing at hearing these elegies and laments about Imam Husain ﷺ as they were surprised by the recitation of the Quran by us Shī'a. The Prophet is reported to have said, '*There is a fire in the hearts of the true believers as a consequence of the martyrdom of Husain that never goes out.*'[32] The heat of this fire has now come to life in the hearts of Umm Majd and Muhammad too.

I feel grateful to be present next to Khānūm Jān's ﷺ neighbours. I feel grateful for the elegies I recited. I feel grateful for the black shirt that I am wearing.[33] I feel grateful for having become a Defender

---

[32] Jāmi' al-Ahādīth ash-Shī'a, 12:556.

[33] [A symbol of mourning for the martyrdom of Imam Husain ﷺ and the other Infallibles.]

of the Shrine. I feel grateful for being able to hold *rawza-khānī* sessions and sessions in which we recite the verses of the Quran, both of which can wash away all of the lies that ISIS has planted in the hearts and minds of these people.

Ja'far had barely left when people start rushing into the hospital. This is what our situation is like every Thursday. Thursdays are distribution day. People line up in the yard from 8 am to get our handouts, which include everything from diapers and soap to towels and everything else having to do with hygiene. We have divided the items inside the Red Cross boxes into individual packages and hand these out to the people on Thursdays. We also give powdered milk to mothers of newborns throughout the week. There is a big commotion in the courtyard. I have put Ja'far to work. All the people of Al-Bukamal are in the hospital courtyard. Around noon, the work is finished, and the closing bell rings. We open the large sliding door of the courtyard, and it is gradually emptied of people as if it were a pool that had a leak. I'm standing on the porch, and it gives me great pleasure to witness this scene. Not the scene of the people leaving, but the scene of them leaving with their hands full of things that they need and which will improve their lives greatly.

When the distribution ritual is over, I go to see what's going on in the emergency room. A dark-complected girl is busy sweeping the floor of the emergency room. Dr. Muhammad and Umm Majd are busy with their work. I had seen the girl in the hospital courtyard today, and wonder why she is holding a broom in her hands. I go up to Muhammad.

'What's up, *habibi*?'

I point with my eyes to the girl who is trying to do a perfect job of sweeping. Dr. Muhammad understands what I mean. I follow him out of the emergency room to hear his explanation.

Her name is Naba'. She is from Al-Qā'im, in Iraq. She lost her parents in the American missile barrages of their city. She walked ten kilometres to Al-Bukamal with her eight-year-old sister, Māria, to reach their aunt's house. Her aunt took refuge from ISIS in Damascus with her family. Now all that is left is Naba' and her sister, their displacement, and their hunger, fatigue, and the loneliness of exile. Muhammad's words bring tears to my eyes. Children are the ones who are affected most by the horrors of war; children like Naba' and thousands of other children like her whose childhoods ended overnight. Muhammad says that Naba' asked if we would let her stay here in the hospital and have her clean the building for us. She has taken on the role of the parents of her little sister; a parent looking for a sanctuary for her child.

My thought is that the hospital is not a suitable place for them to stay, as it is so polluted with germs and other biotoxins. This is especially so in the case of our hospital, which is a paramilitary institution that is faced with other threats and dangers besides. I send Muhammad to go and get her so that I can convince her that this is not a good place for her to stay in. I am prearranging in my mind the sentences that I want to use when she comes in.

'Naba', you are no different to me than my daughter Hāniyeh.'

I haven't finished my first sentence when she bursts into tears. I feel so ashamed; the last thing I wanted to do is to upset her.

She says, 'Doctor! Hāniyeh is lucky to have a father like you. But my parents are now buried under the earth and my sister and I are alone.'

Tears are welling up in me and make it difficult for me to speak. I do not know what to say; all I know is that I have to do everything in my power to prevent this girl from saying that she and her sister are alone. All the words I had arranged in my mind have fallen apart. Where can I send this lonely girl with her little sister so that I don't have to worry about them anymore? If it was Hāniyeh, I wouldn't let her out of my sight. I think of Naba' and her little sister as being a trust that has been entrusted to me by her parents who are no longer able to help them in this world. Damn these untimely tears that have filled my eyes again. I prevent the tears from streaming down my face with difficulty, and say to her,

'For as long as I am here, I will help you find your aunt's family and be reunited with them.' I can see the sparkle of joy flashing in her dark brown eyes. Her natural modesty prevents her from doing so, but I can tell that she wanted to give me a big hug out of the sheer joy she felt.

Threads of Compassion

I ask a lot of questions about the American attack on Al-Qā'im, but am not able to extract accurate information. Al-Qā'im was certainly attacked, but not as Naba' says it was. I go on the assumption that she is not telling the truth, and that they have not come from Al-Qā'im. This is no reason not to help them, of course. They are in need of my help, wherever they might have come from along this seventy-kilometre front line that stretches from Al-Mayādīn to Al-Harī. They are even more in need of my help than Lady Zainab's ﷺ other neighbours. I am sure that the two of them no longer have either of their parents because if either of their parents were alive, they would know as much as their children and would be able to get themselves to this point and to find them and be reunited with them, be it from Al-Qā'im or from any of the other liberated cities around us. Given the tribal setting here, it is not possible to do much lying and play-acting. If Naba' turns out actually to be Syrian, a relative will eventually show up to show her out and put the lie to her fibs. Whatever the case may be, I don't pursue it any further. It is immaterial to me where she has come from; what is important is that she and her sister are homeless girls who do not have any guardian to look after them. What is important is that I have to fill the role of that guardian and do something for them, like the rest of the kids here. I feel strongly that I have to take care of them, so that God will take care of my family, who are also on their own in a strange city.

Threads of Compassion

Chapter Four Photos

Our high school Tawāshī group. Ahmad is seated to my right in the white shirt.

I love this smile of Ahmad's. I know that he will always look out for me with his big smile, and with his loving look in his eyes.

Threads of Compassion

With Umm Ahmad and Khadīja, and one of the newborns.

Next to Husain of the Jahād al-Bannā organization and two Syrian drivers, taken on the ground floor of our hospital.

Threads of Compassion

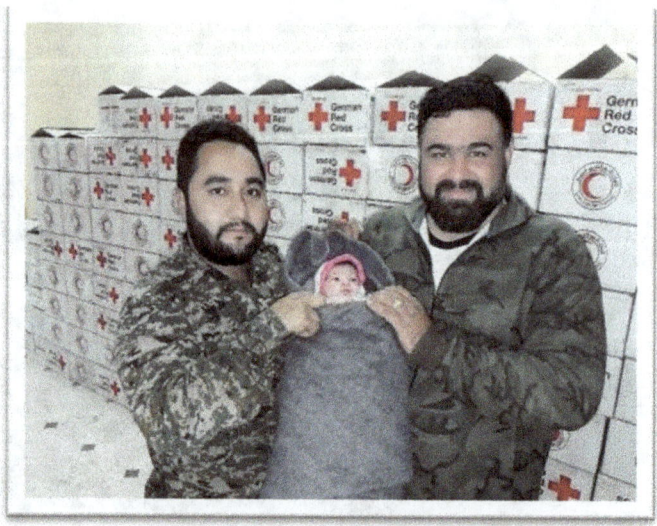

Next to Ābid and one of the hospital's tiny guests, and the relief boxes from the Rd Cross that can be seen in the background. Ābid played a key role in informing me about the geography of the region, as well as the ways to deal and not to deal with the people of the area.

Threads of Compassion

Hāj Rasūl, the commander of the Fātemiyūn Corps in the eastern region of Syria, with whom we sang hymns and psalms in the Tawāshīh groups.

"Distribution Thursdays". A crowd that is several times this size is waiting outside the walls of the hospital to be let in.

Threads of Compassion

My daughter Naba', who was intelligent and well-mannered.

Threads of Compassion

5

I have been out of the hospital for two days now. I'm lying down in some corner of the house. I feel very weak, but as soon as I hear my children's voices and smell the aromas of Somayyeh's cooking, it is as if they have given the world to me. The doctor advised me to keep myself calm as best I could, but it can't be done. The pain of a broken talus bone is excruciating; actually, it is more than broken. It shattered into a hundred pieces. Its pain is with me 24 hours a day, in my sleep as well as in my waking hours. It doesn't leave me alone, even for a moment. The bone of my big toe, my fibula, and some of my ribs are also broken, but their pains are as nothing compared to the pain of my foot. There are only two seconds a day when I do not have any pain, and those are the two seconds after I wake up. Two heavenly seconds. When I open my eyes, I do not have any pain for the blink of an eye. I feel like taking a deep breath and enjoying a body that is free of pain, but as soon as I do, the pain comes around again and grabs hold of my soul and crushes it in its hands.

I become increasingly concerned with every scream Hāmid's wife lets out. We are ten kilometres away from the Moshfi al-Maidāni clinic. Ten kilometres is not far, as long as the expectant mother does not scream in your car. Every few minutes I ask Ābid to go faster. Now Hāmid is like me. His wife's screams have turned into moans; if only we did not have to hear them. I think of Somayyeh. Three years ago, on the night of the birthday of our third child, Muhammad-Hasan, we were in the same situation. Somayyeh was writhing in pain. She kept biting her lips and asking me to go faster. I'm in a state of near panic. My hand is on the horn and my foot is pressing down on the gas pedal.

I have known Hāmid since the first days when the hospital opened. He is one of the guys in charge of the guards' shifts. I feel his spirit becoming more dejected with every moan that his wife lets out. A bumpy road doesn't help matters any either.

Threads of Compassion

God has blessed us after ten years with the birth of Muhammad-Hasan. After Muhammad-Husain and Hāniyeh were born, our house hadn't heard the sound of a baby's crying or the scent of a baby's body. We always wanted our house to be full of the hustle and bustle of children's activities and voices. Now, after ten years, our prayers have been answered. I pray to his namesake for him to be born a healthy child. When we are on the way to the hospital on the night of Lady Fāṭima's ﷺ birthday, I ask her to give us a birthday present. I press down harder on the gas pedal.

Hāmid is eating himself up inside. I know how he is feeling. He's going through what I went through that night. His wife lost one of her kidneys as a child and cannot get pregnant. In her previous two pregnancies, her babies were stillborn. He's more worried about his wife than the baby. The mother must have a caesarean section to stay healthy, but nothing can be done for the child. To get to the operating room in order to perform the caesarean section, we have two options. Either the Deir ez-Zūr hospital, which is 130 kilometres away, and is where both previous unsuccessful deliveries were performed, or the Moshfi al-Maidāni clinic, where Dr. Mas'ūd and Dr. Sādeqī had one condition for admission, which is that the condition should be 'white' during the operation, because the priority for admission to the operating room are wounded soldiers. And tonight, of all nights, just when this desperate mother's labour pains have started and she needs to have an operation, military operations are also ongoing. The rain pounds the windows. The road trembles under the artillery fire from both sides, and my thoughts are on the operation theatre that probably will not be available to us given this level of conflict.

I pace up and down the corridor behind the door of the delivery room. I want Somayyeh and Muhammad-Hasan to be healthy. Three hours had passed since she entered the operating room, and its door still remained closed. My anxiety won't leave me alone. I have resorted to repeating the Yā Zahrā *dhikr*.

God is with us, and we are able to reach the operating room before the soldiers who will inevitably be injured as a result of the artillery exchange. Hāmid, his mother, and I, as well as some of the field hospital staff are gathered behind the door of the operating room. Everyone knows what is at stake and have gathered to see what will happen in the end.

I have brought Umm Munīr and Khadīja with me, along with a big bag of birthing medicines, to have them help Dr. Masʿūd and Dr. Sādeqī. Umm Ahmad is also on standby in the hospital so that if we need anything, he can send it to us by ambulance. Right from the start, we realize we have forgotten to take a vial of metronidazole, which is an antibiotic that is used in such operations to preclude infections from arising. The clinic's phone is on its top floor and the operating room is on the bottom floor. I can't go to the phone because I don't know where the metronidazole is. Umm Munīr and Khadījah are busy, and their hands have already been washed and sterilized, so they cannot go out of the operating room. We have to communicate with the hospital by radio. Umm Ahmad goes to the ambulance's radio in the hospital and Umm Munīr is on my radio outside the operating room.

The hospital continually shakes from the artillery shells exploding in its vicinity because ISIS is taking aim at our artillery battery, which is very close to the clinic. The exchange of artillery fire is escalating by the minute. I feel like taking out my phone and recording everything that's going on so that the child who is on his way will be able to see what people went through in order to bring him into this world. I borrow Dr. Sādeqī's phone and start recording. Umm Ahmad and Umm Munīr are talking about childbirth medicines on the radio when suddenly the voice of the telecommunication operator comes through complaining. He's right. When does one ever talk about childbirth medicines on military radios in the middle of an operation?? And for two women to be carrying on the conversation at that! I quickly dispatch one of the guys to explain the matter to the telecommunications guys over the phone. We've messed up, big time. The poor guys had thought that the integrity of the operation was breached and that ISIS has given radios to a couple of women as their way of poking fun at us. I realize later that if we hadn't explained things to the operator, the whole operation would have been cancelled, wasting all of the time and effort that was put into it.

Threads of Compassion

We are all overcome by anxiety until Umm Ahmad finally finds the vial of antibiotics and sends it over. Everyone is repeating their own *dhikrs* as we all wait behind the door of the operating room. The conflict has continued to rage and has now reached its peak. The ground is shaking under our feet. Hāmid's situation is worse than the rest of us. He paces around, then sits down, then paces again, all the while praying and wiping the tears from the corners of his eyes.

A few minutes before the birth, Dr. Sādeqī determines that the baby has died inside the womb. The news hits me like a bucket of cold water being poured on my head. Were all of our efforts for naught? I turn away so as to avoid seeing Hāmid's face. I can't stand to see him convulsing in sobs like that. We all shed tears for the loss of the life of their baby. It feels as if all of the feelings of fatigue that I have felt in all the time I have been in Syria have come down on my head at once. My heart goes out to Hāmid and to his wife and to their baby who didn't get a chance to open his eyes in this world. If the child was going to be stillborn, why did we bother to come over here? I appeal to Haḍrat Abbās, 'O ye who understands anguish! It is only you who can remove the onus of this anguish from Hāmid's heart.'

Dr. Mas'ūd places the body of the lifeless child, who weighs less than a kilo, next to the stove and massages his heart in the hope that he might be brought to life, but we all know that it is a futile effort because the time of the death of the child in its mother's womb is unknown. But we hold out a modicum of hope, if only because we don't want to let the baby go back without having entered our world.

Finally, the wait is over. Muhammad-Hasan is brought out by a nurse in the cocoon of a blanket. I go towards him excitedly. The warmth of his little body is sweet to behold. Somayyeh is doing fine. I kiss and smell the baby's white lips. He's in a deep and peaceful asleep. I call out his name. My tears of excitement and joy prevent me from being able to see his beautiful face properly. I bend my head down and pronounce the *adhān* (the call to prayer) in his right ear, and weep with joy.

The hospital staff gathered around and read the Quran together. Rasūl is missed. If he was here, he would have sat facing the Qibla and read the Quran, and his voice would echo in the corridors, moving something in the depths of our emotions and releasing our emotional frustrations. Umm Munīr gives a moment-to-moment report of any news coming out of the operating room to Hāmid's mother by cracking open the door, and the old woman sheds tears. I'm exhausted from calling on Haḍrat Abbās, 'O ye who understands anguish! ...', when Dr. Mas'ūd's raised voice is heard saying,

'He's back! The child is back!'

Haḍrat Abbās came through. Hāmid's tearful face is now overjoyed with happiness, as is everyone else's. Hāmid's mother is beside herself, and the medical staff are still reading the Quran. Hāmid kisses all of our faces. He is no longer the Hāmid of an hour ago; he has now become a father.

Umm Munir brings the newborn baby which is wrapped in a blanket out of the operating room. The medical staff and Hāmid's mother send salutations. Everyone's eyes are wet with joyful emotions. The newborn is placed in his father's arms. He is asleep, heedless of this world and its sounds. Hāmid sheds tears and places his face next to that of his newborn. He smells him and kisses him. He is all sweetness and is a sight to behold. He comes towards me and places the baby in my arms, and says, 'As a token of my appreciation for the efforts of the Iranians, I will name him Ehsān.'

Now it's my turn to shed tears and place my face next to that of Hāmid's newborn son's face. Oh, how ISIS would seethe in seeing this naming ceremony.

There are many women who have conditions similar to that of Hāmid's wife in al-Harī: patients for whom we cannot do anything and who must be referred either to the hospital in Deir ez-Zūr or to al-Mayādīn or Damascus.

Sending a patient over who needs a blood transfusion is not a problem, but it is a difficult decision to have to make to send someone who is suspected of collaborating with ISIS. The decision as to whether it is dangerous for them to *stay* is mine, but the decision as to whether it is safe for them to *leave* is Colonel Haitham's, who is the commander of the Syrian Akram

Brigade, which is garrisoned in the region. The number of patients who must be sent to other hospitals is so large that we have set up a weekly minibus service to Deir ez-Zūr. The passengers board this minibus with a ticket that is signed by me and countersigned by Colonel Haitham. There are many requests to leave the area. I am surprised by all the insistent requests of people who want to go to Damascus. How can someone who does not have the means to make ends meet here think that they can survive in the most expensive city in Syria, merely because they have been able to obtain my signature on their exit papers? The situation is even more surprising considering the fact that their treatments will take up to two or three months. I thus feel obliged to ask them where they will be staying so that perhaps putting the question to them will make them reconsider their decision to want to leave. What's interesting is that they all have practically the same answer at the ready, which is that their mother has a cousin in Damascus with whom they can stay. I think I'm being played for a fool. I have yet to learn the principles of tribal life. Everything they have is at each other's disposal, and it doesn't matter whether the person in question is a cousin or brother or a mother's cousin. Nor does it matter how far apart they live, whether it's five kilometres or 500, or whether they live right next door to each other. What's important is that they are of the same blood. They go from al-Harī to Damascus, with their hopes pinned on a blood relative whom they may only have known by name until then. Now a war has started in this country where people take life just as easily as it came to them; a war in which relatives draw guns on each other. Someone whose blood has boiled over because a stranger has shed the blood of a loved one will cool down with the passage of time; but the fire of hatred that is lit by the blood of these people shedding each other's blood cannot be extinguished so easily.

When I'm relieved by knowing the nature of the tribal relationship of people's "cousins", I no longer ask where or with whom they intend to stay for these three months. All I do now is to call Dr. Najmuddīn, the head of the Deir ez-Zūr Hospital, to ensure that there is indeed a cure for a given disease in Damascus, Al-Mayādīn, or Deir ez-Zūr. Now, the only thing I have to make sure of is that the patient is in fact ill, and that he cannot be treated here in our facilities. I'm not strict with any of them anymore, with the exception of some. Some, such as that rich woman who came up to me one day.

The minibus that takes the patients to Damascus, Al-Mayādīn, or Deir ez-Zūr has taken off already, but she still insisted that she needed to go to Damascus. All this insistence for going to Damascus raised my suspicions – the insistence of a middle-aged woman who doesn't have any ostensible illness and always finds an excuse to go to Damascus, excuses that range from seeing her extended family in Damascus to needing to get treatment for her daughters. She thinks that my signature alone is enough for her to be able to board the bus and is unaware of the requirement to have Colonel Haitham's signature as well. Either that, or she has thought about some ruse for that eventuality as well. For several days now, she has been coming to the hospital the first thing in the morning under some pretext, and the minute she sees me on my own, she comes forward and starts insisting on getting her way. One day, when she saw that no matter what she did I would not budge from my decision, she suddenly put her hand in my jacket pocket and placed a small package in it. It contained forty thousand Syrian lira. I was taken aback in surprise as forty thousand lira was the equivalent to a month's salary for a nurse in Aleppo. There was thus not a minute to lose. I quickly wrote a pass in her name and signed it, so that she would come over the following morning after the morning prayers to be sent off on the bus.

She showed up in the early hours of the morning, as expected, together with two sheep that she wanted to take with her, her two daughters, and a stooped-over old man whose head was covered by a red kufi. I point to the old man and say,

'This was not in our agreement.'

She puts a hand on the old man's shoulder and says,

'He's disabled.'

Imād arrives right on cue. I knew he would arrive on time. Concerned looks are exchanged between the woman and her daughters and the disabled old man. Imād takes the kufi off the disabled old man's face and head, only to reveal that he is neither old nor disabled, and no longer bent over either, for that matter. He stands frozen stiff and speechless in a corner. He's been outed in a big way. It's time to check the girls now. All sorts of junk are to be found hidden in the shawls that are tied around their waists, including a lot of dollars. They become Imād's first detainees of the morning. In Al-Bukamal, having [a substantial amount of] money is a kind of crime. Now, here in Al-Harī, among the families of ISIS members and sympathizers, here's a woman who gives 40,000 lira bribes and who has been found with a lot of dollars in her possession. When the city was under ISIS rule, if you had Syrian lira instead of *fulūs* (money minted under ISIS auspices), you were in trouble with ISIS; and if you had dollars instead of Syrian lira now, you were in trouble with us. The rules of an area that is populated by people who had been displaced by the war said that if your case was not problematic, you shouldn't really have any money at all. Or if you did, you would have very little. You would certainly not have as much as to be able to make a 40,000-lira bribe, and a whole lot of dollars besides stashed away in your daughters' clothing. After Imād took his detainees back to his headquarters, I was left with the two sheep which will be confiscated loot that will go to benefit the hospital.

*

Threads of Compassion

Praise be to God. What kind of a trial is this. Here on the front line and right up against ISIS?

I curse Satan and, crumple their bus pass and throw it in the waste bin. When something like this happened the first time, I thought it was another one of the pranks of our own guys, but this has happened several times before. My head feels heavy. My thoughts go back to the first nights when this hospital started its operation, and the words of the blond-haired man to Dr. Karīm. He was right to be so concerned.

I look at a crumpled pass in the bin. Now I finally understand why that cleric at the airport wanted us to avoid going to the homes of the locals. Now I finally understand why that blond-haired man wanted a Syrian man to be in charge of this hospital rather than me, even though Karīm had vouched for me. I feel like taking her bus pass and setting it on fire in the middle of the hospital courtyard so that everyone can see how angry I am. Angry at myself, at this war, at this pass and at the person who authored it, and at the nature of human beings who are so susceptible to error and who so easily jump to the wrong conclusions.

Rahīm's words over the phone put out the fire that was eating me up, just like it did the first time he called from Syria when I was still hesitating and didn't know how to let my family know that my going away to Syria had been confirmed. It seemed as if he was assigned to call me that night to calm me down and encourage me to bring up the subject of my trip to Syria with my family. And tonight, he called from

Threads of Compassion

Aleppo, which is 650 kilometres away, to put out the fire that was eating me up, and to calm me down. He looks out for me. We talk every night; either I call him, or he calls me. He was the one who called tonight. He seems to have intuited that I needed to hear his words. I wish he wasn't so far away so that he could come over just so that we could talk over a cup of coffee. He says, 'Rahīm's reputation is bound up with Ehsān,' and he is right. He has stuck his neck out for me. Well, not his 'neck' exactly, but you know, his reputation, his reputation in the whole region. It is no small matter for the commander of the health services to warrant you in the entire region and to put you in charge of a city full of husbandless women.

Every time I talk to Rahīm, I thank God and ask myself, 'What would I do if I didn't have Rahīm?' Who knows what kinds of things could have occurred if he wasn't around. I think that Rahīm is Khānūm Jān's ﷺ emissary, one of whose functions it is to remind "Doctor" Ehsān that he holds Rahīm's reputation in the palm of his hand, and to remind him why he is here and for whom he is working. In whatever I do, obtaining Lady Zainab's ﷺ approval and satisfaction is the governing criterion. I must always bear this in mind and remember that I have nothing of my own, and that whatever I have is from [the grace of] Khānūm Jān ﷺ.

Rahīm puts the brakes on my emotions so that I don't make a decision in anger. The best reaction to these letters is to ignore them. Now it can be in

Threads of Compassion

anyone's name. All of the men who work at the hospital here feel sorry for these women, myself included. These are women who have suffered a lot and thirst for kindness and affection. Whatever the war is able to destroy, it is not able to destroy people's basic needs. The need to love and to be loved is demonstrated to us here, 800 kilometres from Damascus, in an ISIS-infested area among local women who are suspected of collaborating with ISIS. The person who has caused the pass to be written in her name is unimportant; what is important is the human need that the act represents, which need has hardly been diminished, even under the churning of the heavy wheels of war. And what is even more important is the imperative to maintain one's piety, which, by the grace of God and the grace of Khānūm Jān ﷺ, protects us and her neighbors.

The nurses are busy, and the corridor is crowded with people. I end my call with Rahīm and go to see what's going on. I exit the room, thinking that we might have a case of a mother giving birth to twins or something. But the ruckus is on account of Naba'. She is hugging and kissing all of the female staff. Everyone is congratulating her. She is beside herself with joy. When she sees me, she runs towards me. She points to the middle-aged lady who is with her, telling me that she is her aunt who has returned from Damascus. When she makes the introductions, I can see that her aunt's eyes become filled with everything that Naba' has said about me. The poor child must have sung my praises, and has brought her aunt here to the

Threads of Compassion

hospital to show her who Dr. Ehsān is. Naba' wants to come back to the hospital again to help out. Her aunt has no objection, nor do I, but I say that she should only do so after her school is out. I tell her that she should study hard so that she can achieve her dream of becoming a doctor. I am overjoyed at having made the right decision that day to allow her to stay in the hospital temporarily. Naba' could still have been here, showing me to her aunt, but it would not have been like this. It would have been at a distance and perhaps with spite, with Naba' pointing me out to her aunt saying that this is that same Dr. Ehsān who refused to help me, and who didn't let me stay here. I'm about to invite her aunt to my room for a coffee when the sound of a little girl screaming reaches us from the emergency room.

The poor thing is no more than 10 years old. She is holding her injured arm and screaming continually. When more than a thousand visits are registered in the hospital's registry every day, we expect to see all kinds of issues, from gynecology and obstetrics and internal medicine to skin diseases and burns, and now, fractures. I prevail on her to sit down on the bed with some difficulty. She's bent over her arm and won't allow anyone to examine it. What I wouldn't give for this hospital to have an x-ray machine so that the child could be examined without having to touch her swollen hand and so she wouldn't scream the way she was. The severity of the swelling in her arm tells me she has a double fracture, in both her radius and ulna. I carefully move my fingers under the radius blade of her forearm and the little girl screams out in pain. By the time I align the bones and secure their position with a splint, she has screamed out so much in pain that her voice has become hoarse.

We have set so many fractures and have bandaged them with splints so many times without the benefit of an x-ray machine that eventually, one such machine made its own way to the hospital one day! I don't know if this came about as a result of our prayers or on account of the right of the innocent people who came to us with fractures that needed to be seen to properly. One of the residents pulled me aside and made a good suggestion to me. He said that there is an old portable x-ray machine in one of the hospitals in Sālihīya, and that he can transfer it to our hospital with our help.

We manage to bring the device to Al-Bukamal by hook and by crook, and circumambulate it as if we are at the shrine of some saint, touching it all over. Its arm, keyboard, and lens camera are in good working order. They have also brought the Plexiglas drum and the protective lead coat. The only thing that remains to be found, which is the main thing, really, as it is a consumable, is the imaging solution. The problem is that we don't know what, specifically, to look for, and what the Syrian name for this solution is. Dr. Karīm found a radiologist in Damascus and brought him to a safe distance behind the front line, and we got the owner of the device on the phone to have him explain what we meant by the imaging solution to the radiologist, so that he would understand what we needed to procure, which we were finally able to do with his help.

A week later, we became the only hospital equipped with a radiology lab from Al-Mayādīn to Al-Harī. We cover a range of 100 kilometres, in which patients are brought from far and wide to have their bodies x-rayed, from as far afield as Al-Mayādīn city to the Mahīdhlīyah encampment, which is 90 km distance from us.

We do not keep the device in the hospital because of the dangers inherent in its radiation. We have set up a radiology regimen where we send the patient by ambulance to the "radiology centre", which is none other than the house of the owner of the x-ray machine, who takes the necessary pictures, places the finished images under the patient's arm and dispatches him or her back to us by ambulance. God bless Hasan and Ābid's hearts, who drive the patients back and forth to the "radiology centre" diligently. Most of the patients are from Mahīdhlīyah. I feel sorry for them. We have a relief station there that tries to see to the needs of these people in the tents. Abu Ammār is in charge of the station there. He tries to see to the needs of the civilians in addition to seeing to the needs of the wounded soldiers who are brought there to be cared for. They bring their civilians who have emergencies to our hospital by ambulance for treatment and medication.

Threads of Compassion

It's the last day. None of us feels like working; neither me, nor Muhammad, nor Ali, nor the ladies, who have to return to Aleppo tomorrow and make way for the new team. For the first time, I go and keep them company while they have their morning coffee. Dr. Muhammad's eyes keep welling up with tears due to his seasonal allergies. Umm Majd and Umm Munīr shed tears, but not because of any seasonal allergies. It is the bitterest coffee I have ever tasted.

The new team is supposed to arrive after sunset. Muhammad comes to my room and invites me to dinner upstairs on behalf of the medical team. Since the team has been stationed there, I have avoided the second floor so as not to disturb them. I think it is a good opportunity to introduce the new team; the only thing that is left are the gifts. I want the team members to take a souvenir from us and not leave empty handed. I had entrusted Husain with the task of getting something for them a few days ago, but I have not heard back from him yet. It is not a simple task to find suitable mementos and in the right quantity in the chaos of war. I'm thinking of the gifts, when Husain shows up holding a big box. He has come to my rescue at the last moment, just like what happened with the diapers and powdered milk. He is in a hurry and doesn't wait for me to finish my prayer. He blurts out,

'These are war booty. I obtained the permission to use them too. That's it; I'm out of here. Bye!'

Threads of Compassion

I finish up my prayers quickly and leap up towards the box. It is full of red rechargeable lanterns. This is a great parting present for people in Syria, where electricity goes out for several hours every day. I counted them; there are twenty of them, which means that I now have a gift for the new team members as well as the departing ones.

The new and old team are sitting around the table. I swallow my last mouthful of Umm Munīr's delicious hummus. I clear my throat and take some notes I have jotted down out of my pocket. I wish Abūta was there to help me, as my command of Arabic was nothing to write home about. His leave has been extended, leaving us without a translator. I say a quick *bismillah* in my heart and start my little welcoming speech.

اهلاً و سهلاً بالنفرات الجديد و شكراً من دكاتور و ممرضات القديم. شكراً فى اعماق قلبى. والله هلا انتم نفس اختى و نفس اخى و فراقكم بس اصعب. و انا من بعد دائماً بذكركم. والله لاننسيكم ابداً. انا كثير مشتاقكم. انشاءالله مجدداً شوفكم و معكم فى خدمت شعب المظلوم. لكن انشاءالله فى مره البعد مشفينا فى جوار بيت المقدس و بعد الهزم الاسراييل انشاءالله.

Thank God that the new arrivals are still confused and that the staff who are leaving are over-wrought with emotions, otherwise they would have been laughing until daybreak at the new form of the Arabic language I had invented. I don't know what they understood from my words, but this is what I wanted to say:

> 'I bid the new staff a hearty welcome, and give my heartfelt thanks to the doctors and nurses who are leaving us. I thank you for your services from the bottom of my heart. By God, you are no different than my sisters and brothers, and saying goodbye to you is even more difficult.' I have a lump in my throat. 'I will always remember you; and God will never forget you either. I will miss you a lot. God willing, I will see you again before too long, as you continue your service to those who are oppressed. But, God willing, at a time in the not-too-distant future, we will be providing medical services in the vicinity of Jerusalem after the defeat of Israel, God willing.'

As soon as I was done with my speech, the members of the old team began to believe that they were going to leave, and they each started to break down in tears one by one. They give each other hugs and cry out loud. The lump I have in my throat isn't going anywhere soon. Muhammad comes towards me, and I put my head on his shoulder and start to cry. Anyone who didn't know us would have thought we were brothers

– real brothers. They would think that we are brothers who are going to be separated from each other after having spent many years together, which is why we were crying so hard. Even those who knew we were not brothers still wouldn't believe that Muhammad and I have only spent two weeks together. And even if such a person could get over this, he still couldn't get over the fact that I am Shī'a and Muhammad is Sunni – and a Sunni Muslim who until a week ago believed that the Shī'a do not believe in the Quran. I hug him harder and my sobs get louder. The new team look at us in bewilderment. I don't feel a need to provide an explanation. When they stay here for a week themselves, they'll understand how hard it is to leave this hospital and its hard work and cold nights. Then they'll understand how hard it is to leave these people and the looks of gratitude in their eyes, when they raise their hands heavenward and pray for our continued health and well-being.

Threads of Compassion

Chapter Five Photos

The Mushfi al-Maidāni clinic, which was ten kilometres away from us, to whose operating room we took Hāmid's wife, where she gave birth.

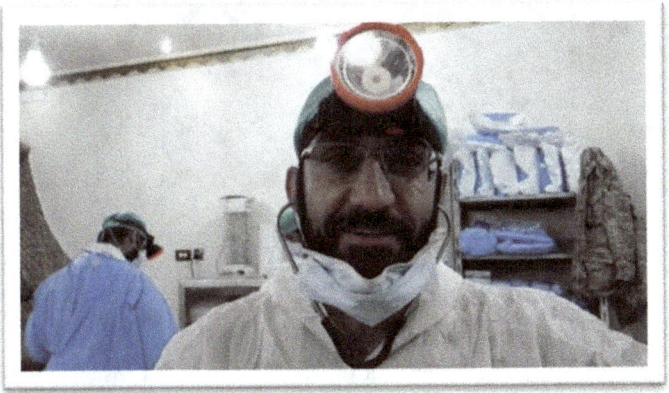

Dr. Muhammad Sādiqī moments before the operation on Hāmid's wife.

Threads of Compassion

Dr. Mas'ūd, Dr. Sādiqī's assistant in the Mushfi al-Maidānī clinic. According to the laws that were in force on the war front, wherever there was work to be done, it was everyone's responsibility to get it done. This included the reinforcement of the walls of the Mushfi al-Maidānī clinic's security kiosk, the responsibility for which fell on Dr. Mas'ūd.

Threads of Compassion

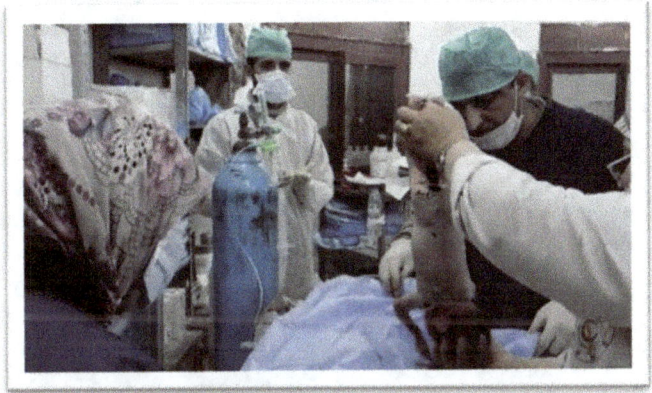

A doctor whose name I have forgotten, and Khadīja and Umm Munīr, reviving little Ehsān, Hāmid's son, and a nurse praying behind the oxygen capsule.

Rahīm, the head of the Aleppo Hospital, who looked out for me from hundreds of miles away.

Threads of Compassion

Naba' would come to the hospital after her school was over and would hang out with us. Here, she can be seen with her sister Māria, together with a midwife from the new team.

Threads of Compassion

Here, Husain can be seen, who was one of the people who worked for the Jihād al-Bannā organization and who never let me down. He would find whatever it was that I needed, even if he had to find it under a rock.

6

I feel pain throughout my whole body. I'm lying in bed at home, staring at the ceiling, waiting for my many broken bones to heal so that I can go back to Khānūm Jān ﷺ. I'm willing to suffer these pains for the rest of my life, as long as I can go back to Khānūm Jān's ﷺ neighbours. Poor Somayyeh has so much work to do. She always looks exhausted but is always smiling. I don't even have one healthy leg so that I could at least hop over to the kitchen to help her out. My talus bone and head start to ache as soon as I move. My brain shoots the pain from my head right to the middle of the talus bone in my foot. And for its part, the talus bone responds decisively, shooting the pain right back up, straight to the middle of my brain. And I am left in the middle of all this, clawing onto the bed.

All of us are feeling hungry together. Before the new medical team has had a chance to get its bearings, we are surrounded by ISIS. It's been a week since we have had anything decent to eat. Instead of eating three meals a day, we are rationed down to eating once a day. Al-Bukamal's communications are cut off from all sides. No one can come in or leave. Both sides of the road are closed: the road that leads south to Al-Qā'im, as well as the other end, which leads north to al-Mayādīn. The fighting on the front line is fiercer than ever. The windows of the building constantly shake with the force of explosions. Every night before going to sleep, we make sure the machine gun magazines are loaded and sleep with our fingers around their trigger guards. I sleep lightly and jump at any sound. The phone lines are down. Nobody in Iran knows anything about our situation. I yearn to hear the voices of my children once more. Don't worry about us, Somayyeh. I don't know if Somayyeh has seen the fact that my phone is no longer on the grid, and whether she has realized that Al-Bukamal is under siege. I don't know whether this would give her a nervous breakdown and whether or not she has been hospitalized for a couple of nights. I know how hard it is for me to be away from her, but I don't know how much harder it must be for her not to know about my status and condition.

I keep the two-way radio with me at all times, as we can receive an order at any moment to head towards Al-Qā'im or to go up to the roof of the hospital. Throughout all this, we have expectant mothers who are on the verge of childbirth. We can postpone seeing to the needs of other patients, but needless to say, we cannot postpone a childbirth. What can we say to a baby who is running headlong to come into this world?

A teenage girl paces around the building wailing. The pain of childbirth has brought tears to her eyes; she is beside herself in pain. I don't go to her so as not to disturb her. Her mother is holding her head in her hands and following her daughter. She looks so much like Hāniyeh.

The day is half over, and the girl is still screaming out in pain. There is so much of this kind of screaming echoing through the corridors of the hospital every day that we have become deaf to them and no longer hear them. But this time it's different. It's the moans of a teenage girl who is not strong enough to give birth to the baby she is carrying inside her; the moans of a teenage girl who is on the verge of becoming a mother. I go up to the door of the maternity ward to make sure of the situation. I avoid interfering with the process of childbirth as much as possible, but I am worried. Three hours have passed since the epidural injection was administered. I don't want anything bad to happen. We have to see to everything right here as all the roads are closed. No one can come in to help, nor can the girl be sent away. Asīla and Saʿīda, the midwives of the new team, urge the girl on.

'Yā'lla mama! yā'lla mama! al-sarīʿ! al-sarīʿ! Come on, mother! Hurry! Hurry!'

I am worried about this girl. I appeal to Khānūm Jān 🕌 to help her. I am afraid that this siege will turn the sweetness of becoming a mother into poison for the girl.

An hour later, the midwives place a black-haired baby boy in my arms so that I can pronounce the call to prayer in his right ear. Heedless of the heat of the battle and drowned in a deep sleep, he moves his chin slightly. Looking at him makes my eyes well up with tears. He is a gift from Khānūm Jān 🕌 in this ongoing siege. I wish I could tell him all about her poor mother who is still shedding tears. When I get to the part in the call to prayer where I testify that Ali is the *walī*[34] of God, my tears start to flow too. I hold the baby boy closer to my breast. I ask Imam Ali 🕌 to help me serve his daughter's neighbours in a way that is worthy and befitting.

The teenage girl sobs. I wish she didn't look so much like Hāniyeh. Her heart is full of sorrow: the sorrow of having to raise her child on her own, the sorrow of a husband who is unaware of her situation,

---

[34] [*walī*: 1. regent, sovereign, lord and master; 2. patron, guardian, protector, custodian; 3. Friend (of God), 'saint'.]

Threads of Compassion

and the sorrow of having to face a world that has shown her nothing but its harshness. Even Asīla's jokes can't bring a smile to her face. Sa'īda bends down and kisses her head, but she continues to convulse with her sobbing. Her tears have broken all of our hearts.

The black-haired baby's arrival was felicitous. With his arrival, the siege was broken, the roads were finally opened, and the telephone lines were reconnected. I pray that his coming into the world will be as felicitous for his young mother. I spend all my time sitting by the phone from morning till night, talking to my family back home. I can't get enough of hearing their voices. An important guest arrived on the day the siege was broken. The guest was so important that I can't name him. He came to check how the hospital was being run. I am busy giving a report to our VIP in my room when Ābid knocks on the door.

'Doctor, Asīla and Sa'īda are looking for you.'

'Why don't they come in?'

'They are preoccupied in the maternity ward.'

I can't leave the VIP alone.

'Tell them that I am in a meeting and will join them in about an hour.'

A few minutes later Ābid is at my door again.

'They need you urgently, Doctor!'

The VIP and I make our way towards the maternity ward. Asīla and Saideh are standing in front of the door of the ward. A woman had come in with severe labor pains. The problem is that she has to undergo a caesarean section but her name is not registered in the hospital register. Caesarean sections are usually sent to Deir ez-Zūr; but only on the condition that they have been seen by us since the beginning of their pregnancy so that we know about their condition and have coordinated their requirements with the Deir ez-Zūr hospital and transfer them there at least two days before their due date. This lady has now shown up at the last minute and states that her previous birth was a cesarean section too. There is no time to drive her 130 kilometres to Deir ez-Zūr. This is even more the case given the physiology of the women of this region who have broken the record of giving birth within five minutes of the start of their labor pains. I have seen many women come in with labor pain, be given an epidural injection, and give birth five minutes later. The Mushfi Al-Madāini clinic is not an option either as its surgeon has gone to Deir ez-Zūr to perform an emergency operation. We are left with a mother who is suffering severe labour pains, and a baby who just wants to be born and is not concerned about the details of how this is to take place. What has exacerbated the situation, of course, is our VIP guest who is following the situation very closely.

I'm concerned about the condition of the mother, and have to make a decision as to whether she should be transferred or should stay here. On the other hand, I'm dejected because everything is always in order in this hospital, but now that we have an important inspector who just happens to be standing in front of the door of the maternity ward, something like this has to happen. Asīla thinks we should deliver the baby right here with a natural delivery. When she sees my surprise, she says,

'Let us do our best and leave the rest in God's hands.'

Asīla is such a skilled midwife that she is renowned among obstetricians, but I still fear to entrust the life of this mother and child to her hands. Even Sa'īda, who is her assistant, is more surprised than me. She tells me, 'Doctor, don't let her, she's gone crazy!'

She shares my fear that a uterus that has been operated on twice before will not be able to withstand the pressure of childbirth and will burst open. No matter how I figure it, there is no other choice but to transfer her out. My brain is overheating. I can't risk it. If, God forbid, something goes wrong during the transfer, it would be the mother's fault for not having come to us sooner and for having left everything to the last minute. But if something goes wrong in the hospital, we will be the ones who are responsible, as we would have failed in our duty, which was to transfer the mother out. I want to get on the radio and have an ambulance prepared for dispatch, but Asīla intervenes.

'Doctor, what is that liturgy that you sometimes recite after the morning prayer?

'I recite the Quran.'

'No, the one you recite together after reciting the Quran.'

'Ah. That's the Āshūrā *ziārat*.'

'I don't know what this Āshūrā *ziārat* is, but I sit on the steps in the morning and listen to your recitation and get positive energy from it.'

I look at her, astonished. Our VIP is just as astonished as I am.

Asīla continues, 'Please recite it together like you do in the morning behind the door of the maternity ward and give me the energy I need, and I will promise to deliver the mother and the child to you safely.'

She says this and takes Sa'īda by the hand and they both disappear into the maternity ward. What else could I say?? Neither had I ever thought that one day a Christian woman would ask me to recite the Āshūrā *ziārat* for her during the performance of her midwifery duties in order for her to get the energy she needs, nor had our VIP ever recited the Āshūrā *ziārat* during the course of any of his inspections, let alone his having done so behind the door of a maternity ward! Ābid and Hasan join our group. I turn to face the Qiblah and put my hand on my chest and begin the recital.

اَلسَّلاَمُ عَلَيْكَ يَا أَبَا عَبْدِ اللهِ، اَلسَّلاَمُ عَلَيْكَ يَا بْنَ رَسُولِ اللهِ، اَلسَّلاَمُ عَلَيْكَ يَا بْنَ أَمِيرِ الْمُؤْمِنِينَ، وَابْنَ سَيِّدِ الْوَصِيِّينَ، اَلسَّلاَمُ عَلَيْكَ يَا بْنَ فَاطِمَةَ سَيِّدَةِ نِسآءِ الْعَالَمِينَ،

Peace be upon you o Abā 'Abdallāh;
Peace be unto you, o son of the

Messenger of Allah; Peace be unto you o son of the Commander of the Faithful, and son of the leader of the inheritors (of the mission and ministry of the Prophet); Peace be unto you o son of Fātimah, the leader of the women of all worlds.

أَلسَّلَامُ عَلَيْكَ يَا ثَارَ اللهِ وَابْنَ ثَارِهِ وَالْوِتْرَ الْمَوْتُورَ، أَلسَّلَامُ عَلَيْكَ وَعَلَىٰ الْأَرْوَاحِ الَّتِي حَلَّتْ بِفِنَآئِكَ

Peace be unto you o he who was killed and whose blood has not yet been avenged – and whose avenging is in the hands of God; and peace be unto you, o son of one who was killed and whose blood has not yet been avenged (Imam 'Ali Ibn Abi Talib) and peace be unto you o he who was (killed) alone. Peace be unto you and also upon those souls who accompanied you to your death.

Emotions well up in me, forming a lump in my throat.

يَا أَبَا عَبْدِ اللهِ، إِنِّي أَتَقَرَّبُ إِلَىٰ اللهِ، وَإِلَىٰ رَسُولِهِ، وَإِلَىٰ أَمِيرِ الْمُؤْمِنِينَ، وَإِلَىٰ فَاطِمَةَ، وَإِلَىٰ الْحَسَنِ، وَإِلَيْكَ بِمُوَالَاتِكَ، وَبِالْبَرَاءَةِ مِمَّنْ قَاتَلَكَ، وَالْجَوْرِ عَلَيْكُمْ وَأَبْرَأُ إِلَىٰ اللهِ وَإِلَىٰ رَسُولِهِ مِمَّنْ أَسَّسَ أَسَاسَ ذَٰلِكَ وَ بَنَىٰ عَلَيْهِ بُنْيَانَهُ، وَجَرَىٰ فِي ظُلْمِهِ وَجَوْرِهِ عَلَيْكُمْ وَعَلَىٰ أَشْيَاعِكُمْ

> *O Abā ʿAbdallāh! Surely I seek closeness to God and to His Messenger and to the Commander of the Faithful and to Fāṭima and to Hasan and to you through love of you and through distancing myself from those who laid the foundations and those who built upon and carried out oppression and cruelty upon you all and upon your followers.*

The mother starts screaming. My heart is in turmoil. All four of us shed tears as we continue our recital.

أَللَّهُمَّ اجْعَلْ مَحْيَايَ مَحْيَا مُحَمَّدٍ وَآلِ مُحَمَّدٍ، وَمَمَاتِي مَمَاتَ مُحَمَّدٍ وَآلِ مُحَمَّدٍ

> *O Allah! Make me live the life of Muhammad and the family of Muhammad and permit me to die the death of Muhammad and the family of Muhammad.*

Asīla's and Saʿīda's voices intermingle with the mother's screams. '*Yā'lla mama! yā'lla mama! al-sarīʿ! al-sarīʿ!*' 'Come on, mother! Hurry! Hurry!' They encourage her to push harder and finish what she started. I close my eyes. Now I am yelling at the top of my voice too:

أَلسَّلاَمُ عَلَيْكَ يَا أَبَا عَبْدِ اللهِ وَعَلَىٰ الأَرْوَاحِ الَّتِي حَلَّتْ بِفِنَآئِكَ، عَلَيْكَ مِنِّي سَلاَمُ اللهِ أَبَداً مَا بَقِيتُ

وَبَقِيَ اللَّيْلُ وَالنَّهَارُ، وَلاَ جَعَلَهُ اللهُ آخِرَ الْعَهْدِ مِنِّي لِزِيَارَتِكُمْ، أَلسَّلاَمُ عَلَى الْحُسَيْنِ، وَعَلَى عَلِيِّ بْنِ الْحُسَيْنِ، وَعَلَى أَوْلاَدِ الْحُسَيْنِ، وَعَلَى أَصْحَابِ الْحُسَيْنِ.

Peace be unto you O Abā 'Abdallāh and unto the souls which were annihilated with you. Unto you, from me, is the peace of Allah for eternity, as long as the night and the day remain; and please do not make this (ziyārat) as my last contact with you. Greetings be unto Husain, and unto Ali, the son of Husain, and unto the progeny of Husain, and unto the companions of Husain.

I beseech the baby who is on the way to endure a little bit longer, and to strive to come into this world and to see it; to come into a world in which the days of war and hard times will pass, and in which life shows its happy face to him and to his mother. I take recourse in my master to intercede on our behalf so that I will not be shamed for not having performed my duty before this mother and child, before these people, before this genuinely Christian woman, and before our important guest. Then the miracle happens, and words of congratulation and felicitation can be heard.

I open my eyes. Sa'īda's happy face says it all, and I am assured of the health of the mother as well as her baby. Sa'īda approaches. Her tone is calm and her tone is jocose.

'By God, Asīla is truly crazy!'

There are many tears and even more smiles. Sa'īda goes back into the maternity ward. I fall down in prostration.

اَللّٰهُمَّ لَكَ الْحَمْدُ حَمْدَ الشَّاكِرِينَ لَكَ عَلىٰ مُصَابِهِمْ. اَلْحَمْدُ لِلّٰهِ عَلىٰ عَظِيمِ رَزِيَّتِي. اَللّٰهُمَّ ارْزُقْنِي شَفَاعَةَ الْحُسَيْنِ يَوْمَ الْوُرُودِ، وَ ثَبِّتْ لِي قَدَمَ صِدْقٍ عِنْدَكَ مَعَ الْحُسَيْنِ وَأَصْحَابِ الْحُسَيْنِ الَّذِينَ بَذَلُوا مُهَجَهُمْ دُونَ الْحُسَيْنِ، عَلَيْهِ السَّلاَمُ.

O Lord! To You belongs all praise; the praise of those who are thankful to You for their tribulations. All Praise belongs to God for my intense grief. O Lord, grant me the blessing of the intercession of Husain on the Day of Appearance (before You) and strengthen me with a truthful stand in Your presence along with Husain and the companions of Husain – those people who sacrificed everything for Husain, peace be unto him.

I wish I could stay in this same position of prostration for the rest of my life and, continually recite the prayer, *and strengthen me with a truthful stand in Your presence along with Husain.* Because everything is in Husain's hands. Everything is in Husain's hands. Everything.

Threads of Compassion

None of us knew that this was Asīla's first experience in this kind of delivery method. To put it the way she put it herself, it was only because of the energy she got from the Āshūrā *ziārat* that she was able to deliver the child safely and to keep its mother alive. We are all delighted, and our VIP is even more delighted that we are. We could have chosen a different path and sent the mother away, and God only knows what would have happened to her in the ambulance on the way. But none of that happened, and we are all left feeling good about ourselves, and it is as if we are floating in the clouds together – a feeling for which I know to whom we are all beholden. The important guest is feeling even better than I am. He feels like we have made him proud before whoever he needs to deliver today's report; before the flag that is raised high on the roof of the hospital and is waving in the breeze; and before those whose blood was shed at the foot of this flag so that it would cast a protective shade over this war-afflicted region.

I feel dejected. I wish that the head of this clan was not coming to the hospital today and I didn't have to invite him for a cup of coffee. I'm talking about Sheikh Hāmid. He has been talking for an hour and I feel like I'm paralyzed. The cup of coffee I'm holding in my hand has gone cold. He's visited the hospital so many times, yet it is only today that I notice the whiteness of his hair. How grand and proud he once was, like a mountain, and how sad and broken he has now become.

I am grief-stricken on account of the sheikh's daughter, who is a young woman who was captured by ISIS. Their family was gathered together one Friday when some ape who knows nothing about God and His ways came and took the sheikh's daughter as a slave. Why? Because they found a black and white TV in their house. I don't know how I can comfort this man. What can I say to cool down the embers of the fire that burns in his heart? Can such embers even *be* cooled down – the grief of losing one's honour?

I had heard a lot of talk about the laws ISIS had; laws prohibiting the use of mobile phones and televisions, laws requiring women to cover their faces in public, the ridiculous ruling that states that a woman can become licit to a man in marriage merely by pronouncing the *takbīr* formula (*allāhu akbar*) three times; and the [compulsory] collection of the alms due (*zakāt*) on Fridays. Hāmid's daughter was captured on one such Black Friday.

I wish I was there that day so that I could break the neck of the ISIS officer and poke his eyes out, and kill him. Hearing the sound of the television set from inside Hāmid's house, the *zakāt* collector ordered Hāmid's daughters to remove their face coverings. He had a preference for the middle girl, who had an infant in her arms and whose husband was working back in

Damascus. He ordered her to sit on the floor, put his hand on her head, and claimed to have made her licit to him in marriage by pronouncing the *takbīr* formula (*allāhu akbar*) three times. Hāmid's shoulders convulse with his sobs and his tears begin to fall; tears which cannot be stopped even by the dignity of his position as the leader of his clan. I shudder to think how many more young women like Hāmid's daughter have had their lives turned black during these *zakāt* Black Fridays. How many other men have lost their honor in this manner? I feel even greater sorrow for Khānum Jān ﷺ who has to witness these things taking place in her city. I remember reading somewhere that after the Battle of Uhud, the Prophet covered the slain body of his uncle, Hamza, with a robe so that his sister, who was approaching, would be spared from seeing Hamza's body in the state that it was. I think how Khānum Jān ﷺ was raised in a house whose bricks and mortars were made of love, and how she had tasted Muhammadan love and seen the kindness of our Prophet, and how she never heard a word that was harsher than the petal of a flower. And then I think about the kinds of things she was exposed to in this city, and how many times a day she has to see artillery craters and fires and the wailing of newly orphaned children. She sees even worse than this, of course. I wish I had a robe as big as this city so that I could cover the city with it to spare Lady Zainab ﷺ from having to see what is happening to her neighbours.

Hāmid's pleas are useless. The ISIS officer looks at him mockingly and says, 'You have paid your *zakāt* for this week. May God accept it from you.'

What are these people doing with the honour of the people, these people who claim to follow the Prophet of Loving Kindness, whose name they have usurped and placed on their flag? Hāmid's grief weighs heavily on my heart throughout the day. I can't stop thinking about him and his grandchildren, children who will never forget that their aunt became a slave of ISIS because they watched a little television. The older they get, the more they understand what happened to their aunt – a woman whose condition is such that even if her body is healthy, will undoubtedly have a badly damaged soul, or one that is already dead. No one knows what has actually happened to her. I think of the remote possibility of her being able to escape the clutches of ISIS somehow, for her to be able to run away, for example, or to be exchanged for a ransom. Where would she go? Would she come back to her home?

Hāmid's coffee has gone cold too. He pulls his robe over his shoulder and prepares to leave. He is like a mountain; a mountain whose insides have been carved out and of which nothing remains but an empty shell. I remember one of the leader's speeches.[35] The development of its human resources is more important than anything else for our revolution because the world is blind and dark without the presence of righteous people. Righteous people are that which gives life and light to this earthly abode. Man is God's *khalīfa,* His vicegerent. I apply this statement to Abu Bakr al-Baghdadi and his claim of vicegerency, irrespective of his so-called revolution and his so-called

---

[35] The following is a statement taken from a speech delivered by Ayatollah Khāmeneī to a group of commanders of the Revolutionary Guards in 1981:

> Truly, this is a fact: that the development of our human resources is more important than anything else for our revolution. If the revolution does not develop its people into new human beings, it has done nothing. If you think about it, the reason for what I am saying will become clear to you. In other words, what I am saying does not really stand in need of any argument, because a world without righteous people is something that is blind, dark, and dead. That which gives life to this earthly abode, gives it value and light, and that which gives rise to meaning is the human being [living out his or her life as he or she was meant to live out his or her life]. [2:30] *"I am going to appoint a vicegerent (*khalīfa*) on the Earth."* Khalīfa (*vicegerent*) is a title given to man by God. Where did God place this *vicegerent*? On the Earth. What kind of land is the Earth without this *vicegerent* and what [inherent] value does it have?

revolutionaries. How are these even remotely connected to human beings and to humanity? How is their behaviour and ideology ever going to give life and light to the world? By violating the honour of others? By shedding the blood of whoever disagrees with them? I search my mind to find even a single good act of theirs that can represent a source of their light. I don't find anything – either in what I have seen, heard, or read. A revolution is a revolution, and it must elevate a nation and enhance its people; it should give life and light to the world. But ISIS has not been able to give life and light even to their own people, let alone to the rest of the world.

> *I feel very depressed. I count the passing of time, not by the day or hour, but by the minute and second. I miss you so much. Even hearing your loving voice from this distance does not give me relief. I wish you were here... My heart desires only you and nothing else. Woe to my heart's desires!*

I put down the pen. As long as I wish it, it will come. Somayyeh's imagination is kind, like Somayyeh herself. She understands how heavily Hāmid's grief weighs on my heart. She sits and listens. I have a whole world of things that I want to say to her. I talk about the people here, about the difficulties of their lives and about the hardships they have endured. I talk about the aspirations I have for them, and about Hāmid's daughter. Somayyeh is the only person who can understand me.

Afāf and Rīma are stocking the medicine shelves with stock from the looted shelves of the ISIS warehouse, whose drugs are being arranged according to various medical indications. Bābā Haidar is hovering above them, causing Afāf and Rīma to double their speed. They quickly empty the cartons and put their contents on the shelves. None of them are tall enough to be able to reach the upper shelves. Bābā Haidar does not even give them a chance to think. He takes the boxes from their hands and places them where they want them, freeing them up to stock other boxes. I was smiling to myself because of this, until a patient arrived in the emergency ward who needed to be seen urgently. I did not call Afāf and Rīma down, as I knew that we could see to the needs of the patient ourselves by the time they came down. Now the shelving of the medicine store has been stocked by Afāf and Rīma under Bābā Haidar's "supervision" in such an orderly way and so quickly that we are all aghast.

It's been a week since Bābā Haidar joined our group. He is a very likable old man. If I don't see him or hear his voice every morning, I feel like I'm missing something all day. I call him 'Bābā', and it is such a sweet moment when he responds by saying, *jān-e bābā*.

He has seen more of the war than the rest of us. His hair turned white during the various wars that he has participated in and witnessed first-hand, from the Iran-Iraq war which started in 1981, to the war in

Libya, in Afghanistan, in Yemen, and now in Syria. Suffice it to say that he has been a nurse in the medical corps for 30 years. He has personally been a witness to anything and everything that we might have read about in books. He is kind-hearted and a jack of all trades, and he has taken over the responsibility for the emergency ward.

Bābā Haidar is so professional and knowledgeable that when our VIP guest tells me on the phone that I need to be away from the hospital for a few days on a special mission, I feel confident that everything will be fine and that the hospital will be in good hands, as I know that Bābā Haidar will run things better than I do. The VIP tells me to be ready after the morning prayer tomorrow for a white Toyota to pick me up.

'What supplies and equipment should I bring with me?'

'Nothing, just bring yourself.'

A thousand questions come to mind, but I cannot ask any of them over the phone. I entrust the hospital to Bābā Haidar the following morning and get in the white Toyota, which had arrived as promised. I expect the driver of the Toyota to make a turn at every alley and side road that we pass, but he goes his own way, heading straight for the heart of the desert. I panic, telling him,

'Brother, you're going the wrong way. If you continue in this direction, we'll be going to Iraq.'

'Don't worry, doc. We'll be coming up to it in no time.'

He has his foot on the gas pedal for a good half hour as he takes us through the sands and the wide expanse of the desert. When I see the barriers at the entrance of Al-Qā'im city [in Iraq], I become convinced that we have taken a wrong turn. I have become suspicious of the driver, as Al-Qā'im is a far cry from Damascus. At the entrance to the city, he turns into a desolate dead-end alley. I keep my hand on the door handle and have my eyes fixed between the driver and the alley. I wish I had asked our VIP friend my questions on the phone yesterday. I wish he had at least given me a description of the driver. I wish I had at least called home yesterday for the last time. I wish... and I wish... and I wish... none of which did me any good right at that moment.

The driver slows down at the end of the alley. The VIP is waiting for me in front of a house, with that characteristic smile on his face. I take in a very deep breath and let out a big sigh. I had been worried for no reason the whole way over, and had fantasized some bad scenarios for myself, and am relieved that that is all they turned out to be.

I can't believe it, but I have been invited to go on a pilgrimage to Karbalā by Imam Husain ﷺ. For eight hundred kilometres, the distance from Al-Qā'im to Karbalā, my heart flutters in anticipation. I still can't believe it, even now that three years have passed. Nor could I believe it at the time that I was sitting in a

Toyota with our VIP and his friend, and that we were going to Karbalā together. After the VIP had witnessed the miracle of the childbirth that day, he said, 'Ehsān, I owe you one.' But I didn't think he would come through like *this!* I figured that when you serve her neighbours, the gift you get will be commensurate with Khānūm Jān's ﷺ generosity. I felt like taking hold of the hands of all of my loved ones and sitting them down on the munificent table spread of this pilgrimage. First of all, my beloved mother.

It had not been our lot to go on a pilgrimage to Karbalā together, and she passed before her time. She was always waiting for Uncle Abdollāh's body to be returned home for all of the twelve years that remained of her life after Uncle Ali and Uncle Abdollāh were martyred. When Abdullah's body was finally returned, she finally found peace and was gone before we had a chance to find out who we were. Now, it is as if she's by my side. I see her holding her *chādor* tightly around her face now, just as tightly as she held it when we were at Uncle Abdollāh's grave. No one saw her in an agitated state that day. We didn't even see her cry. She just sat quietly next to her son. She reached inside the coffin and opened the straps of the shroud one at a time. After ten years, there was nothing left of Uncle Abdollāh. Our wailing could be heard for hundreds of yards within the Martyr's Cemetery, but Mom was very calm that day, just as calm as she was on the day she was told that both her sons [who were fighting on the front line in the Iran-Iraq War] had been martyred.

Threads of Compassion

Uncle Ali's body was returned a year after his martyrdom, Uncle Abdollāh's was returned ten years later, in 1997. We wailed louder every time Mom's hand moved over his shroud. It was as if we wanted her to cry and to wail and to shed tears, but she was calm; very calm. And her peace calmed us down too. One by one she called out our names, and we went quietly to see what she wanted to say. When we became silent, she took his skull and a couple of his bones in her hands and said,

'Send salutations of peace and blessings (*salawāt*) for the health of Agha Khāmeneī.'

Stunned, we sent *salawāt*, as requested. We were looking at Mom in stunned silence, waiting to catch her if she passed out, so she wouldn't fall over. She paused for a moment, as if she was no longer worried about something after having been worried about it for ten years; as if she had reached something that she was heading towards for ten years, and wanted to pass it by; as if she wanted to say something that was on her mind for ten years. She placed the bones back in the coffin and said,

'Their lives were a worthy sacrifice for the health and safety of Agha Khāmeneī (*fadā-ye sar-e khāmeneī*).'

She then gathered her *chādor* tightly around her face, got up, and left the Martyr's Cemetery; calm and resolute, and without any [undue] connection to the coffin that was in front of her feet; without any [undue] connection to what she had given in the way of God.

I cover the 800 kilometres of the hot desert road from al-Qā'im to Karbalā with thoughts of my mother. I miss her so much. For who she was; for her Mashhadī accent; for the aroma of the locally produced clarified butter that she used to make the fried eggs that she made especially for me; for her martyred sons, Uncle Ali and Uncle Abdollāh, who I am sure are now with their mother, accompanying me on my way to Karbalā.

When I got out of the car, I found myself in the middle of the *bayn al-haramayn* (the paved walkway between the shrines of Imam Husain ؏ and Haḍrat Aba'l-Faḍl). I hear the voice of Husain al-Ajami singing in my head:

تجب صلاه الخسوف بكربلا على من حضر
أنّ بين الحرمين جُمع الشّمس والقمر

> *Praying the Prayer of the Eclipse is religiously incumbent on anyone who makes the pilgrimage to Karbalā, because the Sun and the Moon are at one on the path of the bayn al-haramayn.*

What an atmosphere God inspired this poet to create. The poet put together the sentiments one feels when one is in the *bayn al-haramayn* word by word, carving them out, polishing them, and washing them with his tears. I sing along with Husain al-Ajami. I don't know what I would do without Husain, or where I would go without Aba'l-Faḍl. Without Husain, my day is dark; and without [Aba'l-Faḍl] al-Abbas, my night is dark. I sing and I wail.

عباس و الحسين کتمام رکعتين
انا من دون ابالفضل ای من دون الحسين

> *[Aba'l-Faḍl] al-Abbas and al-Husain are like two rakats (cycles) of prayer, which become meaningful when they are together. When I am without Aba'l-Faḍl, it is as if I am without Husain.*

I wish I could stay in this state of amazement for the rest of my life. Amazement at these two brothers. I take a few steps towards the Sāqi (Aba'l-Faḍl) and a few steps towards my master (al-Husain). The air is clear and light. I fill my lungs with the fragrance of heaven. Everything is shrouded in a mist of uncertainty. I close my eyes. I give [the blessings of] this heavenly pilgrimage as a gift to my martyred comrades. There is nothing better for me to offer them than this. I whisper their names: Muhammad Husain Bashīrī, Rezā Sanjarānī, Ahmad Dāvarī, and Javād. I know that they hear me and respond to me. I wish I wasn't deaf to hearing their voices. I ask them to remember me to my Master by name. I wish they would say that I have been left behind and am stuck in a fire of longing.

Threads of Compassion

A force draws me to the Master. I feel so much lighter, like a dream, like the perfume of the shrine. I go down the entry stairs. A corner of the hexagon [housing the sepulcher] fills the frame of my vision. I place my hand on my chest and recite the formula,

'Peace be unto you, o my lord and master, o Abā Abdallāh.'

The sending of this salutation is all that remains of my individual existence, after which I turn to dust, prostrating myself under the feet of my master. I testify that the hexagon of God's heaven is a place on Earth.

I open my eyelids with difficulty. It takes me a while to realize I'm in the hotel. As soon as I am assured of where I am, I quickly close my eyes and turn onto my side so I can go right back to sleep without missing a beat. The sweetness of the morning's pilgrimage is still coursing through my being. My thoughts become hazy. I saunter in and around the shrine, from one courtyard to another. I pray. Then I walk over so that I am under the dome. I have been left behind, sir, have mercy on me. I am floating in space. I now make my way towards the Sāqi's (the Cup Bearer: Aba'l-Faḍl al-Abbās') shrine. A pigeon walks around on the carpets, pecking intermittently. I send my *salāms* and enter. A throng of people are circled around the shrine, their fingers holding onto the protective metal latticework of the sepulcher. I know that my aspirations will not be dashed here. I pray, 'O ye who

Threads of Compassion

understands anguish, and who brought Hāmid's son back to life, bring *me* back to life!'

My foot hit something. What's my duffel bag doing on the bed? I stretch out and push it with my foot. It makes a dragging sound. This strange bag is not my duffel bag. It feels like they have glued my eyelids shut; I open them with great difficulty. I have cottonmouth from sleeping. I sit up on my bed. There is a big black duffel bag on my bed. I don't know which of my roommates it belongs to. I feel its contents, then look inside. My sleepiness disappears as fast as lightning; the bag is full of money.

My roommates have woken up from the rustling of the bag full of money. I'm curious to know who the guy with all the dough is. Both of my roommates deny it's theirs. The thought crosses my mind that maybe the bag is another gift from Lady Zainab; its material aspect. I'm starting to like the thought of such a "material aspect" when my roommate suggests I ask the hotel manager about the bag; so I put the bag under my arm and we head towards the hotel's reception counter.

We are full of questions, but the manager is cool and indifferent. He looks at the bag and its contents, and asks, 'Have you seen the image printed on the notes?'

He places a bundle of bills in front of us, each of which has a picture of Saddam staring back at us with bulging, angry eyes, as if someone had stolen his father's inheritance and he wanted it back, the scoundrel. Seeing his picture made me nauseous and depressed. The hotel manager explained that finding these worthless bills are actually not that infrequent an occurrence. But in any case, he doesn't know how they ended up in our room. It's no longer an issue. Maybe it was left by one of the hotel staff, or the previous occupant wanted to take these worthless bills for his children to play with and forgot and left the bag in the room. I look at the bills again; at Saddam's image. I see a man with a pretence to a hollow grandeur with epaulettes on his shoulder. He was supposed to be the Conqueror of Qādisīyah and the Conqueror of Tehran. He lined up the men of Iraq against the Persian "*majūs*" (Magus; "fire worshippers"). Now the children of those very men are part of the Hashd ash-Shaʻbī (Iraq's Popular Mobilization Forces) and under the command of Hāj Qāsim [Soleymani], and are fighting ISIS alongside the Iranians. The day when they line up for the liberation of al-Quds (Jerusalem) is not too far in the future, God willing.

I arrive at the hospital at 7 pm, weary from the wear and tear of travel and still feeling the high from a pilgrimage that was as short and sweet as the taste of honey in one's mouth. The hospital staff have gathered around. They stand in front of my room to welcome me back and say their goodbyes. I thought that I was the

Threads of Compassion

only one who knew that I was going to be sent back to Tehran tomorrow; but everyone knows. I look at Bābā Haidar and smile; it's his doing. I haven't left yet, but I miss him already. I will miss everyone. I will miss this hospital and the never-ending work that is here. I will miss its cold nights. I will miss the innocent look of the children who come to the hospital with their mothers. I will miss the Quran and Āshūrā Zīārat recitations after the morning prayers for the tired Dr. Ehsān who collapses at night after a hard day's work. And I will miss the angels who are born in this building each day. Frankly, I really don't want to leave.

Everyone has put the tasks that need to be done in writing so that I can go on vacation with peace of mind. They answer my questions before I even ask them. I flip through the pages of the register to check the birth statistics one last time. The names and dates of birth of all the babies born in the hospital are recorded. One out of every three names that I read is Ehsān. I flip through the pages and go back to check again. My name is written on each page three or four times. I have chosen the names of many of the babies myself, after reciting the call to prayer in their ears, but I don't remember giving my own name to any of the children. This same phenomenon has occurred in the case of the names of the female babies too. Somayyeh's name can be seen being repeated once every three or four names. Asīla was the only person who knew my wife's name. I call her into my office. I point to the register, and as soon as I am about to ask about the names, she laughs and explains,

'They name their children like this as their way of thanking the Iranians, so that you know they will always remember you.'

I mention the fact that Somayyeh appears in the register too. She laughs some more and says,

'For the people here, it is common knowledge that between Iranian husbands and wives, the wives have the upper hand. That's why they think you'd be happy with this arrangement.'

I laugh at the way these people think and at their way of showing their affection. And I laugh at the fate of ISIS, which is seeing heavier and heavier defeats every day. These are the same people who did not allow us to approach their children in the first days of the hospital's operation, or to even put our hands on their children's heads.

The phone in my room is ringing. It's Mustafā from the Deir ez-Zūr Hospital. Every time we talk on the phone, I am comforted by the sound of his voice. He is calm even in the most critical situations. This last call of his was no exception.

'If you want to fly to Damascus from Deir ez-Zūr airport, brother, get yourself here within the hour.'

That sounds crazy to me. I say, 'Mustafā, are you crazy? It's two and a half hours to Deir ez-Zūr from here. How can I get there in an hour?'

'That's out of my hands, bro. They just made the announcement that the flight has taken off from Damascus.'

I feel like banging my head against the wall because of Mustafā's cool-headedness in this situation, the long distance from here to Deir ez-Zūr, and my worse luck, which has just run out. This is the situation of the flights in Syria: their schedules are chaotic and everything is an emergency. Mustafā's sense of humour is acting out. He says,

'But there is a way.'

A glimmer of hope.

'What way is that?'

'I'll go and lie down in front of the wheels of the plane and say that the plane can't leave until Dr. Ehsān is on board. But the problem is that the pilot doesn't understand Persian.'

Now my head really needs a wall to bang against. I put the phone down and run to the car. The driver knows that there's no way we'll get there in time, but he does his best anyway. Looking ahead is like seeing an unattainable mirage, so I look to our rear every few minutes. All I see is a funnel of dust, just like in the action and adventure movies. The plane that I'm trying to reach landed in Deir ez-Zūr airport an hour ago, and we have been on the road for two hours. My heart is filled with anxiety. If I miss the flight, I have to go to Damascus by road, which means I won't have time to do a farewell pilgrimage and will have to go

Threads of Compassion

directly to the airport. I repeat all of the *dhikr*[36] formulae that I know so that the flight to Deir ez-Zūr will not take off until I get there.

We finally arrive. The plane has been delayed for an hour and has not taken off yet. The more beautiful way to put it is that my prayers have been answered, and Khānūm Jān ﷺ has stopped the flight so that I can board it and make the farewell pilgrimage.

This is the first time I'm boarding a military plane, and a Russian one at that. Ja'far has held a seat for me, one of those folding benches that runs along the windows. This military plane has no seats as such. Other than twelve of us who are sitting on this folding bench, the rest of the passengers are lying around on blankets on the floor of the plane, all friendly and like comrades in arms. Mansūr is here too. I saw him on the first day I came to Syria, and am seeing him again now on my last day. He is a good-humoured and knowledgeable person who has been in charge of the Fatemiyūn Corps' medical station in Al-Mayādīn, where I had dreamed of being stationed. Mansūr is always on the front line, which is always active. I'm talking about this very same skinny, well-mannered and witty young man, Mansūr. During the period of his tour of duty, his girth has been reduced by half and he is standing a little taller. I wouldn't have recognized him if he hadn't started talking and telling me all of the tales of his adventures.

---

[36] [Invocation of blessings.]

Threads of Compassion

The most memorable moments of this flight were the moments of its take-off and landing. When the plane started its take-off, the passengers who were sitting together on the floor in an orderly and polite manner suddenly started to fall on top each other and all over the place. There were no belts to hold us in place, or any seats for us to be fastened to. There were just a few woven canvas grab-handles attached to the fuselage, and all of those were lined up above the bench. We give in to the force of inertia that is dragging us to the back of the plane. The force of inertia is a cousin of the force of gravity. Those of us who are seated on the bench and hanging on to the canvas grab-handles almost fall on the heads of the people on the floor. The situation of the passengers who are sitting on the floor of the plane with blankets that slide to the back of the plane before they do is truly a sight to behold. Only the wounded are immune to the ravages of this force as they have been tied down to their beds and are immobile. But they do let out loud moans with each shaking of the plane, especially one of the members of the Fatemiyūn corps who has a bullet lodged in his spine. The poor fellow lets out terrible screams at the slightest movement of the plane. In addition to the wounded, the martyrs do not move either, as their coffins had been arranged in the back of the plane from the start, and they have no place farther to go. So it's just we who are the ones who have to worry about spilling over. We are more concerned about the guns and grenades that are hanging on our persons than about ourselves; concerned that they will go off in the middle of all the chaos and put an end to us. We laugh at each other and how we each deal with this inertial force, and the martyrs laugh at all of us.

The plane finally gains altitude and stabilizes. We stick to our spots, sitting politely and in an orderly manner. The number of Iranian passengers is small; most are Arab. And the distribution of the coffins is the same, with there being few non-Arab coffins among them. All of them are wrapped in the Syrian flag. Two of the coffins are different from the others. The coffins of the Fatemiyūn Corps martyrs which are draped in their signature yellow flag. These two soldiers were martyred two nights ago in Al-Bukamal. I can't stop thinking about them. Where are we flying to, and where are *they* flying to?! I wish someone would recite a funeral dirge for them, and talk about the valor of the Fatemiyūn soldiers. Of their innocence and courage. Oh, how my heart goes out to them. I wish someone would recite a liturgy in honour of Haḍrat Abu'l-Faḍl al-Abbas. I wish I had the nerve to do so myself. Like that day when I recited a liturgy for Ja'far, and Dr. Muhammad and Umm Majd heard the liturgy through the door of my room, and heard what we were chanting in honour of our master [Imam Husain ﷺ]. I wish I could recite a liturgy here and be taken back to that mood, next to these companions who are reposed in their coffins. I am sure that I will not have the fortune to be in such company on any trip again. What a feast is awaiting them in the heavens now. What a welcome they will have received. I think about how their bodies will be received and welcomed in Iran. If they have a little girl as I do, what language will she be able to use to express her emotions to her father's body? What if their spouses cannot make ends meet on their own? What if they have parents who are elderly? I take in a deep breath. They knew all this and came to Syria anyway. They must be laughing at my thoughts from above, thinking, 'Dear Doctor! May all of this be as a ransom for a single thread of Lady Zainab's ﷺ *chādor*.'

Mansūr started to talk about his experiences. Both of our tours in the region have not been for more than 50 days, but Mansūr has so many tales to tell that it is as if he has been deployed here for five years. He talks about his friend, Abdul-Karīm, who has not seen the child that his wife was pregnant with when he left for Syria. Two days before his martyrdom, he expressed his longing to see his two-year-old son; but it was not his lot to be able to hold him in his arms again. The way Abdul-Karīm was martyred was that he was giving fire cover at an important point on the Al-Bukamal to Al-Mayādīn road, enabling his comrades to make their retreat. I remember the cold nights in the hospital. The night ISIS crossed the Euphrates. The night when the hospital was in a deep sleep. The night when the commanders were asking for help over the radio so that the Al-Sukhna[37] tragedy would not be repeated. The night Abdul-Karīm saved so many lives on the Al-Bukamal to Al-Mayādīn road. The night when Abdul-Karīm's sons became orphans. The night we slept comfortably until the morning. The night when Abdul-Karīm's head was cut off from the rest of his body. I turn and look at the coffins. I feel ashamed. The 45-minute flight with the martyrs passes like a quick sleep. We prepare for landing, by which I mean we wiggle around a bit so as to get a better purchase of our seats. But it is to no avail anyway. This time we slide to the front of the plane. Inertia doing its thing again.

After fifty days, Mansūr, Ja'far and I have seen the shops but don't know what to buy. We stroll up and down the corridors of the Shām Center several times, window-shopping to see what colour headscarves and which model toys will be most suitable for our loved ones who have not seen us for almost two months. We dig in the bottom of our pockets to gather all of the money we have, and dig in the bottom of the place we keep our best tastes, and meet up again in an hour in the middle of the Shām Center shopping mall with

---

[37] An area between Deir ez-Zūr and Palmyra which fell to ISIS, who proceeded to cut the heads of upwards of a hundred people when they took it over.

souvenir bags in hand, tired and hungry. Well, if the truth be told, we were already hungry before we did our souvenir shopping, as it had been fifty days since we had eaten a decent meal. We walk towards the supermarket on the ground floor to see if we can find something to placate our stomachs. The colourful soft drinks in the refrigerator outside its door are alluring. Whatever we were able to get our hands on during these fifty days, we definitely didn't have access to any soft drinks, that's for sure. Various cans and bottles of different sizes and colours are lined up and are winking at us politely. Their prices are puzzling. They are basically the same thing in terms of their content and quantity, but their prices vary, depending on the shelf they are on, varying from 15 liras to a thousand liras. I splurge on a thousand lira can, which is the approximate equivalent of 15 thousand tomans[38]. The guys agree that we should treat ourselves to the best soft drinks after not having had one for so long. The coldness of the can alone is enough to quench my thirst. I open it and gulp down about half the can in a single breath. Its sweet and fizzy. Mansūr and Ja'far finish the rest of the can, and we are off again, satisfied with having served the needs of our stomachs.

We're still in the supermarket when I feel my blood rushing to my face. My head feels hot and my heart is beating fast. I think it might be travel fatigue, but it is not really a feeling of fatigue. It's closer to a

---

[38] Approximately $0.75 AUD/ $0.5 USD at the time.

sense of elation than fatigue. I look at Mansūr. His face is covered in sweat. Ja'far is like the two of us as well. He puts a hand on his forehead every few minutes and tries to figure out what is ailing him. The three of us focus on the empty can of soda that Ja'far is holding in his hand. Mansūr cries out,

'Oh my God! After all this service to Lady Zainab and her neighbours, did we just drink some alcohol??'

We are on the verge of tears. I can't bear to look at Mansūr and Ja'far's faces anymore. They feel the same way. I curse myself for this self-inflicted wound that I afflicted us with.

We try to read the ingredients on the can to at least understand what percentage of it was alcohol, but it does not give us that information. I head towards the refrigerator from Hell that has placed us in this bind to try to figure out what we can do.

Ja'far says, 'That was the only blight that hadn't befallen us, which we now brought on to ourselves with our own hands.'

His voice is saturated with sadness. He's right. How can we return to Iran with mouths that are ritually unclean (*najis*), and for people to come to the airport to welcome Defenders of the Shrine whose mouths smell of alcohol!

We stand like refugees in front of the soft drink refrigerator. The cans stare back at us with a defiant look on their faces. I regret not having chosen one that costs 15 lira; at least the percentage of alcohol would have been less. There is nothing we can do. We are sorry for having committed a sin whose passing sweetness we didn't even have the time to enjoy. One of the supermarket employees comes over to see if he can help us find anything. I show him the empty can and explain to him that all three of us have drank from it and are not feeling well. He understands our predicament, but says,

'No, brother. This is non-alcoholic. It's just a high-energy drink with a lot of calories.'

I read the can again, and it finally dawns on me that we drank an energy drink, not an alcoholic one. No wonder our bodies reacted the way they did. The "best" food we had had for the last fifty days was packets of instant noodles, so having an energy drink now was like doping our bodies. We are miraculously sobered up in an instant, and make haste to leave the supermarket before we get ourselves into any more trouble. Mansūr and Ja'far cannot stop laughing, and I am happy to join them too. Now all that is left of that "alcohol" is the memory of the few minutes of our "drunkenness".

We have reached the Zainabīya [the shrine of Lady Zainab ﷺ]. The shrine is quiet, as it was when I first came fifty days ago. It has the loneliness of exile written all over its walls, just as it did fifty days ago. Emotions well up, causing a lump to form in my throat, just as it did fifty days ago. I was so eager to come to Syria when I first entered Syria, but now I feel a sense of shame. I had asked for martyrdom, but now I am being returned all safe and sound. What can be a worse fate than this? I apologize. I ask Lady Zainab ﷺ to forgive me in her munificence if I have failed in my duties, which plea I know she will look upon with favour as I have always tried to live in accordance with the mode of conduct that is in accord with [the following words of Imam Hādī ﷺ's]: 'Doing that which is good is your manner of living, and generosity is your habit'.[39]

I sit facing the *ḍarīh* (the protective metal lattice around the sepulcher of the shrine). I have so much to say to Khānūm Jān ﷺ; I have as many words to tell her as the number of people I have seen on this trip. I have as many words to tell her as the number of babies born in our hospital. But I don't say anything other than this single sentence: 'Accept the service of this servant of yours.'

---

[39] The Ziārat-e Jāmi'a al-Kabīr (attributed to Imam Hādī)
(عَادَتُهُمُ الْإِحْسَانُ وَ سَجِيَّتُهُمُ الْكَرَمُ)

Threads of Compassion

Chapter Six Photos

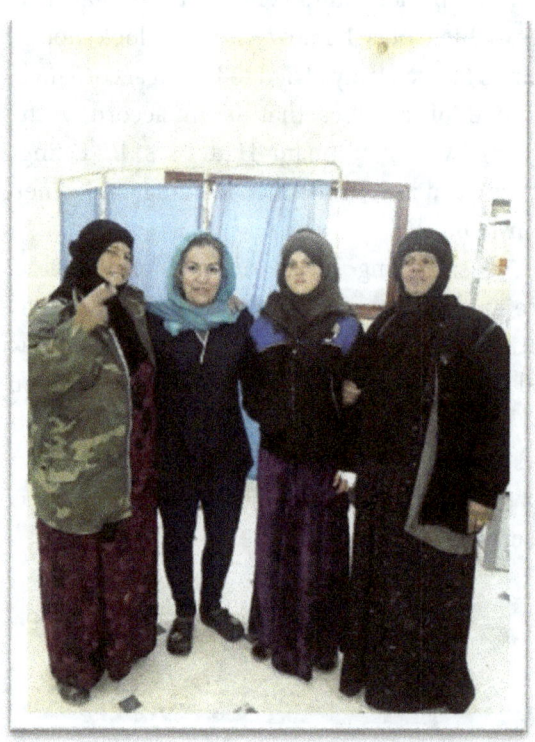

The youngest mother who gave birth in our hospital. She couldn't stop crying after she gave birth. She is standing between her mother and her mother-in-law, and next to Asīla. A few hours have passed since she gave birth, and she wanted to be discharged already, but her eyes were still red from having cried so much.

Threads of Compassion

Bābā Haidar, the likeable old man of the front lines.

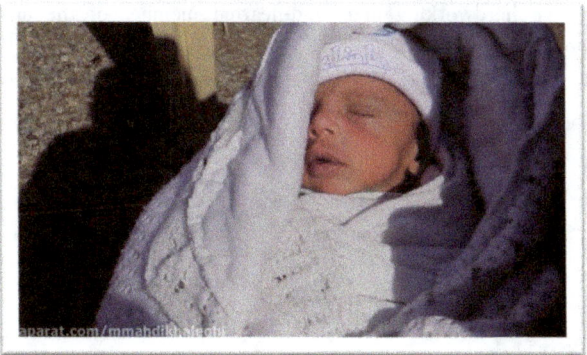

A baby whose name and gender I do not remember. I only know that its mother said, 'I would like to send this child to Iran to study to become a doctor, because he would not have survived if it were not for the Iranians.'

Threads of Compassion

Ja'far; a hardworking and kind-hearted member of the army support staff.

Mansūr in the Al-Mayadīn station. Shab-e Yaldā (the winter solstice) is being celebrated, and everyone's share of fruit is arranged on their plates.

Threads of Compassion

My memorable trip to Karbalā.

Threads of Compassion

Deir ez-Zūr Airport, a few minutes before that memorable flight. Ali can be seen here on the left. He is an operating room technician at a field Hospital.

Shahīd (Martyr) Abd'al-Karīm Parhīzgār and his son, whom he missed during his last days.

Threads of Compassion

7

It's only this kind of pain that I like. The pain of my fractured ribs that course through my soul every time I turn from side to side. It's similar to the pain one gets in the side of one's torso; that's why I like it. I sing an elegy to my mother under my breath, and the pain helps to bring tears to my eyes. My body is trapped in this hospital bed, but my heart is in Syria; in Khānūm Jān's  shrine. To stand in a corner of her shrine and give all I have to sing a eulogy in her honour. My heart pines to be in the Baqī' Cemetery so that I can stand in front of Khānūm Jān's  father's shrine and sing an elegy for his daughter. I don't want Somayyeh and the kids to see me crying. I pull the blanket over my face. I can't stand this situation anymore. I can't stand being away.

It's 3 am, Wednesday 10 January 2018. I've climbed four flights of stairs non-stop, carrying my navy bag. I'm sweating profusely. I am so excited that even if the elevator was not broken, I would still have used the stairs. A shard of light makes its way through a thin crack in the door. A faint sound can be heard from within the house. It's Hāniyeh's voice. I sit on the stairs. My dearest loved ones are awake and waiting for me on the other side of this door. Something stirs in my heart, a longing, together with pent-up emotions. My shoulders convulse as I start to sob, my tears finding their way down my cheeks. I shed tears for all of these fifty days that I felt ashamed before Khānūm Jān  [to return to my family]. I don't hold anything back. How I miss hugging my children.

All of us are up all night: me, Somayyeh, and even the children. Even if we run out of words, we can't get enough of looking at each other's faces. I just can't get enough of each of their beautiful faces. It's just us, the baklavas I have brought from Syria, and the glasses of tea that keep getting filled, emptied, and filled again in rapid succession.

When I was in Syria, seeing the mothers and their children in the maternity ward reminded me of home and my own children. And now, seeing my own children here, I am reminded of the children in Syria. It's been a week since I've returned, and I already miss them a lot. I leave the house so that I can maybe feel a little better but to no avail. I head back home so that I might feel better, again to no avail. I am in search of myself; the Dr Ehsān who was left behind in Syria; the Dr Ehsān who is wandering the streets here, lost; the Dr Ehsān who cannot survive for long when he is away from Khānūm Jān ﷺ and her neighbours. My pent-up emotions continually weigh down on my chest. Syria and Khānūm Jān ﷺ and her neighbours have become a distant dream that I can no longer reach. I have become like children who are fixated on one thing and don't want anything other than that. No matter what I see, Syria is what I want. It seems that the task of returning to Syria is even greater than the task of reaching her in the first place. Now that I want to go back, I can't bear to be away from her even for five more days, let alone five years. I keep asking myself what I'm doing back here? I'm concerned that Khānūm Jān ﷺ may no longer give me her permission to engage in *jihād* and to continue to serve her community. Could it be – God forbid! – that I will have to remain behind closed doors again like the five years I had to wait? Could it be that I will never see Syria again? Should I not have come back on leave??

After the morning prayer, I stand in front of the window. The city is covered with a thin layer of snow. The piercing cold has gripped my heart. I'm worried about the Syrian children who don't have warm clothes. They will surely catch colds with this snow in the dilapidated houses and cold tents of Al-Harī. I start to sob. My heart is as full of sorrow as the sorrows of the world and all of its people's sorrows; as full of sorrow as this gray, snow-laden overcast sky. I wail as I am standing by the window looking out, and the angels in the heavens are probably laughing and saying, 'Are you kidding doc? Al-Bukamal and Al-Harī have never yet seen the colour of snow!' I had forgotten that it does not snow in the desert. There is just the rain and a wind that chills to the marrow of one's bones.

Somayyeh did not go back to sleep after the morning prayer. She comes and stands silently next to me by the window. She has understood what I am feeling. She says,

'Ehsān, do you want us to go to Mashhad?'

A smile makes its way through my tears.

'How did you know that I needed to go on a pilgrimage?'

The road is endless. I feel like going somewhere where this heart of mine can find peace. I feel like going to the Goharshād Mosque, to the Maqsūra courtyard, to open my heart under the dome so that perchance I might be cured of the incurable pain of the loneliness of exile. I feel like going to a corner of lot 30 of the Behesht-e Rezā Cemetery, to where Javād is buried, and tell him everything that is on my mind, and be reminded of his great sense of humor and all the jokes he used to make.

The air smells like it's going to rain. Would that it would pour down and wash away all the dust of the sadness that is in my heart. The children are sleeping in the back seat. Somayyeh's stories always make the journey shorter, but this time, there is a bitterness in her words. Her pent-up emotions have formed a lump in her throat, but she resists the urge to break down and cry. The bitterness is showing through all the more in her words, causing my head to want to explode. I can't imagine how she kept all these words to herself and didn't tell me anything before this. The more she talks, the more my heart goes out to the children of the Defenders of the Shrine and most of all for the children of those who are fighting in the Fatemiyūn Corps.

Hearing Somayyeh's words takes my thoughts to Mashhad's Golshahr neighbourhood, among the Fatemiyūn volunteers, among the houses of the volunteers who make up Khānūm Jān's ﷺ Lashgar-e Abbās (the Abbās Brigade) – a brigade whose members' only wish is to offer up their lives [in defence of the cause]. They don't want anything else, not from Khānūm Jān ﷺ, nor from anyone else.

Somayyeh's heart is full of blood from the wounds of the hurtful things that she has heard, as is mine. Not for myself and the huge sums of money [that I am supposedly making for each day of my tour of duty in Syria] whose first red cent I have not even seen.

Threads of Compassion

But for the volunteers of the Fatemiyūn Corps who are always accused [in this way]. I hear the voice of Muhammad Kāẓim Kāẓimī singing in my mind.

غروب در نفس گرم جاده خواهم رفت

پیاده آمده بودم، پیاده خواهم رفت

Come evening, I will depart in the warm breath of the road.
I came on foot, and that is how I will leave.

I walk the streets of Golshahr looking for the house of a veteran who was a Defender of the Shrine whom I have been told is in need of money to pay for his medical treatment; the house of a family whose members are suffering the depravations of extreme poverty. I am ashamed to look into their children's faces.

منم که نانی اگر داشتم، از آجر بو

و سفره‌ام ـ که نبود ـ از گرسنگی پر بود

Even if I had a piece of bread, it would be as hard as a brick,
and my non-existent table-spread was full of nothing but hunger.

I feel like wailing with each and every verse of this poem. To read each of its verses a hundred times over. To read it and melt away in shame because of the meaning of its words. I remember the half-burnt notebook that Imād found in the underground warehouse of ISIS's medicines that contained the names of Iranians who supported ISIS and cooperated with them from within Iran. True; the Defenders of the Shrine do get paid, of course they do; but there is no comparison between their salaries and what these traitors get paid. The Defenders of the Shrine are paid for putting their own lives on the line, whereas these others are paid for selling other people's lives [to the enemy]. I hear Kāẓimī's words again.

من از سکوت شب سردتان خبر دارم
شهید داده‌ام، از دردتان خبر دارم

> *I know all about the silence in which you pass the cold night,*
> *My dearest loved ones have been martyred, so I do feel your pain.*

It seems that this poem was written about pain. No, it was written *in* pain. I remember those two coffins of the martyrs of the Fatemiyūn Corps that I saw on the plane. If they arrived with me, the seventh-day anniversary of their martyrdom has just passed. Their families are still in mourning. Mourning the loss of a loved one. Mourning for the loneliness of exile. Mourning for invectives and hinted insults. Emotions well up inside me as I remember Javād, who got himself to Syria to serve Khānūm Jān ﷺ by saying he was from Afghanistan. I remember all of my brothers in arms in Syria who go without a decent meal or proper sleep each and every day. I remember the Golshahr neighborhood of Mashhad, which is full of noble people who have forbearance and longanimity in spades, but who are accused of being 'aliens'. I sing along with Kāżimī.

من از سکوت شب سردتان خبر دارم

شهید داده‌ام، از دردتان خبر دارم

به این امام قسم، چیز دیگری نبرم

به‌جز غبار حرم، چیز دیگری نبرم

> *I know all about the silence in which you pass the cold night,*
> *I came on foot, and that is how I will leave.*
> *I swear upon the honour of this Imam, I will not take anything.*
> *I will not take anything other than the dust of the Shrine.*

Oh, how scathing the words of this poem are for me, for I have lived with these people. Hasan left his ten-month-old son in Herāt and came to defend Khānūm Jān's ﷺ shrine. No matter where I turn the beam of my flashlight, I still haven't come across the limits of the huge cavern that is ISIS's medicine warehouse; there's no end to it. I was told that the baby who was born in the hospital a week ago died of malnutrition. Hāmid talks about his daughter and how she is completely unaware of his situation. Abdul-Karīm misses his two-year-old son and gives fire cover to that vital junction on the road until daybreak so as to ensure that the operation does not fail. I let out my sadness with a deep sigh. I hold Somayyeh's hand. Now that I'm here, I won't let her feel the pain of sorrow.

The police signal us to stop. I pull over on the unpaved shoulder and get out. The young officer comes forward, offers his *salāms*, and asks,

'How many of there are you?'

'There are four of us.'

He hands me four food coupons and says, 'Pray for us too, when you are in the shrine.'

I wish Hāniyeh and Muhammad-Husain didn't have exams and could have come with us, so that we could all sit at this divine table-spread together.

For those of us who are from Mashhad, Imam Riḍā's shrine is like our own father's house. We are just as at ease there and even more at ease. I feel like a burden has been lifted from my shoulders when I am in the Goharshād Mosque and its courtyard. It is as if my body has been left behind at the Bāb al-Jawād portal and that I have been freed within the environment of the shrine. I feel as light as the scent of the frankincense perfume rising out of the burner that is being held by the hand of one of the shrine's custodians next to the shrine's entrance. I feel as light as the breeze that circumambulates the dome, making its flag flutter in its breeze. I get lost in the twists and turns of the squinches and complex geometric patterns of the Maqsūra courtyard, and the lapis lazuli garden depicted in the tilework of its walls. I float in a deep trance while facing the dome. I have a whole world's worth of words [to share with the Imam], with eyes that can't get enough of the goldest of golds [of his shrine's golden dome].

How much whiter has my father's hair become over these last fifty days? But the change that Somayyeh has undergone is huge. She dotes over me, kisses me, takes in my fragrance, and feeds me; she does all of that, but stops short of telling me not to return. She is reconciled with my wanting to go back. I ask her to pray for my being reassigned. In the afternoon, she goes to the shrine with my father, and when she returns, she laughs, saying,

'When you go back to Syria, give our *salāms* to Lady Zainab.'

I have a lot of work to see to in Mashhad. I go from this religious group (*hai'at*) to the next, from the shrine back to our house, from our house to the Behesht-e Rezā Cemetery. I wish Ahmad was here with me, or Javād, at least. I will go to the Behesht-e Rezā Cemetery to see them. I sit down next to their graves and start telling them all of my tales. Now I too have tales to tell about my adventures in Syria. I tell them everything, spending a lot of time with them. Suddenly I go quiet, as if I have remembered something. I turn to both of them and say,

'But where you are at now is better than where I am, you rascals!'

My phone is ringing. It's that famous number that is full of zeros.

'Your name is on the list for Saturday. Be at the Imam Airport at 7 pm.'

Threads of Compassion

I am so happy that I have stopped breathing. They had called to say that Khānūm Jān  has recalled me, and that I should answer her call. I feel certain that it's because of my mother's prayers. I feel like kissing her hands a thousand times.

My vacation in Iran has taken longer than everyone anticipated, and their grumblings reached my ears. The poor man, Bābā Haidar, has taken on all of the burdens of my responsibilities for these past two weeks. He's waiting for me with bated breath to reach Al-Bukamal, so that he can hand the hospital back over to me and go back to Iran. I miss him so much., especially his shooing everyone out of the building at the end of the work day at four o'clock. It is his habit to come over to the emergency room every afternoon when office hours are over, wave his hands from side to side and make shooing sounds, like shooing animals out of a barn.

Naba' had learned how to imitate him and does so to everyone's amusement and delight. Bābā Haidar's shooing had become like the tolling of the hospital's bell. When they hear Bābā Haidar's shooing, the people who had come to be seen know that business hours are over and it's time for them to go back to their homes; and the nurses would laugh and close up shop. Bābā Haidar himself would come to my room with a tray of

Threads of Compassion

tea for a tea break. Now Bābā Haidar is waiting in the hospital for the hospital bell to toll for him, waiting for me to go and shoo him out so that he can return to Iran.

We have had lunch and are on the way to Palmyra with Abu Abdo and his passengers. Besides me, there is Ja'far and Masīh, the medical officer of one of the Fatemiyūn brigades, and Shahrām, who is an anesthesiologist. We arrive at Palmyra before dusk. Ja'far has brought something that had been entrusted to him in Tehran for one of his friends. He looks high and low to find his friend to give him what has been entrusted to him, and he eventually finds him in the Heydariyūn barracks. We were supposed to avoid moving in the darkness, but night has already fallen. When we reach Al-Sukhna, the portion of the road that is susceptible to Kornet missile fire begins. We have to drive 120 km through this road to Al-Shūla in the dark. Even if we are not targeted by Kornet missiles, the bumpy road and its twists and turns in the dark will be the end of us. The bridge at the entrance of Kabājib has been destroyed, forcing us to make our way through the alleys of the village. Behind Kabājib is an ISIS-infested desert, out of which they crawl at night, attack, kill, loot, and leave, and disappear back in the desert like a handful of sand. Abu-Abdo has the "pedal to the metal", trying to pass the danger zone at maximum speed. He has armed his weapon and given it to Ja'far. Masīh has loaded a bullet into his pistol's chamber and is at the ready too. Even if I didn't know about ISIS and the traps that they set here, the sound of weapons being armed would have been enough to put fear into us. It was only a few weeks ago right here in Kabājib that eight Hezbollah soldiers were killed. Darkness is everywhere and sticks to everything like tar. The bumps of the road have made us all feel nauseous. Everyone constantly prays and repeats *dhikrs* and sends *salawāt* to help us make a safe passage through this ISIS-infested road and to avoid our being hit by a Kornet missile. 500 kilometers later, we finally arrived at the Ferāt Hospital in Deir ez-Zūr. The hospital used to be a large, two-story empty orphanage that has now been converted into a field hospital. The rooms of the orphanage will undoubtedly be filled to twice their original capacity and even more than that as a result of this war. This is where we have to spend the night.

At bedtime, Shahrām apologizes to everyone for the snoring that he will be subjecting us to. We don't take it seriously. We laugh it off, saying that we are so tired that even if they came at us with cannons and tanks, we wouldn't wake up. We were so exhausted, both physically and emotionally, that we just plonked down and went right to sleep.

A high-pitched sound like one that would be let out by the rusty tracks of a tank wakes me from a deep sleep. I push the gray military blanket away from my torso and sit up. It's 3:00 am. I'm very groggy from sleep, as are the rest of the crew, who are also sitting up and looking at each other's bloodshot eyes. Shahrām is the only one who is still sleeping, letting out loud snoring sounds.

Threads of Compassion

After making our morning prayers, we got into the car and headed out in the direction of Al-Bukamal. Fifty kilometres later, our hopes of arriving on time are deflated when we find out that the road is closed. It is the worst thing to have happened to me during the entirety of my stay in Syria. I want to get there, but we are told to go back. An Iranian soldier and a soldier from the Fatemiyūn Corps were captured on this road earlier in the morning, after the morning prayer. That's why the road is closed. And so we return, very dejected. I busy myself in the emergency room of the Furāt Hospital to pass the time. I'm not happy; either with myself, with the road that is closed, or with Deir ez-Zūr, which has kept us against our will and won't let us pass. I have no choice but to sleep here against my will, and to grin and bear it.

We're in the middle of the second day in which we have stayed in the Furāt Hospital when they say that a guest has arrived. And what a guest; one for whom many will mourn. It is the body of the martyr Shahīd Gholam-Rezā Langarī-Zādeh together with one of his companions. These were the two martyrs who had fallen into ISIS's hands early the previous morning. They headed out on foot yesterday morning and have now been returned minus their souls, bloody and burnt. Everyone is dejected. It is a normal occurrence to see a burnt body with a severed limb that is covered in blood in a hospital, and this does not in itself upset anyone. But seeing a burnt body that is missing its ears and nose, and a head that has been half cut off and separated from the body with a kick is what really ruined everyone's mood. What I have seen has left a very bitter taste in my mouth and has completely upset my emotional state. What possible good can cutting off the ears and nose of a captive do? What cathexis will such an act release for its perpetrator, and what pain is it supposed to alleviate?

There is such a wide divide between these two warring fronts. Here *we* are, and arrayed against us is absolute malice and hatred. We go from door to door, frantically trying to reach Al-Harī in order to be able to serve children, one or more of whose fathers might well have been responsible for bringing this calamity to our compatriots. It might well be that we might ourselves be captured by their fathers one day, in which case they will kill us with the same depth of depravity and hatred they displayed in their killing and mutilation of Shahīd Gholam-Rezā Langarī-Zādeh. Ja'far is holding on to the two-way radio wherever he goes, monitoring it to make sure we don't miss the announcement of the opening of the road. Naturally, my ears are perked up for the same information. We thirst for reaching the hospital and the opportunity to serve Khānūm Jān's ﷺ neighbours.

After making the noon prayers, we are back on the road again. This time, we're headed to Sālihīya, on the other side of which all of our business and livelihoods lie. When we get there, we are as insistent as our strength and propriety allow, so it is finally decided that we will pass through the mouth of the lion being escorted by a military squadron consisting of ten to twelve Toyotas equipped with man-portable and fixed artillery guns of various calibres. Their august presence is strangely comforting and strengthens our hearts. What is stranger still is that we have all gone quiet in their presence!

The road is littered, full of shrapnel from various skirmishes. We have to pass as quickly as possible, but at the same time, we have to navigate carefully through all the sharp shards of shrapnel that cover the road. I try to imagine what the last words were that the martyrs who were captured on this road exchanged. What was the last thought that crossed their minds? Did they miss their homes and families? Were they sending salutations to Khānūm Jān ﷺ? Were they smiling at their lord and master who came to welcome them?

As these thoughts are going through my mind, one of the Toyotas gets a flat tire. But this is no place to stop. Another armoured truck with man-portable artillery stops to help, and the rest of our convoy continues on its way. We will be escorted all the way up to Al-Bukamal's environs, which is about 70 kilometers distance.

The news of my arrival has preceded me. The locals and medical staff, and above all, Bābā Haidar, have come out to welcome me. The display of so much love and affection brings tears to my eyes. I shed tears because of the love and affection that the locals have for me, and more importantly, because of Khānūm

Threads of Compassion

Jān's ﷺ love for me, which is what has caused me to become so beloved in the eyes of her neighbours. There is a great commotion in the hospital's courtyard. People are stomping their feet and shouting their welcomes, and letting off machinegun fire in the air, which has filled the courtyard with the scent of gunpowder. I take in a deep breath. I take in the cold and the smell of the soil. I take in the cold and the smell of gunpowder, the cold and the smell of the Euphrates. I like the smell of this city. Tears wet the corner of my eyes. I turn my face towards Khānūm Jān's ﷺ shrine and say,

'Peace be unto you, o wise one of the Arabs.'

And I think to myself, 'Take my hand and guide me aright, as everything is transfigured by the will of the transcendent.'

The medical team has just left. It is just me and a hospital that is as deserted as it was on the first day we were open for business. I'm waiting for the new team to arrive. Over the phone, Dr. Karīm promised to send me a specialist nurse. I'm waiting for the team to arrive so that I can see this Ms. Fātimah Duba and the rest of her staff. I go from room to room, like one who has returned home after years of absence. I check the storeroom where the medicines are shelved; I check the registers where the births are recorded; I check the guards' room. Everything is in order, except for one thing: Bābā Haidar is no longer here. Something is amiss without the presence of this old man and his warm sense of humour. Hasan and Ābid have gone, too, being replaced by Ahmad and Jamāl. I regret not having been here to give them a proper send-off. It doesn't take Ahmad very long at all to become my right-hand man, filling the void left by Bābā Haidar's absence. If it weren't for him, I would not have been able to sustain myself. He's the jack of all trades of the hospital. There's nothing he can't do, be it finding a vein and inserting a catheter and starting an IV drip, to repairing an electric motor, to cooking. This Mashhadī Afghani of the Fatemiyūn brigade is a true godsend. Jamāl is also an Afghani of the Fatemiyūn brigade and is a lion of a man, who has come to Syria and taken up arms to defend Khānūm Jān's ﷺ shrine.

When the work at the hospital is over, Ahmad and Jamāl fill the car full of donated bread, milk, and yogurt and go to the outskirts of Al-Bukamal and distribute everything that has been donated to us among the indigent that populate the outskirts of the city. The most delicious yogurt and milk I have tasted in my whole life are those that these people bring to us as their way of thanking Dr. Ehsān and this hospital. I am proud of the fact that we are able to raise Iran's flag above the hospital's rooftop, and of the fact that our relationship with these people is improving every day; and proud of a bowl of milk that is donated to us, which might well be the entirety of the wealth of the family that donates it during that whole week, a wealth that they have decided to share with us.

The team finally arrives late at night. The team of Fātima Duba's team, which includes Waʻd, Hamīda and Wahīda. Their presence is fecund; before they have had a chance to settle into their room, not one but two pregnant women come to the hospital, needing to be seen to. I stand aside to see how well they can perform their duties, and am pleased to see that there is no need in the least for me to interfere. By morning, both births have been recorded in the register and all of the needs of the mothers have been seen to, with the midwives taking the weariness of the seven-hour journey from Aleppo to Al-Bukamal in their stride. They were so energetic and their energy so infectious that I didn't feel sleepy either.

The second mother to have given birth is released from the hospital after the morning prayers. She holds her newborn in her arms and goes back to her home. Here, it is not customary for mothers to stay in the hospital until they have recuperated; they are in a hurry to go back home and get back to their daily lives. It is only after she leaves that we can think about getting some sleep, of which we can only get about an hour's worth, enough to be somewhat recharged so that we can work for the rest of the day until closing time. I get ready to head in. I can hear Fātima's and Waʻd's voices coming from the corridor. They're chatting and laughing. It seems their tiring work has not tired them out, because they have each other. Oh, how much I miss Husain when I see the two of them together. He's no longer here to see that it has not become a habit for me to make my morning prayers at the top of its hour, and that not only do I not sleep after having made my prayers, but that we also do communal recitations of the Quran and of the Āshūrā Ziārat now. Husain believed that all five of the appointed daily ritual devotions were to be made in congregation [whenever possible]; and that it was important for the morning prayer to be made in congregation as well, and this was a goal that we needed to aspire to. When he was here, Husain used to make me get up and participate in the congregational morning prayer. On days when I was really tired, I would pretend to be asleep. No matter how many times he called me, I pretended I didn't hear him, and he eventually felt sorry for how tired I was feeling and relented. After he had made his prayers, he would come back and see that I was still asleep, and he would say,

'Still sleeping?! Get up! Your sloth deprived us of the benefit of praying in congregation again.'

Fātima's husband was martyred in Aleppo and Wa'd's was martyred in Latakīa. They have both experienced the same hardships. The adversities that they have suffered have made them so kind and full of longanimity and forbearance. They treat their patients and those who accompany them as if they were members of their own families. They are so kind to their patients that if you didn't know which is which, it would be impossible to tell whether Fātima or Waʻd was the mother of the child who was being treated or whether it was the woman who came in with the child. Both Fātima and Waʻd live in the doctor's room of the hospital in Aleppo. The two of them are together from morning till night and again from night until morning, just as Husain. I lived and worked when we were undergoing a supplementary specialization course in 2009 – a year that stands out from the rest of the years of my life because of the memories I have of having spent time with Husain.

    Fātima gives the child a hug and sits him down on the examining bed. He has a fungal infection whose symptoms cover his face. His mother talks about the outbreaks, which discharge an infectious puss. Fātima places her hand on the child's head with a smile. It's as if she cannot see the scabs and puss. My heart goes out to the poor child, not because of his wounds, but because of the state of the hygiene of the people of this area, which has brought this pestilence onto the head and face of this child. No matter how much effort we put into our work, and no matter how many essential health services and goods we provide to them, there is still a disconnect several kilometres wide between the state of their health and hygiene and where it needs to be. Waʻd talks to the child's mother to reassure her that her son will be fine. Blood and the puss that has been discharged from the wounds have made his hair stick together in clumps. Fātima insists that the child's hair be shaved off, even if we have to do it ourselves in the hospital, because she knows that if the child is allowed to go home in the condition he's in, no one will do anything for him, and he will end up coming back to us with the same wounds a little later. One of the guards has an electric hair clipper, but he refuses to lend it out for such purposes. And who can blame him? He's concerned about the infections discharge that will get on the clippers. He relents when I promise that I will disinfect his shaver after we have finished using it. Luckily for the boy, there is a loving doctor present in the hospital as well. It is Dr. Muqayyim, who is a resident at the Mushfi Al-Maidāni clinic, who often comes to pay us a visit. Dr. Muqayyim was the doctor who was my roommate on the first night of my arrival in Syria and who taught me how to call Iran. Dr. Muqayyim, who used to be a professor in one of Iran's prestigious universities before he came to Syria, now does volunteer work in our hospital. Every time I see him, I am reminded of Somayyeh's words and the huge sums of money they say the Defenders of the Shrine are paid. What possible need does a doctor like Dr. Muqayyim, for example, have for money, so that such an incentive would induce him to leave his prestigious social position and job to come to Syria for money? There is no question that it would be much easier for him to earn that same amount of money in Iran.

If he sees there is some work to be done, he doesn't ignore it, whether this be the stocking of shelves with medicine or the treating of a boy's infected wounds with medicine. In this case, many different medications have been tried on the child, but his fungal infection is persistent. As we don't have specialty skin medications, the doctor mixes some ointments together and tells us to apply the mixture to the boy's face and head without bandaging the application so that the mixed ointment can dry up the infection. After having shaved the boy's head, Fātima applies the special ointment to the boy's infected areas as kindly as his mother would have done for her own son. Three or four days after Dr. Mohhebī's concoction had been applied, the boy's fungal infection is finally vanquished.

To me, this current medical team is truly a golden team. The need for my making rounds to the emergency and maternity wards has been reduced to a minimum. Within a matter of a few short days, the new team members have taken over the running of everything as if they have been working here for several months. They don't even ask me where this or that medicine can be found. Even in the maternity ward, Hamīdah and Wahīdah do everything, from pregnancy examinations to setting the [approximate] date of delivery, to the registration of the births, to seeing to the needs of the mother after childbirth. They are energetic and compassionate. They share everything and do not claim anything exclusively for themselves; and they are devoted to seeing to the needs of the people. That is enough for them as long as they are supplied with their cappuccinos. Besides that, they keep their noses to the grindstone.

They spend their days together doing what I was doing eleven years ago, when I was 26 years old, full of dreams, and working alongside Husain. Those were the days in which I was taking the supplementary specialized course. They were such special days with such sweet memories that I know they will never be repeated again. I miss those days and feel certain that this period of my life will take on a similar hue and flavour and that it will become an unrepeatable period in my life that is full of rich memories. Would that I was close enough to them to be able to tell them to appreciate the times we have together while they last.

After making our morning prayers, we quietly get ourselves to the gym. This is what Husain and I used to do every morning for the seven months I was stationed at the Imam Rezā Education Center. From the very beginning of the course, everyone knew that Husain and I had become bosom buddies. We were always together. Whenever I was feeling sad, he would show up and talk to me and tell me as many jokes as it took to make me feel better, and it was only then that he would rest at ease. Only then would he ask what I was upset about.

The large front yard of the hospital, where there is so much toing and froing, is unlandscaped; with all this running back and forth, a much sturdier kind of footwear would have been much more suitable than the two-bit sneakers that I'm wearing. My shoes are giving me calluses and blisters and are no longer serviceable. But I can't go to Deir ez-Zūr or Damascus even to buy a new pair of shoes. Although I am not concerned about leaving the hospital in the charge of the new medical team, I still can't leave the hospital to carry out a personal errand.

It is early in the afternoon, and Ahmad and I are prowling around all of the basements of the abandoned houses on the hunt for an incubator. The blister above my heel is giving me hell. We look high and low, but no incubators are to be found. An incubator is a glass enclosure that acts as a cradle for prematurely born babies until they are ready to enter this world. If we were to find one, it would bring down our infant mortality numbers significantly.

Everywhere is pitch black, and there is a foul smell everywhere that fills our throats as soon as we enter. I turn on my flashlight. We pass from one shelf to another, and from one corridor to another, and all we are confronted with is darkness and the nauseating stench. Two packages of chest tubes catch my eye. A chest tube is a hollow, flexible tube placed into the chest (between one's ribs and into the space between the inner lining and the outer lining of one's chest cavity) in order to drain blood, fluids, or air from around one's lungs, heart, or esophagus. I grab them, as leaving with them is better than returning empty-handed. As our hospital has no need for them, I will send them on to the Mushfi Al-Maidāni clinic, where they can use them in their surgery operations on wounded soldiers.

I can't stand the stench anymore, and Ahmad feels the same, so we return the way we came. The beam of the flashlight illuminates a corner of the corridor that had been hidden from our eyes previously. We figure, now that we have come this far and put up with the stench for so long, it would be a pity not to see what's at the end of the corridor. The stench gets worse the farther on we proceed down the corridor. It is impossible to breath. I raise the collar of my shirt in front of my mouth and say,

'Ahmad, believe me, it's the smell of a rotting corpse.'

Ahmad nods his head in affirmation. He is too afraid to speak and let the stench invade his stomach. My foot hits a heavy but pliable object. I shine the beam of the flashlight downwards. Both of us stop breathing at witnessing the scene that is under our feet. If we weren't trapped in darkness like this and could see where to place our feet, we would have run back to the hospital without making a single stop or looking back. What we saw were a couple of half-decayed corpses which, from the look of it, had been lying there for more than a month. I felt like not just my last meal, but everything that I had eaten over the last week was gurgling up at the back of my throat. Ahmad felt the same way. He said,

Threads of Compassion

'Doctor! Let's go and have the authorities come and gather the body and put this place back into some semblance of order!'

I agree completely. The hell that surrounded those two corpses was no place to tarry. One of them was lying on a special stretcher for carrying corpses. They were probably killed in the fight to liberate Al-Bukamal. Their comrades had left their bodies here in the hope of coming back and getting them as soon as they took the city back from us, a hope that thankfully turned out to be false. My eyes catch the sneakers that are on the feet of one of the corpses. Frankly, the way he was prone in this dark basement, he no longer had any use for them! I hate to even touch them and want to forget about them, but the calluses above my heels won't let me and the gaping mouths of the new sneakers are too inviting. I hand the flashlight to Ahmad, kneel down at the feet of the corpse, and get busy on the laces.

At the same time that Ahmad and I enter the hospital, a young girl comes in with a bloodied face. It is past our working hours, but her wound needs immediate treatment. It is a deep transverse cut that runs from the side of her nasal septum up to her cheek. Wa'd disinfects her wound. I'm still trying to recover my senses from the stench and condition of the corpses.

Would that I was able to guzzle a bottle of Betadine to wash away the stench that still surrounds me. Fātima starts stitching up the girl's wound. When she takes up the needle and starts to ply it, I see that she is just as skilled at this task as she is in the rest of her work. She works delicately and carefully to make sure that the two edges of the wound do not overlap and to ensure that the skin does not become deformed or over-stretched. It's as if the needle in her hand is saying,

'I am in the hands of a skilled person. One who is skilled and considerate.'

It occurs to me that this medical team is a godsend that has been sent to help me implement the plan that we have of localizing the medical capabilities of the hospital. I consult with Karīm. He likes what I have in mind and gives his permission for the plan to be executed. I want the people here to be served by a team that is fixed and tied to the area, and is not rotated out once they serve out their tour of duty. This is especially important for the maternity ward. A mother who is being seen by a certain person who is in charge of monitoring her progress cannot accept a condition whereby the midwife that she was seeing has suddenly been changed out on the eve of her delivery. The skillset and temperament of this team encourage me to implement this plan; the plan of the 'girls of the hospital'. The plan entails girls who are living in Al-Bukamal who must learn everything there is to know about nursing and midwifery from Fātima and her team. Thankfully, the locals completely welcome the

Threads of Compassion

plan. It enables some of them to have jobs in an economically blighted region of the country. They want to cooperate with us, but on one condition: that ISIS does not become aware of the fact that they have cooperated with the Iranians.

I wade through all of the potential candidates patiently until I finally whittle them down to the four people who have the quality that I was looking for: Mirāl, Tahrīr, Hadya, and Isrā'. Four people who know that there is no longer any need to fear the return of ISIS.

Threads of Compassion

Chapter Seven Photos

The Furāt (Euphrates) Hospital in Deir ez-Zūr, whose staff made us stay the night. Here Dr. Sādiqī can be seen with one of the likeable drivers of the region who is named Sādiq.

Threads of Compassion

Shahīd (Martyr) Gholām-Rezā Langari-Zādeh, whose burnt and mutilated body made us all feel bad. I like this photo. I think he was just as eager for attaining martyrdom as he is shown in the picture.

Threads of Compassion

The kind-hearted Dr. Mohebbī, seen next to Fātima Dubā's professional staff, as well as seen arranging medicine on the shelves. From left to right: Fātima, Vāʿd, Dr. Mohebbī, and Vahīdah.

Threads of Compassion

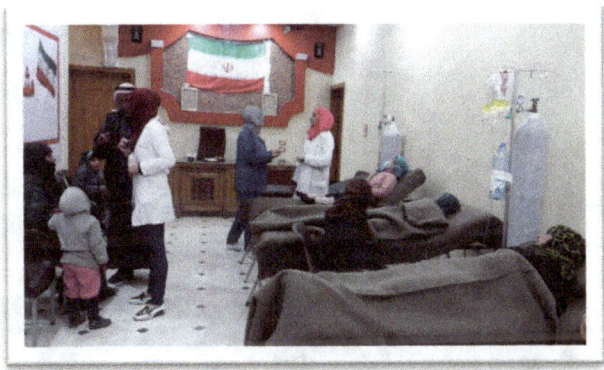

The in-patient ward which was empty most of the time if we had childbirths, but was even more crowded than this if we had emergency patients.

Ahmad, one of the soldiers of Mashhad's Fātemiyūn Corps. Ahmad became my right-hand man after Bābā Haidar left.

Threads of Compassion

Jamāl; one of the kind-hearted Afghani soldiers of the Fātemiyūn Corps.

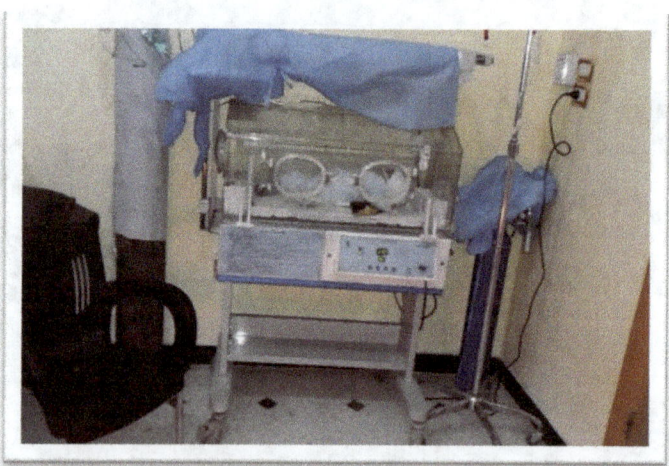

This is the incubator that I was finally able to find from "under a rock" and bring to the hospital.

8

Fātima is clutching onto my legs and cane, beseeching me to pick her up and hug her; but this is not something that is within my powers to do. A lump forms in my throat. The child is standing on her tiptoes and is insistent. This battered leg of mine can barely support me, let alone any other weight. Muhammad-Husain comes over and picks her up and gives her a hug, but this only sets her off crying. She wants to be in her father's arms and no one else's. My convalescence is taking forever, and it seems as if I'm never going to get better. I have become weary. Weary of this body of mine that has been lying in a bed for four months. I wish I could leave it behind and go back to performing my service. My service to Khānūm Jān's  neighbours.

Threads of Compassion

The locally recruited medical team in training was able to get going sooner than any of us thought they would. Each of them has picked up a part of the tasks that are to be performed. Mirāl has taken on the responsibility of receiving the patients and maintaining the registry; Tahrīr has taken charge of the pharmacy; Hadya is working in the emergency room; and Isrā' has become a midwife in training. None of it is willy-nilly either, of course. Tahrīr has a bachelor's degree in English and excellent reading skills; Mirāl maintains the registry with her good and legible handwriting; Hadya is fast on her feet; and Isrā' is a born midwife. Hamīda and Wahīdah can't believe how much talent for midwifery Isrā' naturally has. Every day, they describe the progress of their students to me, whom they have thereby made the principal of their school.

The trainees arrive at the hospital first thing in the morning and work closely with the nurses. They learn everything from our medical team, from starting an IV catheter to learning the names of all of the various drugs to making sutures and splints. It doesn't matter which ward is busy at any given time; they need to learn everything, as they might need to transfer their knowledge to others at some point in the future.

When a patient arrives, before doing anything else, Fātima calls the trainees. She adjusts the girls' fingers on the vein and the syringe when they are being trained on how to administer an injection. They insert the needle under the skin together, causing blood, as red as cherry syrup, to fill the capsule. The same procedure is repeated if an expectant mother arrives. The trainees must be at Hamīdah's and Wahīdah's side from the first examination to the delivery and the recording of the birth in the registry so that they can observe and learn what needs to be done.

We have officially become a University of the Medical Sciences, with an emphasis on the more practical side of things. We take the trainees through every step of every task, taking pleasure in the hustle and bustle of their learning. I feel like someone who has carved a kind-hearted angel out of the raw material of a stone; an angel who goes back and forth between the emergency room and the maternity ward and doesn't let anyone leave the hospital without getting their satisfaction. The trainees' temperaments are such that even if they are not able to do anything for a patient personally, they never fail to comfort them and to give them plenty of their loving kindness. These nurses in training are young ladies who might have ended up in that miserable building in Hamdān village, but whose souls have become pure by performing a good service here on our side. Instead of cutting off heads and blowing people up, they are learning the necessary skills to love their fellow human beings, irrespective of whether that human being is Iranian or Syrian, Shī'a or Sunni, or Christian or Druze. What is important is that someone is in need of help, and that he or she should therefore be helped. This is the kind of help that is taking place under the auspices of the

Iranian flag that is flying high on the roof of the hospital.

The second decade of the Fātimīyah[40] has begun, and even though we are a stone's throw from the shrine of Lady Fātima's ﷺ daughter, we are unable to have a *rowza-khānī*[41] ceremony to mourn her loss. I'm feeling dejected. I feel like hanging black flags on the walls of the hospital and starting a mourning ceremony. When I start to tell Ahmad how I feel, he jumps in,

'And why shouldn't we? Leave all the work with me; you just worry about inviting the guests.'

Ahmad doesn't let the words come out of my mouth; he knows instinctively what I was thinking and agrees with me.

'So then I'll first call the folks at the field hospital.'

I pick up the phone and begin calling.

'Hey, how are you? How are things? ... We're holding a *rowza-khānī* ceremony tomorrow night here at the hospital in honour of Lady Fātima ﷺ, and you are invited.'

I tell everyone the same thing as if I have an army of young men at my service to see to everything

---

[40] [The ten-day period (of mourning) for the martyrdom of Lady Fātima ﷺ, the august daughter of the Prophet of Islam.]

[41] [*Rowza-khānī*: a highly stylized ritual where elegies are recited in honor of Shi'a Islam's fallen heroes and heroines.]

that needs to be done in order to be able to serve all these guests that I have invited. I was so excited I invited everyone I could think of, without thinking of the consequences. When I had finished making all of my calls, I counted the guests written in the list. There were over fifty people. It was only then that I realized just what I had done. I looked at Ahmad and asked,

'How on earth are we going to prepare dinners for so many guests?!'

'Doctor! The person in whose honour the *rowza* is being held will arrange everything herself!'

I wake up early in the morning thinking about the dinner that we will be serving that evening. I am filled with anxiety. A dinner in honour of Lady Fātima ؑ is nothing to trifle with. I send Ahmad to the check the warehouse of the armed forces support staff to see if he can maybe find something that we can serve for dinner there. While he is doing that, I make all of the prayers and *dhikrs* that I can think of. I ask Lady Zainab ؑ to help me not to be ashamed before her mother.

An hour later, Ahmad arrives with two big sacks of rice; and prime-grade, fragrant Iranian rice at that. I look at him in stunned surprise. He says,

'Doctor, the rice for the dinner has been provided!'

'Provided *by whom*??'

'One of the guys of the support staff had brought these sacks of rice from Iran for his own consumption because he has a weak stomach. But as soon as he heard about the *rowza-khānī* ceremony in

Threads of Compassion

honor of Lady Fātima ﷺ, he offered up his rice for that purpose in fulfilment of a *nadhr* (a sacred vow).'

Without seeing and knowing him, I believe that his stomach troubles will be resolved due to his donating these two large sacks of rice. I head towards the shelving where the canned goods are stored. I count excitedly and find that we have enough canned beans for fifty people. So far, so good. But canned beans and Iranian rice, no matter how premium the rice might be, is still not befitting of a *rowza-khānī* ceremony in honour of Lady Fātima ﷺ.

By now it's almost noon and there are enough butterflies in my stomach to fill a rainforest. I can hear Hamīdah's and Wahīdah's voices coming from the maternity ward.

'Come on, mother [-to-be]! Push! Harder!! Hurry up!'

The mother-to-be's screams are endless. I think that there must be a problem, as the birth process never takes this long. I go up to the door of the maternity ward and call Isrā'. She says that all the screaming was for the first of the twins, and that the second one is now on its way. I step out into the hospital courtyard. I look at the Iranian flag waving on the roof and I look in the direction of Khānum Jān's ﷺ shrine. I'm stuck, wondering who I can turn to for help. Everyone who could have done something has already done what they could. Besides, all of the resources that I could think to draw from have all been invited, so what kind of invitation would this be if the guests are asked to pitch in? What would I say if I were to call them up? That they have been invited to a *rawza-khānī* dinner, but please bring your own dinner, if it's not too much to ask?! I wish I had one more day to deal with the problem; if I had one more day, I could eventually think of something and would be able to do something. I feel the weight of the world on my shoulders. Isrā' comes out of the building to give me the news that the second twin was born, and that he is a boy too. The twins' mother's mother-in-law has also stepped out with Isrā'. The old woman sighs and says something in Arabic. She kisses Isrā' on her forehead and goes down the stairs swiftly and leaves the hospital. The miracle of birth makes me feel better. A miracle that is repeated every day in this hospital, but which despite this, still retains its miraculous character. I go inside to recite the *adhān* or call to prayer in the ears of the twin boys, [as is the Islamic custom].

After the prayers, I sit facing the Qiblah. I can't stop thinking about dinner, a proper and righteous dinner worthy of Lady Fātima ﷺ. It is to be our Mother's assembly, an assembly for the Lady of all ladies. In my imaginal world, I fly to Damascus and the shrine of Khānūm Jān ﷺ to see if she can do something for me. "Who is it that can fulfil the needs of the distressed?"[42] I then take flight to Qom and Iran's Khānūm Jān ﷺ [Lady Ma'suma, Imam Riḍā's ﷺ sister,

---

[42] This is a reference to a hadith report that is attributed to the Twelfth Imam: (أَمَّنْ يُجِيبُ الْمُضْطَرَّ إِذا دَعاهُ وَ يَكْشِفُ السُّوءَ).

whose shrine is in Qom]. I will lose face if I am not able to serve [Lady Fāṭima ﷺ] properly after a lifetime of wearing [the] black [clothing of mourning on these various religious commemorative occasions]. I'm distressed. My honour and reputation are at stake. My imagination next takes flight to the Baqīʿ Cemetery, to beseech our Mother herself to provide the necessities of this *rawza*. I rest my head on the steel grates. What kind of protection is this [that the Wahhābis have put around the graves,] instead of the metal protective latticework around the sepulcher (*ḍarīḥ*). It's like a hard cold slap in my face. I hear Aqā Mujtabā Tehrānī's voice in my mind's ear saying,

'They beat you in the middle of the street.'

Would that I could die right now! I can't take it anymore. I take the rest of the *rawza* back to Lady Fāṭima's ﷺ daughters in Damascus and in Qom. It takes a woman's heart to understand suffering. Women understand the meaning of a *chādor* covered in dust. Women understand the heft of a slap in the face. Women understand the weight of the next stanza, which I cannot even bring myself to recite. How many tears I have shed on account of these words! I put my face in a corner of her *chādor* and wail. I smell the scent of dust.

Ahmad is busy in the kitchen cooking all the rice. Their fragrance has spread all over the building. The sound of a sheep can be heard coming from the yard. I think the sound is coming from one of the nearby houses. The sound gets closer, a long and stretched-out bleating sound. I step outside. I see that there is a brown sheep seated in a wheelbarrow with its chin resting on its front legs, chewing on something. The mother-in-law of the mother of the twin boys is holding the arms of the wheelbarrow, trying to navigate it up the ramp that leads to the entrance to the hospital. She has brought the sheep as a present. It's her way of thanking us for the healthy delivery of her grandchildren. So now we have the meat of the stew to go with the rice and beans of tonight's dinner, which walked in on its own legs, in a manner of speaking.

When the hospital doors close, the area goes to sleep. The taste of the *rawza* we had two nights ago is still coursing through my soul. I recited elegies and beat my chest and wailed to my heart's content, and my recitation of these elegies brought tears to other people's eyes too, just as they would have done if they were recited by any other elegy reciter (*maddāh*) during the Fātimīyah. My tears would not stop flowing. They were tears of thanks for being able to hold a *rawza* here on Syrian soil, in the neighbourhood of Lady Fātima ﷺ's daughter, next to her neighbours, and for the dinner that she had provided for the gathering in such a miraculous fashion. They were tears of thanks for everything I had asked for, for this *rawza*, which she had arranged herself. They were tears of thanks for the good situation we were in. They were even tears of thanks for seeing Abūta back, who had finally returned after a two-month leave of absence. Although he was not going to be stationed at the hospital and had to go somewhere else, but even so, seeing him again was worth the world to me. I embraced him tightly and we shed a sea of tears on each other's shoulders. That's what *rawzas* do: they soften the calcifications of the heart, and are cathartic in that way.

It's dark out now. I wish I could hold *rawzas* for ten days on end instead of for just one night. The cold forces its way through the window. The medical team has gone upstairs. They are so tired that they must have fallen straight to sleep as I don't hear them making any noise. Ahmad and Jamāl are in their own room. The light of the guards' fire has illuminated the far end of the courtyard. I pour myself a cup of tea. I wished these teas could wash away one's loneliness as well as one's fatigue. I place a cube of sugar between my lips. The first sip does not give me the taste I'm looking for: the taste of the teas that Somayyeh used to bring me. The second sip saturates the sugar in my mouth. How I miss my home. I remember telling Somayyeh to sit down next to me whenever she brought me tea, as her presence adds sweetness to the tea.

Somayyeh sits in front of me. I recite some poetry for her, and take a third sip. I have so much to say to her. The words that are going around in my head have started to line up so that they can pour out in some sort of order when a heartbreaking scream of several women hit them like a missile and scattered all of them away. The women's wailing dispels all thoughts of homesickness, tea, sugar, and Somayyeh at my side. I run towards the courtyard. A white pickup has pulled up to the bottom of the ramp at the hospital's entrance. Several Arab women are in the bed of the pickup, and are flailing themselves in the agony of grief. There is a dead body wrapped in a blanket lying between them; the lifeless body of a young girl. Her wet black hair clings to her throat and cheeks. It is as if they have taken her body out of the Euphrates River. Her lips are white and her face is discoloured. I take her arm out of the blanket, and check and see that she has no radial pulse. I place my left hand on her neck, only to see that she has no carotid pulse either. Her chest does not move. I open her eyelids. Her left pupil is fully dilated. I check her right eye, and see that it is still normal. We have less than five minutes before complete pupillary dilation, which is an indication of irreversible brain death.

We grab the corners of the blanket and run to the emergency room, carrying the body on our shoulders. Every second counts in such a recovery operation. We place the girl on the examination table just as she was, wrapped in the blanket. Fātima inserts a catheter and gets an IV line going. Lung medicine is injected into the infusion fluid. I clamp a mask on her face and start the process of oxygen being pumped into

Threads of Compassion

her lungs by opening the valve of the oxygen tank to its fully open position. I instruct Wa'd to start the massage process quickly and vigorously. Wa'd interlaced hands pump up and down on the girl's chest. We are told that the girl did not drown in the Euphrates, and find out that fumes from a coal fire that had accumulated in the closed space of a bathroom have sent her lungs into a state of shock. The people of the region use water that is drawn from a tanker, and have to heat the bathroom with a pan of molten coal. The girl's lifeless body was rescued from the bathroom and brought to us wet and wrapped in a blanket. After two minutes of Wa'd's administering a vigorous pump-action massage, the girl's radial pulse comes back. Her level of consciousness is still very low. Her chances of being successfully resuscitated are very low, given the fact that we have no specialist doctor and no resuscitation-specific drugs, and that we are only four kilometres from the front line of the war with ISIS. I have no choice but to use the stimulant of pain. I give her a hard slap on her face. She clinches her eyelids. Tighter and tighter. She lets out a weak moan, sending a wave of relief through me. I step back. The women who accompanied the young girl said that these kinds of bathroom-related incidents happened a lot during the time of ISIS's reign, but that there was nothing that they could do about it. My heart goes out to them. To think that people died because of a simple case of lung poisoning that could be remedied with rigorous massage and oxygen, just as this girl almost died, is heart-wrenching. It was less than an hour ago that the young girl was brought in wrapped in a blanket and without a pulse, and now she is walking out of the emergency room on her own two feet wearing a long Arabic dress. Her face is still pale, but she is alert and is smiling. Her companions gather around her and cheer her on. They leave the hospital noisier than when they entered, but this time, the sounds are happy sounds. How narrow indeed is the gap between life and death.

I put a spoonful of chicken kabse in my mouth and delighted in the taste of chicken, which I had almost forgotten about. When chicken breeding and the production of chicken meat is disrupted down to 20% of its original capacity in a war-torn country, it goes without saying that what chickens are still able to be produced will not make it to the front lines of the war; thus, it is no wonder that we have almost forgotten what chicken tastes like. But things changed for us thanks to Hāj Majīd's chef burning his hand the other day. The chef, who is a portly and good-humored Syrian who works in the Syrian Army's combat service support (CSS), comes to our hospital every day so that Fātimah and Waʿd can change his hand's bandage. Everyone knows that our hospital only serves the locals here, and that everyone else has to go to the

Mushfi al-Maidāni clinic. I have made an exception in the case of Hāj Majīd's chef on account of Hāj Majīd himself, and so that the chef can get back to work as soon as possible. This is why he brings us gifts from the CSS every day. And what gifts! Frozen nuggets of chicken for a chicken-hungry crowd such that we are. I put a second spoonful of kabse in my mouth and send prayers of blessings for the Syrian cook and for the steam of the pot that burned his hand. The tradition of the women doing our cooking has remained with us from the first medical team, which consisted of Umm Ahmad and her friends. This tradition is the most delicious goodbye present they could have left for us before they left. It is a tradition that has been handed down from one team to another as each complete their tours of duty. I have yet to get to the bottom of the pot of kabse that Fātima has cooked when the screams of expectant mothers are raised. They came in before we started our dinner, and finished their childbirths before we had finished our dinner.

The rain hits the window like a whip, fast and relentless. It is a loud desert storm. The entire yard has become covered in a layer of sticky mud. The Euphrates River has overflowed its banks and has flooded the roads because of this rain, and the floods have cut off our communication with everyone: with the field hospital, with our headquarters, and with everything else that is Iranian in the region. In the midst of all of this, we have an important guest tonight. An Iraqi surgeon is coming to al-Bukamal to become

Mushfi al-Maidāni's resident surgeon. Dr. Mustafā is the famous American-educated doctor of the Axis of Resistance. If the news of the rainstorm and its flooding reaches him, he will definitely postpone his visit. But he will not be able to reach the hospital even if he crosses the border, given the rainstorm and the conditions of the dirt roads leading to the field hospital.

Hamīda and Wahīda have loud voices, which they put to use urging the expectant mothers to work harder. I think about how many interesting stories these mothers will have to tell their children about the rainstorm and the flooding that occurred on the night of their birth. The sound of the ambulance's sirens overshadows the screams of the birthing mothers. They are probably bringing more expectant mothers to the hospital. I put a hat on my head in lieu of an umbrella and step out. The courtyard is riddled with large puddles.

The noise of the guards' complaints reaches the building. It is a military ambulance and according to my standing order, it must go to the field hospital. But the driver of the ambulance insists on entering. When I go to discuss the matter with him, I see that the driver's passenger is none other than Dr. Mustafā, the renowned Iraqi surgeon. The road to the field hospital is flooded and he has no choice but to stay with us for the night. Dr. Mustafā is a well-dressed and tall young man. He steps out of the ambulance, carrying a backpack with a leopard skin pattern, and boots and a hat that are designed for special desert operations. He is a guerilla in every sense of the word; a guerrilla who is ready to perform surgery at any moment. He introduces himself, saying that he is Dr. Mustafā from Baghdad, and that he is at my service.

He transfers his M4 carbine to his left hand and squeezes my hand warmly and firmly with his right hand.

Mustafā is up at dawn and hangs around the various wards of the hospital, completely unphased by his arduous journey to Al-Bukamal of the previous night. He travels a lot to Iran, but he cannot speak Persian, so we have to resort to my terrible Arabic. We are trying to communicate in this extemporaneous manner when the two-way radio starts to squawk loudly. It is the voice of Hāj Majīd, the warehouse or supplies quartermaster from CSS.

'Nobody move!!'

He is shouting anxiously.

'Didn't I say nobody move?? Husain! Sit the hell down!'

He says sit down with such vehemence that I sit down too! The voice of Hāj Majīd's forces can also be heard now.

'*Hāji!* One of them was shot, but we can't see the other one.'

Hāj Majīd shouts again.

'Don't go after them! They have snipers who will shoot you.'

Threads of Compassion

The sound of gunshots and explosions are not strong enough to mask Hāj Majīd's screams. He is worried about his forces.

I am gripped by anxiety. The flood has divided Al-Bukamal into two halves, an eastern half and a western half. The field hospital is in the western half and our hospital is in the eastern half. The eastern half is under fire and the support forces are pinned down and cannot move. I jump in on the conversation to see if Majīd is on our side or on the Mushfi al-Maidāni side. Dr. Mustafā has understood the situation perfectly. In the blink of an eye, he is dressed for the operating room, and is ready and waiting for the injured party to arrive. I pray to God that Majīd is on the side of our hospital and that he will send the injured soldier to us. Mushfi al-Maidāni is for injured soldiers and is better equipped than our hospital, but what good is a well-equipped hospital without a surgeon? Their surgeon Mustafā is here with us, and the road to the field hospital is closed. I call out to Hāj Majīd. He responds,

'We are sending the injured party to you.'

'Wait, I'll send an ambulance out.'

'He has lost a lot of blood. I've already sent him to you in a Toyota.'

I call up the team and have them prepare the operating room. I call the guards to have them leave the hospital door open. A few minutes later, the Toyota has backed up onto the ramp with a 45-year-old wounded fighter who's losing consciousness by the second due to his loss of blood. We put him on the delivery bed and circle around him. One of the nurses inserts a catheter and starts an IV drip, and Dr. Muṣṭafā checks the trajectory of the bullets he has taken.

Fāṭima puts a temporary dressing on the head wound to stop the bleeding. Waʻd is busy controlling the bleeding of the injury to his arm. But the main problem is the two bullets that have cleaved his ribcage and lungs. We need a chest tube to prevent various bodily secretions from entering the lungs. If we cannot prevent that from taking place, there'll be nothing else that can be done to save the patient's life.

Dr. Muṣṭafā looks around. There is everything to be found in the medicine cabinet other than a chest tube. Not having a chest tube in a maternity ward is not strange, but not having one in an operating room with a patient whose lung has been punctured is awkward.

'I need a chest tube,' Dr. Muṣṭafā says, as he continues to examine the wounds.

I send Taḥrīr to the room where the drugs are stored. Aḥmad follows her. I know we don't have any chest tubes, but I demure from telling the doctor this to give myself time to think of something. I'm calculating how long it will take if I send Aḥmad to the field hospital in an ambulance and have someone meet them half way from the other side, when Aḥmad and Taḥrīr come in holding a chest tube.

I want to shout, 'It's a miracle! A miracle! We didn't have any chest tubes! Where did you get these?'

But Aḥmad beats me to it.

Threads of Compassion

He says, 'Doctor, it was so fortuitous that you took these chest tubes that day we were searching around in ISIS's underground warehouse!'

That jogged my memory. I had found this chest tube in that basement the same day that I removed the sneakers from the feet of that rotting ISIS corpse; the chest tube that I wanted to send to the field hospital, but was somehow left behind here in our medicine storeroom to be on hand in order to save the life of a wounded Iranian fighter. I keep the feeling to myself that I felt a miracle had happened a moment ago. I just nod and say,

'Yes, thank God.'

Everyone else might not know, but Khānūm Jān  and I know why the chest tube is here, and whose will it was that wanted the life of one of the Defenders of her Shrine to be saved. When the chest tube is inserted and in place, the injured soldier starts to breath more normally and starts to revive, and before too long, we start feeling assured that he will survive the operation. Isrā', Wa'd, and Fātima are attending to him, and Hamīdah, Wahīdah, and Tahrīr are also busy at the foot of the bed disinfecting and dressing the soldier's wounds. When he regains consciousness, he looks around and says,

'Did I become a martyr?'

Laughter explodes among us like firecrackers.

Threads of Compassion

A month has passed since the arrival of Fātimah Duba's medical team and the golden period their arrival inaugurated. All of the medical teams stay for no more than two weeks, but this team has stayed for a month. They wanted to stay for the third week, and the fourth week was extended at my request. Whatever it was, it passed quickly; as fast as the first two weeks; as fast as the seven-month period that Husain and I spent together. I have a lump in my throat again. It's always the same on the day that the medical team leaves. But this time it's different. None of us want this period to end.

    I felt the same way in 2007. I'm talking about the time when I was taking the supplementary course together with Husain. When I open my eyes in the morning, I feel a yearning for Husain, for the way he used to talk and the things he used to say, for his poetry readings, and even for the way he signed his name. He would take a green pen and write MHB under his prescriptions, the initials which stood for Muhammad Husain Bashīrī. I miss him signing his name and then following it up with a "Yā Zahrā". Husain is also feeling down. All we have done since the noon prayers is to shed tears. The chaplain of the barracks, Hāj Āqā Mohsenī, envies us, because he hasn't seen anyone have this kind of relationship since the nights of the offensive operations [in the eight-year Sacred Defense against Saddam's Bathist Iraq]. He envies the pure emotion of the moment of separation of friends who have become half of each other's beings; friends who know everything about each other; and friends whom God has placed on each other's paths: heavenly friends. We cry until the railway station to Mashhad. Husain has a ticket that will take him back to Hamedān. Our tears won't leave us alone. The image of his face behind the train window has been burned into my memory more than any other image and memory. He tidies himself up a little, smiles, and waves at me. The train blows its whistle and slowly pulls out of the station, completely unconcerned about the fact that it is putting a distance between me and my friend with each turn of its wheels – a very long distance. Longer than all of the wagons of the train that have been arrayed in a single line. That train was the train of Husain's life. He left, and I stood and watched. There was nothing I could do but cry.

That autumn night of 2016 was the same: there was nothing I could do but cry. I was on shift duty at the Khātam al-Anbiā Clinic in Tehran. At 1:30 past midnight, I came to the break room to drink some tea and lie down for a while when Mehdi called. He had just come back from Syria and had a whole lot of stories to tell. For my part, I was eager to hear what he had to say, as I felt left behind, so he talked for an hour.

'So you went and became a doctor! If you were still one of the vanguards (*takhrībchī*), you would have been martyred by now.'

I chuckle bitterly.

'I don't deserve martyrdom, bro. That's my problem, and it has nothing to do with whether I have become a doctor or am still one of the vanguards, as you put it.'

'Two weeks ago, one of my comrades who was martyred was one of the vanguards. Hāj Qāsim [Soleimāni] loved him very much.'

'Who was this?'

'Muhammad Husain Bashīrī.'

'Was he from Hamedān?'

'Yeah.'

'Was he light-complected?'

'Yup.'

'And bald?'

'Yup.'

At that point, I just lost it. I didn't know what I was saying anymore or where I was at. I let out a moan and shouted,

'Oh, my dear Husain, my dear, beloved Husain!'

I struck myself on the face.

'Would that I was buried under the dust of the earth!'

I am burning up inside for having been left behind. I am burning up inside because my brother and soulmate left so quietly that I wasn't even aware of his passing. I am burning up inside because I was not even allowed to be one of his pall-bearers. I am burning up inside because I don't have Husain as a friend anymore. Mehdi is confused on the other end of the phone. He calls out my name anxiously. All the doctors and nurses of the shift have poured into the room because of my wailing, but it is Husain that I would like to see come in through the door, wearing that same blue tee-shirt he used to wear, and to laugh as he always did and say,

'Why are you acting up again?'

I want him to embrace me and lay my head on his chest, and for us to cry together again. But everyone came in, except Husain. Husain never came back, ever again. Even in my dreams. But nevertheless, he is always by my side. When I speak, he listens. When I make a joke, he laughs. When I recite elegies, he cries. When I cry, his heart goes out to me. His heart aches for mine and with mine. His heart aches for the conditions I am subjected to, for my knees, which are sore from running so much and scraping them. Hussein is present; my kind brother who understands me and worries about me. He is present, but distant. The train of his life has gone somewhere far away that is out of my reach; to a place where no matter how far I run, it will be out of my reach.

Threads of Compassion

Chapter Eight Photos

My dear friend and brother Muhammad Husain Bashīrī, whom I love more than life itself. He is laughing, as always. He was as uncomplicated as the writing on the column next to him. [The writing states: 'Martyrdom will be our lot in life, God willing.'] And that is how he was martyred: simply and quietly. So simply and quietly that I found out about it two weeks after the fact.

Threads of Compassion

From right to left: Vaʻd, Fātima, Wahīdah, and Hamīda. Jamāl is to my right, and Ahmad is to my left.

Threads of Compassion

Fātimah and the delicious Kabsas she has cooked for us with chickens donated by the chef of the Tepil Support Services.

A *rawḍa-khānī* ceremony in honor of Ḥaḍrat Zahrā (Lady Fāṭima ﷺ). Ahmed can be seen sitting next to me.

Dr. Mustafā, a skilled Iraqi surgeon who was a guest of our hospital on that rainy night.

Threads of Compassion

Hāj Majīd, who was in charge of support services in the days when it flooded.

Threads of Compassion

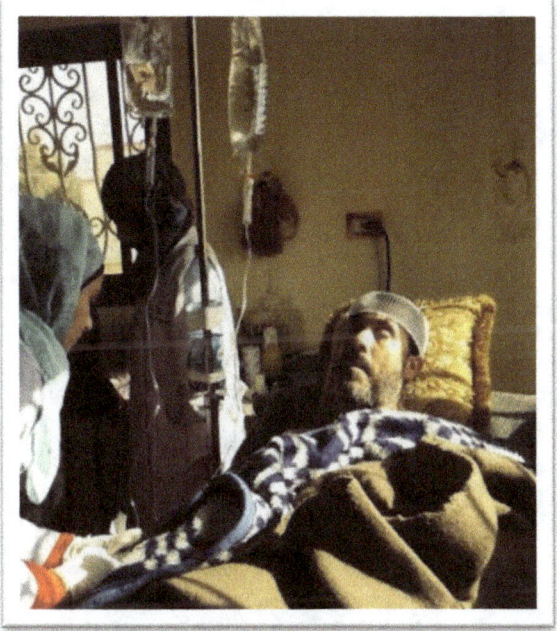

Suleimān the rider, who was injured on that rainy night, and whose life was saved with the use of some adhesive.

Threads of Compassion

A cute boy who was brought to the clinic one day with a wounded leg. Fātima and the other female staff fussed over him and dressed his wound. A few days later, he came dressed like this to thank the kind nurses.

Threads of Compassion

9

Karīm has come to Al-Harī. Seeing him reminds me of the first day we came here together. He seems to me to have lost a lot of weight since then, and it is no wonder, given all his hard work and constant moving around in the region. The time has gone by so fast. That day, I was so concerned that I should not be posted here for my mission, but now I get anxious when there is any talk about leaving. Maryam, Karīma, and a team of documentary film-makers have accompanied Karīm. They plan to make a documentary about the medical teams that come out here from Aleppo, and Maryam's and Karīma's stories will play a central role in their documentary. They stayed here with the purpose of serving the people from the first day they arrived, even though at that time they didn't have the necessary facilities to carry out their work properly. They must have had a great deal of purity of purpose in their work in order for an independent documentary filmmaker to want to make a documentary about their activities in the region. The absence of Dr. Ali and Ismāʿīl, who were colleagues of Maryam and Karīma, will be sorely felt in the documentary.

When Fātima Duba's medical team was leaving, I thought that my work with the next team would definitely be more difficult because I had become used to their professionalism and the high quality of their work. But God sent me Asīla back, whose return puts my mind at ease about the activities of the maternity ward. A veritable hustle and bustle has started up in the building as a result of the presence of so many guests, especially since Maryam and Karīma are staying overnight. Maryam roams around the building, checking everything out. She can't believe that so many facilities have been added in just three months. And in fact, there really is no comparison between our present emergency room, pharmacy and maternity ward, and that clinic that she left three months ago where everything that we had and did could have been done in a single room.

The womenfolk are happy and talking up a storm, but Karīm is angry because of the Al-Sūʿīyah clinic which Dr. Najmuddīn was supposed to have opened up two months ago, which hasn't happened as of yet. Al-Sūʿīyah is a village near Al-Harī. As such, if there was an emergency clinic there, our workload would have been cut in half, and people would be referred over there for their medical needs, and our hospital would turn into one that operates solely as a maternity ward. Karīm lays it down for Dr. Najmuddīn on the phone, giving him till 10 am tomorrow to get to Al-Harī with his hospital staff. What is interesting is that the head of Deir ez-Zūr province's School of Medical Sciences abides by the law that Karīm has laid down, and is in the hospital yard at ten the following morning along with five ambulances, making a field day for the documentary filmmakers, whose cameras don't stop rolling.

In the midst of all of this hustle and bustle, Karīm and I and some other people are invited to lunch by a tribal chief of one of Al-Bukamal's tribes. The chief has sent his son twice to extend the invitation, but we are not allowed to accept any such invitation. And rightly so; this is a necessary precautionary measure. Extending such invitations to us by people who are residents of a city whose loyalty to ISIS is a proven fact makes no sense. Around noon, an old man in a white robe and skullcap enters the hospital, followed by an entourage. He is an Arab sheikh in every sense of the word. He looks to be over seventy but is slim and light on his feet. The big knife he was holding in his hand captured my attention. I approached him with caution. He stops a few steps away from me and casts a glance at his companions. At this cue, two of the young men who are standing behind him quickly bring a sheep that they have brought with them up to the old man, then take their positions behind him again. Our guard, who is a Syrian, says,

'Doctor! What's going on here is this. If the man puts the knife on the ground and leaves the sheep and walks away, he will not talk to you for the rest of his life; but if he cuts the sheep's head with his own hand, what that will mean is that he will become your enemy for the rest of his life.'

I now realize that the fellow is the head of the tribe whose invitation we have twice turned down. We are caught in a stand-off. He stares in my eyes like they do in Texas movies before a duel. His six-shooter is the big knife he is holding in his hand, and my six-shooter is my ability to accept his invitation. I can neither risk accepting his invitation, nor can I risk allowing the fire of a grudge being started.

Before I know it, he has wrestled the poor sheep to the ground and is holding the knife up against its throat. I run towards him and hasten to accept his invitation with my broken Arabic. Satisfied with his victory, he proudly stands back up again. He looks at his companions, as if to take in their acknowledgement of the feat he just accomplished where they had failed to do so. He sheathes the knife back in its sheath and leaves the sheep in the hospital yard as a gift. Karīm and I, Dr. Najamuddīn, and the documentary team sit in the van and head towards the old man's house, like chastened obstinate schoolboys who have to take a beating before they can learn their lesson. Thank God

Threads of Compassion

Hāj Salmān is around. He is the security officer of the area, who always looks out for me. He visits the hospital every afternoon and doesn't leave before reminding me to take care of myself. Today is no different than every other day. He came around, and learned about the dinner party we were forced into attending. Before we leave, he checks the political leanings of the chief, as well as the address of the old man's home and its various points of access in order to ensure that nothing untoward will happen.

We are sitting around the edges of a red carpet that is spread out in the courtyard, like a group of well-mannered children. The courtyard is arid and dusty. We wash our hands with water that is poured out of an urn by the chief's son, who at the same time also holds a plastic tub underneath our hands to gather the runoff. Dr. Najmuddīn acts as the arbiter between the guests and the host. I don't know much Arabic, but there is a sentence exchanged which is full of praised and admiration for Dr. Karīm and Dr. Ehsān. I am not familiar with the customs of the Arabs and their hospitality. When the big trays of food are brought out, I expect the young men who are our hosts to sit next to us so that we can begin the meal. But they continue to stand above us with their arms crossed, at our service. A large sheep roasted whole has been placed before us, and they indicate that we should start eating. The sheep's front legs are in one tray, and its hind legs rest in another. Both trays are filled with rice and vegetables. I look back and forth between the table-spread and our hosts, and consider the situation: me, Ehsān Jāvīdī, sitting here on the border of Syria and Iraq, at the table-spread of a real-life Arab sheikh! If we were to meet under different circumstances anywhere else in the world, we would have had to go back and forth for years, with various Dr. Karīms and Dr. Najmuddīns acting as go-betweens and mediators between us, before we could sit at the same table together, because we don't have a single star in common in any of the seven heavens. But now everything is different. All of the calculus is centered around a single star. We are Khānūm Jān's ﷺ servants, and the sheikh and his fellow citizens are Khānūm Jān's ﷺ neighbours. Can there be a brighter star than this?

I don't know if it's just because I haven't had a decent meal in so long or whether the food is really greasy. I finish eating sooner than usual and wait for the others to be sated so that we can go and take a look at the building that Dr. Najmuddīn is supposed to turn into a clinic. Following my lead, everyone else gradually stops eating prematurely too. The food is too rich for them too. After we have finished eating, the turn of the host's young men comes. They collect the remains of the meal and go a little farther out and start eating on a straw mat in the middle of the yard. I don't feel good; both because of the over-richness of the meal, as well as because of this custom; I suppose that after the young men have finished eating, it will be the women's turn, who will gather what is left on the trays and will finally be able to eat their meal.

Karīm and the documentary filmmakers and Maryam and Karīma are leaving, leaving me and my hospital. It has been decided that a warehouse is to be added to the hospital. Hussain, who is the manager of the Jihād al-Bannā warehouse, wants to go on leave in two months, and there is no one to replace him who can run the warehouse. If I don't accept the responsibility of running the warehouse, Husain will not be able to return to Iran. Even if he could do so officially, his heart would still be here, concerned about what would happen to the warehouse. On the other hand, if I accept this responsibility, our situation will become even more difficult. As it is, we have a difficult time seeing to the needs of the day to day running of the hospital. And if we add the burden of responsibility for the warehouse onto our shoulders, who knows what will happen. I look at Ahmad, and then at Husain, who is sitting in front of me waiting for an answer.

Husain's responsibilities have to do with people's food. He divides a given quota of flour and sugar between them every week. Food is not like medicine, which is only needed when one is ill. It is a daily need whose supply cannot be interrupted. I want to be there for Husain and for these people, but if I accept this responsibility, I will only be able to sleep three hours a night instead of the five hours I get now. The thought occurs to me that, Oh well, let it be a sacrifice for a single thread of Khānūm Jān's *chādor*.

Threads of Compassion

What use is a couple of hours of sleep to me, if I can set her mind as ease that her neighbour's food staples will be supplied. What if I don't accept the responsibility for the warehouse? What would we say to the people: that the warehouse manager has gone on leave and has taken the key to the warehouse with him?! That is obviously out of the question. People must eat if they are to survive. It would not please God if even a single morsel of food is taken from the table-spread of these people. What kind of neighbourliness would it be, and how would I be able to face Khānūm Jān ﷺ? If I don't accept this responsibility, all of Husain's efforts while he was here will have been wasted. The people who have worked under him have worked hard and lost a lot of sleep so that the affairs of the warehouse are put in order and for it to become a place where people know they can fall back on if they don't have anything to eat; knowing that they will not be sent away empty handed.

I say a "Yā Ali" and put Husain's mind at ease.

An hour later, I am checking the various storerooms in the Jihād al-Bannā warehouse. Husain is accompanying me so that he can clue me in to the ins and outs of running the warehouse. The warehouse consists of a large house with many rooms, each of which is dedicated to a specific commodity, from clothes to cooking oil and bottled water to ready to eat meals and flour and sugar. The largest room and its covered porch are full of large bags of flour. The mill of the region produces a hundred bags of flour daily. In a province that has just been liberated from ISIS and is 800 kilometres from the country's capital, delivering this amount of flour to the hungry stomachs of the region's populace is a praiseworthy activity that has its rewards in heaven as well as on earth.

Two days later, when Husain has gone, we are left with a world of work that we neither have time to do, not have the experience to perform properly. Asīla is managing the girls in training and everything having to do with the emergency room, and I am trying to figure out how to run the warehouse with the help of Ahmad and Jamāl, for whose help I thank them a hundred times a day. At the same time, some new areas have been liberated and the women and children of those areas are brought to Al-Harī by the truckload every day. The task of recording the vital statistics and settling these new immigrants in tents alone is a full-time job for three workers, let alone the rest of the work that their addition adds into the mix. And while it is true that our services are provided without any expectation [of financial compensation], there are, nevertheless, limitations on what we can do.

A certain minimal share or ration had already been determined for each family, and it is just enough to keep them from dying of starvation. With the arrival of the new wave of immigrants, that share will have to be decreased in order for everyone to have a share of the limited supplies. The rations are so paltry that one is ashamed to even characterize them as any kind of aid. Any "aid" which doesn't make its beneficiary open his or her eyes in surprised delight isn't really aid, is it? What possible good can a kilo of flour do for these starving people? Who is going to eat it, and who all will just sit and watch? As if my yearning for medicine was not enough, a yearning for flour and sugar has now been added to my needs. I have become the perfect example of a servant who is never satisfied. Until yesterday, I was sitting before God's house asking for medicine, and saying that we need a lot of it; that He should provide a lot from His limitless capacities. Now my prayers are to be able to fill the stomachs of these wretched people; to fill them with a delicious Iranian dish whose taste should be so good that they will always remember it. What's wrong with that? Those who know more than we do and are greater stakeholders in this heavenly business have always advised us to ask for great things when we pray and not to limit our requests to measly items, so I don't think I asked for too much. These things that I aspire to are not unattainable for me, as my prayers are directed to One who is all-powerful. If He so wills, all He has to do is say, 'Be', and it will come into being.

I drag my exhausted body to bed. My whole body is aching with fatigue and the soles of my feet are hot and swollen. The intensity of my need for sleep doesn't even allow me to make sure that the breech of my pistol is loaded before I go to sleep. Sleeping with a loaded weapon is a nightly ritual for all of us. The first day we set foot in the region, all the experts told us to be sure to sleep with a loaded weapon by our sides; that we should be armed and alert. And they are right, of course, because we are sleeping in the gaping mouth of a dragon, between our headquarters and ISIS territory. I clutch the cold barrel of my pistol and pull the blanket up to my ears, and feel the intensity of the pleasure of the onrush of sleep.

The sound of machine gun fire jolts me up from my sleep. It is 1:30 past midnight. I make sure my pistol is loaded. The sound is very close by, as if ISIS forces are shooting in the courtyard of the hospital. I pull the pin out of a grenade and start running. Ahmad and Jamāl are standing by the entrance and watching. I'm shocked at their nonchalance, and shout at them,

'Don't you hear the sound of gunfire??'

Jamāl sees the grenade I'm holding in my hand and tries to calm me down.

'I swear to God, it's nothing. We saw that you were very tired and didn't want to wake you.' A whole tribe-full of people have gathered in the middle of the courtyard, cheering and kissing each other's cheeks in celebration. Our guards have also joined in the fun, firing volleys of gunfire in the air from time to time. I'm wondering what's going on. Jamāl says that while I was sleeping, the daughter-in-law of Bashār, the head of this clan, gave birth to twin boys, and that the ruckus is the birthday party of the twins. So now I'm left with a grenade in my hand whose pin I have pulled, and Bashār and his whole clan in the hospital yard. Bashār's two sons were killed by ISIS, so he is certainly

Threads of Compassion

well within his rights to celebrate the birth of these twin boys in this manner.

I turn away from the celebrations and am making my way to the embankment in front of the hospital to get rid of the grenade when Bashār calls me over and invites me to join the circle of the menfolk. I cannot refuse the invitation of the chief of the tribe; but just as urgently, I cannot ignore the grenade that is ready to explode as soon as I let go of its lever. I squeeze down on the grenade's safety lever harder, and go and join the men. I kiss them all and congratulate them. Poor Jamāl probably thinks I intend to tell them to stop making noise with the grenade that I'm holding. He runs over amid the cheers and the shots in the air and shouts,

'Get *down!*'

No one present understood any Persian so they just ignored him.

When the face-kissing and congratulations are over, my hand has become numb from the intensity of the pressure I had been applying on the safety lever. I quietly step away from the crowd and make my way to the embankment in front of the hospital, toss the grenade, and *boom!*

In the morning, Bashār's daughter-in-law is discharged from the hospital and Bashār's clan vacates the hospital with her. Our eyes sting from a lack of sleep and our ears are ringing from all the barrages of machinegun fire. Bashār pulls me aside and wants to thank me; to thank me, my team, and the Iranians. I place my hands over my eyes and forehead as a sign of respect, indicating that it is an honor for us to be able to be of service here. His dignified countenance becomes wet with tears. He pulls his *abā* robe up over his shoulders and leaves without saying another word.

    Bashār showed up two days later. When I saw him, I prepared myself for another sleepless night of machinegun barrages and celebrations. I figured he must have another bride whose turn has come to give birth. He wants to say something, but is hesitant, chewing on what he wants to say. He then starts to talk about his sons who collaborated with ISIS and were killed as a result. His trust in ISIS caused their lives to be wasted. He feels responsible for the death of his sons and for the death of many members of his tribe who were beheaded by ISIS. He tells me that if he had not cooperated with ISIS, at least he wouldn't be feeling this burden of guilt now. He says that not only has he spent in treasure, but he has also lost the lives of loved ones, as well as lost honour and standing. Now he is ready to trust the Iranians. And how is he going to do this? By revealing the location of ISIS's food warehouse. A huge warehouse full of sugar and rice and beans and pulses. I know all of the basements of the area like the back of my hand by now, and know that there are no basements left that we haven't gone through. Bashār says the same thing, in a sense. He is sure that no one has had any access to the warehouse. He says that in any case, the Iranians haven't come across it yet, because if we had, we would have given everything in it to the people by now. These words of his make me happy and proud. What a good feeling it is for one to come to an area of ISIS supporters after seven years of ISIS rule and raise Iran's flag among its supporters, and then be recognized as being true to one's trust in such a significant sense.

The location that Bashar gives me of the ISIS warehouse is near the Euphrates and in the direction of the desert. I get Hāj Salmān on the radio. I have to consult him in order to reach this dream warehouse that is stocked with 50 kilo bags of rice and beans and pulses, most of which are chickpeas. In our warehouse, I would be satisfied if there was only flour instead of all of these things. Half an hour later, Hāj Salmān has mustered a number of our elite forces to accompany us to the warehouse. No matter how much I insist, he refuses to take me along, and this is because no matter how many contingencies we take into account, there is still the danger of this being a trap. Ahmad goes with them instead of me. I am so excited that I can barely sit down. But time is something that I do not have, so I force myself to sit down and write up a plan for dividing and distributing the flour and sugar and beans and rice that I have only heard of and dreamed about. I draw all sorts of tables and charts and while away the time by multiplying and dividing the various possibilities. It is getting dark. I think about how delighted and surprised Husain would be if he came back only to see that we took delivery of his warehouse when it was full, but delivered it back to him ever fuller. Finally, Hāj Salmān's Toyota enters the hospital grounds and sounds its horn. I see the beams of the headlights of the convoy of cars, and Ahmad's head sticking out of a window. He shouts excitedly,

'Doctor, congratulations!'

I run to the car and hug Ahmad excitedly. He is as sweet as sugar.

The warehouse is even larger and better stocked that what we had been told. There is so much sugar in it that we have enough to send to other cities as well. There are enough legumes and beans and pulses to meet the needs of the whole of the city of Al-Bukamal. The blessings of this find are so great that they will even reach the camp that is in the environs of Muhidhalīya. There is only an aid station in Muhidhalīya, and their situation is still so dire that they dispense medication one pill at a time, and one spoonful of syrup at a time. This is done, of course, as a supplementary service to their main task, which is providing medical services to wounded soldiers, and is a boon to the people of the area despite the paucity of their medicine. I have seen the people of Muhidhalīya making their way to our hospital ever since the x-ray machine was added to the facilities of our hospital. They are wearier and more enervated than our clients here in Al-Harī. I also know Abu Ammār, the Iranian official in charge of that camp. Knowing all this, why should these people not be helped now that it is in our power to help them?

Threads of Compassion

I tell Abu Ammār to come over with a big truck. He arrives before noon with a big truck. I don't know how he was able to get his hands on a truck so fast. We fill the truck up to its full capacity, loading it with everything from sugar, chickpeas, and flour to clothes and medicine; a load that was made possible by the grace of Lady Zainab ﷺ so that it will reach the hands of a mother living in a cold tent in Muhidhalīya, and perhaps a hungry child whose eyes are peeled in the expectation of the loving-kindness of a father whose whereabouts and date of return he is unaware of.

The find of the warehouse has multiplied our work. Jamāl, Ahmad and the guys from the elite forces spend their time in the ISIS warehouse from dawn to dusk, transferring the materials to our warehouse, which has no more room. What am I saying? Not only is there no more room in the warehouse, but all of the rooms of the hospital are full too! I am grateful for the abundance of this blessings, for the white flour dust that covers our clothing, and for Khānūm Jān's ﷺ grace, which enables us to hold on to our honour before her neighbours. And I am grateful to God who answered my prayers for filling the stomachs of the hungry and said 'Be', and so it came into being.

Threads of Compassion

Fātima is sitting up on my shoulders, clutching onto my hair and melting my heart as she does so. I play football with Muhammad-Hasan. Every time his forceful shots on goal get by me, he runs around the room in celebration of having beaten me. It is my turn now. I plant the ball and make a valiant effort on goal, only to be woken up by the vigor of my shot on goal and to see that there is no goal, there is no ball, no Muhammad-Hasan, and no Fātima. I feel like I'm carrying the sadness of the whole world in my heart. I haven't seen them for two months. I close my eyes quickly to at least try to get back into my dream, but it's too late. My dream has packed up and is long gone. I sit up in bed, dejected. My throat itches from the morning cold; a cold that will only be ameliorated by the presence of my family.

My heart cannot be contented either by my being away from here or by being away from home. Its appetite knows no bounds and wants to see my family in Syria, which is a privilege that is granted only to those who have completed five tours of duty. The permission can be granted only then, at which point one would still be responsible for paying for one's family's trip. So in such an eventuality, half of it would be up to one's commander and whether or not he grants you his approval, and the other half would be up to your budget and whether or not you can manage to pay for your family to fly out. Neither half of this privilege applies to me, so what am I daydreaming about?

Threads of Compassion

The guards open the sliding door quickly, making a lot of noise, letting in four Toyota pickups that are used as escort vehicles. One of the commanders has come to make an inspection, and Karīm is accompanying him. The commander inspects every quarter and listens to what everyone has to say. Karīm talks about the condition of the people and how it has changed from the time of ISIS's reign to our time. He talks about the fact that news of the services we provide has spread beyond a 50-kilometre radius from the hospital and that there are no longer any mothers giving birth in tents anymore. He talks about the skin and infectious diseases of which there are no traces left anymore. The commander listens carefully. The questions he asks make me realize that he not only knows the region better than I do, but that he is fully aware of all of ISIS's underground warehouses and knows those better than I do too. I have a good feeling about his presence. It reminds me of the times when my dad asked me how I was doing and asked specific questions about what I was up to. I used to tell him about what I was doing with gusto. He would just listen, but I would think how great the things I had done were, and how interested my father was in the plans that I had in my mind. Our commander are like our father. When he says something like "God be with you," one feels ashamed at the sleeplessness one sees in his eyes, and at how exhausted he looks. It's too bad that I don't have the boldness to bend down and kiss his hand to thank him for his presence, not in the hospital, of course, but in Syria.

By the time of the *maghrib* or evening prayers [at sunset], the hospital is quiet again. I can't stop thinking about Somayyeh and our children. I sink into the solitude of my room, and try to content myself with just their thoughts. If they are not themselves, at least I will be happy with their memory. Today, in the hospital, everyone told the commander everything they needed, but I demurred, as I was too ashamed before Khānūm Jān ﷺ to ask for anything for myself. If the truth be told, I felt too ashamed before the commander as well. How could I look in the eyes of a man who hasn't been home for at least six months and tell him that I miss my wife and children? I believe that being able to face these difficulties is a part and a parcel of any *jihād*, in addition to other considerations such as being hungry, sleepless, tired, and lonely. I am searching the depths of my mind for a verse or couplet in support of the notion that the greater the length of one's tour of duty, the greater its heavenly and earthly rewards, when the phone rings. Doctor Karīm is on the other end of the line. He asks, 'Ehsān, do you want to bring your family to Syria?'

Tears well up inside me. Oh, what a master is this Doctor Karīm in making one feel good, and also in taking that good feeling away.

I leave the hospital in Ahmad's hands for 24 hours and board the dilapidated ambulance of the Mashfi al-Maidāni Clinic, whose front end is all crumpled up and has been waiting for ages for someone to take it to Damascus and get it repaired. Who else does the job fall to but me? I have to go to Damascus and do the administrative work of getting Fātima's passport at the Iranian embassy. I'm already on the road at dawn. The cold and dry wind tunnels its way through the glassless windows. My nose is red and my eyes are watering. No matter how much I want to deny it, I can't avoid facing the fact that I'm freezing. I only last ten more kilometres in this junk heap, with my fingers frozen stiff around its steering wheel. I wrap whatever crepe bandages that I can get my hands on in the first aid kit around my face and hands, so that only my eyes and mouth are visible. I have become a moving mummy. I open the bandages one at a time at every checkpoint so that the guys manning them will recognize me and not riddle me with bullets. When I reach the Mayādīn checkpoint, I don't have the patience to open the bandages anymore. I suspect that the guys at the previous checkpoint have radioed ahead to let the guys here know to expect me and let me pass, so I put my foot on the gas pedal and proceeded forward. Meanwhile, this turned out to be a bad assumption on my part and the officer at this checkpoint thinks that an ISIS suicide bomber is headed towards him.

With my face bandaged like a mummy, it is no wonder that he is suspicious, and I'm grateful that he has not opened fire on me. After he has made sure that I'm just a moving mummy and not a cannibal, he offers me a very welcome hot cup of tea. The cells of my body revel in the heat given off to them by the tea, which courses between them and embraces them.

I finally reach Damascus after sunset, tired and stuttering, like the ambulance that got me there. I am only a few signatures away from seeing my family in Syria, and the thought of this prospect drains away the fatigue of this long, cold journey from my body. Dr. Karīm has performed the necessary correspondence for me to have become an officially recognized nurse. I just have to prove to the embassy that I am Fātima's father, who is going to get a passport in Iran and come here to climb up on my head and shoulders. This only takes up half the day. I spend the rest of it in the shrine.

But I want to keep this pilgrimage for myself. I won't say anything about it, and will keep it to myself, like a secret that is in my heart; at its very depths, where no one can reach it. If my heart, which is a metaphor for my soul, was my body, the place I would bury this secret would be a space between the left and right ventricles whose width is less than the length of a finger joint. It's called the myocardial wall and it is an interventricular wall, a small and crooked and irregular wall, but interesting for all that. Not because of its shape, but because of the memories that are secreted away in it. That's actually the reason God placed this wall where it is: so that people can secret away memories that are dear to their hearts in it. And so that is where I will secret away my memories of this pilgrimage, with respect, and after having made my ritual ablutions. I want the blood that my heart pumps out to have a good taste. I want my blood to have the flavour of the tears and words and supplications and promises of this pilgrimage every time my heart contracts and expands and pumps my blood through the valves to the cells that are the farthest from the heart.

Early the next morning, I get in a car and hit the road in the direction of Al-Harī, returning all the way back the same way I came. But this time I'm in a Toyota pickup with Sayyid Ali, who is a health worker from the Fatemiyūn Corps. There is an ambulance waiting at the Palmyra aid station for us to take to Al-Bukamal. This is one of the laws of war zones. You can't just go anywhere by yourself; you either have to take something with you, or you have to bring something back. I take the ambulance, and Ali follows with the Toyota. Yesterday, ISIS hit a Syrian military vehicle with a Kornet missile in Kabājib. We have to ride fast so that the Kornets don't eat us for breakfast.

    I tell Ali on the two-way radio that I'll be going full speed ahead, and that he should follow me. I have one eye on the dirt road which is an obstacle course, and the other eye on Ali following behind me. I don't know how many twists and turns I have passed when suddenly I can no longer see Ali behind me. I'm afraid something has gone wrong. I call him up on the two-way, and he responds,

'Doctor, I've got a flat.'

That takes the wind out of my sails. Ali insists that I should continue on my way, but I can't leave him alone like that. I turn around and head back towards him. I reach him five minutes later. He's busy putting on the spare tire in a blind spot between two buildings. My jaw drops to the ground like a flat tire when I see how fast he has been able to fix the flat tire. His alacrity is the result of contests that are held at headquarters to see who can change tires the fastest. These kinds of competitions serve us well in urban warfare situations where the roads are paved with shrapnel, but besides these competitions, which are voluntary, testing soldiers' abilities to read maps and compasses are obligatory.

We have put Kabājib behind us. By the time we reach Deir ez-Zūr, the time for performing our prayer will definitely have lapsed, so I stop somewhere between Al-Sukhna and Al-Shawlā. Ali tells me this is no place to stop, and he is right. I send him on to wait for me at the Deir ez-Zūr hospital. I start searching for a source of water and a place to make my prayers in the adobe houses of the desert that are quite literally in the heart of ISIS territory. An old man comes out of one of the adobe dwellings. Even if he is an ISIS supporter at heart, his appearance is harmless enough. When I roll up my sleeves, he understands what I am looking for. He guides me to a crooked faucet sticking out of a small cement-lined basin. It is nothing short of a miracle that when I open the faucet, water comes out and splashes the basin in several directions. He indicates that I am welcome to go into the room for making my prayers. It is an adobe hut that I am afraid will collapse on my head if I bow down or prostrate myself too quickly. The old man stands in a corner of the room, looking at me for the entire duration it takes for me to perform my prayers. He is right to be concerned, as I don't look as harmless as he does in my desert camouflage commando pants and holstered radio, and the Toyota that is parked in front. After I finish sending my salutations, which signals the end of the prayers, he asks,

'Are you a doctor?'

He probably figured that out from the ambulance which Ali took to Al-Bukamal. I nod in affirmation. He asks me to examine his wife. I follow him to another adobe room. A sheet of polyethylene has been nailed to a wall and hangs lifelessly from it. Its purpose is to act as a barrier against damp when it rains, and to act as a barrier against dust when it is dry when one sits up against the wall. There is a pan full of ashes in the middle of the room in which fires are lit, a brazier of sorts; but the ashes are cold. The old woman is leaning against the wall and sits up a little when she sees me enter. He wraps a black cloth patterned in the Arabic style around his head says some things to his wife that I don't understand. She has become immobilized by back pain, and this is torture for a

Threads of Compassion

Bedouin Arab woman. I take her pulse. It is very weak; barely there at all. She is anemic. There is a sheet of ibuprofen in my pocket, and it will have to do for her back pain. I don't have anything else and nothing else can be done for the back of a woman who has worked hard all her life.

The old man appreciated my quick and easy examination and my dispensing of the medication. He wants me to examine his son as well, who is a 17- or 18-year-old young man who says that he has problems moving his deformed hands and feet. The old man makes me understand that he also has psychological issues. My heart goes out to these people who are stuck in some corner of this desert. And here I am, having been drawn here from two thousand kilometers away, so that I might lay a hand on the young man's head and perhaps massage his tired body so that his father can get some satisfaction that he was at least able to bring a doctor to examine his wife and son. Truly, what a strange thing war can be sometimes. I administer a massage for the boy with all the love that a nurse can have for a patient. With a lump in my throat, with a smile on my face, and with a kiss that I plant on his head at the end of the massage. I promise to follow up his case, and for our personnel to bring him the special medicine he needs. I am about to get in the car when the old man asks,

'Where are you from?'

Threads of Compassion

I put my hand on his shoulder and say, 'I'm one of "the friends".' [*isdiqā'*. That is what the pro-government Syrians refer to Iranians as, "friends".]

He expected me to say anything other than that I was Iranian. Something boils up in his soul and can be seen in his eyes. Something like a heat that has been separated from the bottom of his soul. He throws himself in my arms and starts to wail.

There are still more than 500 kilometres to Al-Bukamal and the heart of ISIS territory. In the middle of this desert of God's, here's an old man living in a squalid shantytown who is led to believe that if the Iranians come, they will kill everyone in sight. Seeing this old man and the ghoul that has been made of the Iranians in his mind, I can't really blame the people of Al-Bukamal and the displaced women gathered in Al-Harī for taking their time to open up to us and trust us enough to allow us to approach them. Equally, you should not blame me for admiring the ideological propaganda and intellectual brainwashing that ISIS has been able to carry out on this population. It is highly effective. Their brainwashing has been carried out to such an extent that its effects remain with the people, even if they are starving to death. It is an ideology that they have inherited from ISIS and its collaborators and sympathizers, and it is an ideology that they will pass down if we fail to penetrate their ossified hearts and minds.

Night has fallen. I can't stop thinking about the old man and his family. I turn on my side in my bed, sliding my gun to the side under the blanket. The old man is still with me. The scent of separation that could be felt in the adobe room of his house, the taste of the two cycles of prayer that I prayed in fear and hope under his watchful gaze. It was a fear and hope in which hope predominated, as I knew that a guest in the house of an Arab has a certain sanctity, and Bedouin Arabs consider the life of their guests to be dearer than their own lives. I can't stop thinking about how his sick son looked and how his own eyes welled up with tears when he found out that I was Iranian. My eyes become heated. Why did I have to become obsessed about making my prayers on time, which in turn caused me to stop right outside his house? I hold the old man's hands in mine. They are rough and arid, the hands of a toiler. I tell him that I have brought medicine for his son. His eyes sparkle. Sleep washed over the fatigue of the journey like a flood. My breath warms the space under the blanket and keeps me warm.

I wake up with the sound of the windows of my room breaking. The bullets whiz past each other and pass over my head. The walls become riddled with bullet holes, and plaster and dust fall all over my head and face. My heart is beating frantically. I grab my pistol and crawl out of the room, holding the pistol close to my chest. The womenfolk have also been awakened by the sound of gunfire. They wander up and down the stairs and scream uncontrollably. I shout with all my might, ordering them to go back upstairs to their rooms. The gunfire is coming from behind the hospital. Imād and Hāj Salmān have told us on numerous occasions that the hospital rooftop is safe, and that we can resist an attack for three or four hours behind its high walls until reinforcements arrive if an attack occurs. Jamāl and Ahmad are armed and have come to the yard. Jamal's other self can be seen now. The self that he kept concealed in Syria for 18 months, in defense of Khānūm Jān's shrine. Gone is that well-educated and calm person whose clothes always bore the sharp lines of being well-ironed. He has switched his machine gun from single- to multiple-shot mode, and is responding to ISIS's gunfire with barrages of his own. The guards are doing the same. I call up Hāj Salmān on the radio. The attackers are not equipped with heavy weapons. If they were, they wouldn't have given us a chance to be afraid and would have brought down the roof over our heads already.

I go up to the roof with Jamal. Ahmad goes to the street that runs behind the hospital and opens fire on the attackers that we can't see. The trail of the bullets can be seen in the darkness. The shooting of the attackers originates from three points. The exchange of machinegun fire has intensified when Hāj Salmān and his forces arrived, throwing water on the fire of the attackers and the fire that was raging in my heart from worry. Worrying about the medical team, worrying

Threads of Compassion

about the guards, and worrying about Jamāl and Ahmad, who have put their lives on the line by standing up to the attackers and returning their fire in kind. By daybreak, two of the attackers have been arrested and have been taken away by Hāj Salmān's forces. Sleep is out of the question for us. For us, for the medical team, for Hāj Salmān and his men, and for the guards. I have a coffee and look at the bullet holes in the walls of my room; bullets that were not destined to hit me.

The morning sun rises and shines from the horizon of the dirt road, red and golden. I return alone on the road I took with Karīm four months ago. This road is no longer a stranger to me. I roll down the window. A cold wind and the smell of the soil embrace me with both arms. Somayyeh and the children are coming to Damascus today. We will stay with Khānūm Jān ﷺ for three days, then return to Iran.

Last night, I didn't feel like bidding farewell to anyone. Not to Asīla and her team, nor to the nurses in training. Goodbyes are meaningless to me. It is not as if I'm leaving. I will be returning to this city. I'm just going to catch my breath, freshen up, and then come back. I *have* to return. I have work to do here. What am I supposed to do, with all this work here that still remains to be done?

Threads of Compassion

I wish that Somayyeh was here with me so that she could sit in the passenger seat and accompany me to Damascus. I would show her everywhere I'd been and tell her all about everything I know. I would take her to the house of the old man whose son was sick who started crying when I told him I was Iranian. I could take more medicine for his son, and Somayyeh could sit with the man's wife and have a good heart to heart with her. We would be going to the home of one of our Muslim brothers. What could be more normal than this? We would give them our phone number and invite them to Iran. We would become friends, just like the friendships that are forged between Iranians and Iraqis during the Arbaʿīn commemorations.[43] What could be more normal than this?

As I approach Palmyra, I see a series of green buses lined up in train formation. My gaze continues to be focused on them as I pass them, on the number of seats there are in these buses, all of which will be occupied by women, children, and old men who will be leaving a 'cauldron' or area under siege [before the street-to-street and the door-to-door fighting begins]. The number of seats available on these buses will determine how many families will be able to reunite with their loved ones. The first time these green buses were used in Syria was to transfer the people of the two Shīʿa towns of Fuʿa and Kafraya. The inhabitants of

---

[43] Arbaʿīn is the commemoration of the fortieth day of the martyrdom of Imam Husain ﷺ.

these towns were supposed to be exchanged with the families of ISIS forces who were besieged by the resistance forces in Maḍāyā and Zabdāni.

Why were Fuʻa and Kafraya besieged and for no less than two years? I'll tell you. Because these two towns are at a strategically significant point near the Turkish border. Because in war, taking control of border crossings is a significant victory. The Takfiris surrounded these two towns in a tight siege for two years, from April 2017 to April 2019, in order to attain this strategic advantage.

When I say 'two-year siege', read 85 thousand mortar shells exploding in the midst of civilian populations, and two thousand civilian deaths. Now the next question is, why was this siege not broken, despite the use of tunneled underground explosions and shooting down planes that took food supplies and medicine to the two besieged towns, and despite the cutting off of their water supply, electricity and gas? I'll tell you. Because the lions of the Haḍrat az-Zahra Battalion resisted the breaking of the siege from within the towns, under the rain of mortar shells not just on their own heads, but on the heads of their wives and children too. They ate the roots of trees in lieu of food, but they didn't put down their guns and didn't give up land and houses to their enemies. After two years of this, it was decided that an exchange should take place. The women, children and old men were taken on green buses and they were exchanged with ISIS families who were besieged in Maḍāyā and Zabdāni.

Threads of Compassion

My imagination takes me on its wings... to where the prisoner exchange is to take place. The people with the Red Crescent and journalists have been waiting for three days for the recalcitrant residents of Fu'a and Kafraya to come out and throw everything they have at their feet. But no matter how long they wait, there is no sign of them. The news spreads by word of mouth. For three days, the passengers of Fu'a and Kafraya have been kept in the buses. Everyone has run out of patience, mainly for the sake of the children, who have suffered enough. There are mothers who are worried about their children's hungry stomachs; and there are old men who cannot bear to sit in one place for more than an hour, and who have now been confined to sitting on bus seats for three days. The leaders of the takfiris cannot come to an agreement among themselves with respect to the conditions and ways and means of how the exchange is to take place, and this has made everyone concerned about the kind of decision they are going to make.

My imagination takes me on its wings to Rashidīn, which is an area where the buses of Fu'a and Kafraya have come to a stop. I see the tired faces from behind the bus's windows. I see people's cheek bones protruding as a result of two years of hunger and unimaginable hardship. I see anxious looks on the faces of people whose loved ones are still under siege in Fu'a and Kafraya. Finally, the doors of the buses open. The passengers have been allowed to leave; passengers who are either women, old men, or children. I see these children and it breaks my heart. Children, here in the middle of the war, in the heart of a siege, under the guns of armed men, and more than thirty hours in a bus. These children haven't had a decent meal for two years. They've either eaten tree roots, or small portions of the aid that was dropped on the city by planes which the takfiris tried to bring down, sometimes successfully. A car pulls up to where the buses are parked and distributes packets of chips among the children. They are so happy to receive these gifts, and can't wait to get their hands on a packet. They alert each other to what's happening and run to get their share. The packages are handed out by the children in front to the children in the back over their heads. All of the children have gathered round. They have big smiles on their faces or are laughing and enjoying the taste of potato chips which they haven't tasted in two years. Eating potato chips is the first taste of happiness that these children enjoy after being able to leave the two-year siege; and what can be more enjoyable that this pleasure for a child? The adults don't interfere with them, and let them have their fun and enjoy their pleasure.

A small blue pickup makes its way through the crowd and approaches. I wish I could run in front of it. I wish I could lay down before its wheels to stop it from going any farther. I wish there was time for me to shout and disperse the children from the terrible menace it poses. I wish... I wish... I wish a hundred wishes.

Threads of Compassion

The pickup reaches the place where the children are gathered and suddenly we hear the sound of an explosion, sending blood, body parts, and shrapnel and smoke and screams among the children instead of chips; instead of happiness and pleasure.

My imagination cannot take it anymore and comes all the way back at the speed of light. Who can bear to see children's pleasures and excitement be bloodied and become lifeless and fall on the ground in a bloody mess? If anyone can bear it, me and my imagination certainly can't. Who can bear to see a child dragging his foot on the ground as he is dying, without even having had the chance to open the package of chips he is holding in his hand? Who can bear to hear the wailing of parents who are bent over their children, whose dead bodies have been riddled to pieces by the shards of shrapnel? They wanted to get out of the siege for the sake of their children, but now their hands have been emptied of their life's most precious assets. Now they are outside the circle of the siege, but without their children.

The lump in my throat won't let me speak. I look for the buses in the mirror. The only thing I can see is the dust that they have raised. From where have they come? Who are its passengers going to be exchanged with? Which besieged people, and from which region, will they be ransomed for? My heart trembles. And that is only right: one's heart should indeed tremble when one's enemy has no fear of the consequences of his actions before God. What if they perform another one of their atrocities again?

My mind divides the war into the two halves of us and our enemy, placing each of the halves in the pans of a scale. On one side, there is the sound of explosions and the wailing of children and their mothers, and on the other side, there is us, by which I mean Hāj Salmān, who called me up on the radio last night. He was on his way to the hospital, bringing me a patient. I put on my jacket and go out to the hospital's courtyard. I am taken aback by [the identity of] the injured patients and even more surprised at Hāj Salmān and the fact that he preferred not to wait until the morning to bring these two ISIS combatants to the hospital to be treated. It was just two nights ago that they had sworn an oath to do everything in their power to inflict casualties on the members of the hospital staff, and indeed, their barrages of machinegun fire that were aimed towards us never stopped for a single moment. The contrast up to this point is sufficient for the pan on our side of the scale to tip the scale in our favour. But I'll say the rest of it too.

Hāj Salmān gets out of the car. Two ISIS combatants are behind the Toyota in a cage. I enter the cage. The feverish look of one of the ISIS combatants in the darkness spews pure hatred towards me. I guess it's understandable, as his expectation is for us to pronounce their death sentence, and spill their blood right there in the cage where we have them. After all, that is precisely what they have done to our prisoners on numerous occasions. The prisoner doesn't want to show weakness in his dying moments. I signal to him that he needs to roll up his sleeve so that I can insert a catheter in his vein. He hesitates to carry out what I have asked him to do. The other prisoner is in worse shape and in no shape to do what I need, so I roll his sleeve up myself. He is wearing a *thawb*.[44] I think about the number of our soldiers that have been martyred by the bullets fired by this man. How many heads has he cut off with his own hands? How many children have become orphans at his hands, and how many mothers and wives have his machinegun barrages put to grief? I think about what the situation would be if our places were reversed. Would he be inserting a catheter in one of my veins and starting an IV drip that has the medicine I need in its infusion fluid? Or is a bullet or two, or three strokes of his dagger on my jugular vein all that he would be willing to expend on me?

    I put a hand on my jugular vein without thinking about it. I guide the needle into a vein. My gaze catches the engraving on the carnelian of my ring, which reads, *Jānam Hasan*.[45] Behold the heart of this family! They have the murderer of their father [Imam

---

[44] [An ankle-length robe, usually with long sleeves, that is closed in the front.]

[45] [This expression is equivalent to something like, "I give up my soul for you, O Hasan." Or, "Would that my soul were sacrificed as your ransom, O Hasan."]

Ali ﷺ] as their prisoner, and my lord and master shares with him some of the milk that has been brought for his dying father. He is duty-bound to meticulously carry out his father's orders regarding their prisoner, and this he does. A prisoner is a prisoner and must be treated as such, irrespective of whether he has struck the blow with his sword in the Kufa congregational mosque that will eventually kill your father, or whether he has killed your friends and brothers in arms in Sālihīya, Sa'd al-Wa'r, or Khāntumān. I kiss my lord's name on the carnelian of my ring and open the slider clamp on the IV drip. Would that this infusion fluid that is coursing through his veins now would transport my question to his brain and cause him to ask himself what he would be doing if the roles were reversed and this nurse was his prisoner?

I give Hāj Salmān a bunch of pills and medicinal syrups to give to them at set times throughout the days ahead.

He smiles and says, 'So much for seeing to your final patients in this hospital;' – two sworn enemies from ISIS, who have been taken prisoner.

I have finally reached Damascus. There are still a few hours left before sunset, and I want to drive on a little farther, as there is not much farther to go for me to get to my main destination, which lies at the end of the Tehran to al-Quds (Jerusalem) road, as Hāj Qāsim [Soleymāni] used to say: Start in Tehran, go to Baghdad, then to Damascus, then to Beirut, and from there to al-Quds. The highway goes through Al-

Threads of Compassion

Bukamal. That same highway that America lost in the fight to gain mastery over it. That same highway over which Uncle Sam failed to create a 55-kilometre no-fly zone, the desire for which still remains in his treacherous heart, a desire that had been nestled in his heart for seven years. That same strategic junction of the highway in whose environs we recited the call to prayer in the ears of the newborn babies of its residents, whose names we chose for them.

I have come as far as Damascus, and Beirut and al-Quds still remain. I feel like keeping my foot on the gas pedal and continuing on to Beirut; al-Quds I'll leave for later, for when its time is right. But why not go to Ḍāhiya and the Rawza ash-Shahīdīn Cemetery, and rub the dust that has settled on Imād Mughnīa's tombstone on my face to take away the weariness of my journey, and be energized by the exemplary model of resistance against Israel? Imād Mughnīa was an exemplary model who, for 25 years was like a sword and a wraith for the occupiers of al-Quds. He would land like a sword and disappear like a wraith. Why not pray two *rakats* in the Rawza ash-Shahīdīn Cemetery and ask the martyrs buried there to help me to continue to participate in the war against Israel, like Hāj Imād? I would like to pay a military tribute on behalf of all the martyrs to the living symbol of God, Sayyid Hasan Nasrallah. I would then get back in my car and proceed to the Marūn ar-Ra'is border, to pick up a few largish rocks, and write the names of my friends on them: Javād and Muhammad-Husain, and a few others, and my own name on the last one. Say a *bismillāh* and throw them across the border into the occupied territories, and have them land next to the foot of an Israeli soldier, on the other side of Marūn ar-Ra's; and take pleasure in hearing the sounds they make at his feet, knowing that he has heard them too. We are no more than a stone's throw from making these Zionist occupiers disappear from the pages of history. Less than 25 years from now, five years of which have already passed. And how quickly the seconds of this countdown go by, bringing ever closer the conquest of al-Quds, the destruction of the state of Israel, and the taking of our revenge for the spilt blood of Hāj Imād and Haj Qāsim and all of the others.

The shrine is not the same as it usually is. Pilgrims consisting of families of its Defenders can be seen in and around its environs. What a good feeling it is to see their movements and hear their chatter. Many people have placed requests to have their families join them here during the Nowruz holidays (the Iranian New Year). I am excited to see crowds in and around Khānūm Jān's ﷺ shrine, but a bitter taste pervades my soul: the bitter taste of loneliness. Now that I see other people's families in and around the shrine, I understand just how lonely I am without them and how much I miss them. It'll only be a few more hours now for Somayyeh and the children's flight to land, but

Threads of Compassion

I still have a big lump in my throat. It is not on account of my own loneliness and my separation from my family. It's on account of the bitter taste of loneliness that pervades my soul; the bitter taste of exile that Khānūm Jān ﷺ had to endure in the crowded streets of Damascus.

السَّلاَمُ عَلَيْكِ يَا أُمَّ المَصائِبِ يَا زَيْنَبُ وَرَحْمَةُ اللهِ وَبَرَكَاتُهُ

> *God's peace and blessings be unto you, o mother of the afflicted, O Zainab!*

Tears start to flow with the utterance of the first salutation. I recite the words and mourn for the lady whose troubles and afflictions can never become normal and will always weigh heavily on me.

السَّلاَمُ عَلَيْكِ يا مَنْ نَطَحَتْ جَبِينَها بِمُقَدَّمِ المُحْمَلِ إِذْ رَأَتْ رَأْسَ سَيِّدِ الشُّهَدَاءِ وَيَخْرُجُ الدَّمُ مِن تَحْتِ قِناعِها وَمِن مُحْمَلِها بِحَيثُ يرى مَن حَولَها مِن الأَعْداءُ

> *Peace be unto you, O you who thrust her forehead with the front part of the howdah, when she saw the severed head of the Chief of the Martyrs (Imam Husain ﷺ) and caused blood to flow from beneath her veil and from the howdah in the view of the enemies.*

I mourn for the sorrows that suddenly befell her when she became a prisoner in exile with nothing but grief as her companion. Can there even be anything more bitter than Khānūm Jān's ﷺ captivity and exile? Woe to the emotions we hold in our souls that are exposed by this *zīārat-nāmeh*.[46]

السَّلَامُ عَلى مَن رَكِبَتْ بَعيراً بِغَيرِ وِطاءٍ وَنادَت أَخَاها أَبَا الفَضْلِ بِهَذا النِّداءِ: "أَخِي أَبَا الفَضْلِ، أَنْتَ الَّذي أَرْكَبْتَنِي إِذْ أَرَدتُ الخُروجَ مِن المدينَةِ

Peace be unto her who had to ride a saddleless camel and then called on her brother Abu'l-Faḍl (al-Abbās), saying, "O brother! O Abu'l-Faḍl! It was you who helped me ride on a camel when I left Medina."

Among all the verses of this *zīārat-nāmeh*, this one verse in particular wrenches my soul. It's as if Khānūm Jān ﷺ is reciting an elegy for herself. She is searching in a sea of *nāmahrams*,[47] and calls on her brother for

---

[46] [A liturgical form of supplication or ritual prayer recited specifically during one's pilgrimage to a sacred shrine or location.]

[47] [*Mahram* is a category of people in the sacred law of Islam (the *sharī'a*) who are related to each other by blood or marriage such that they are not allowed to marry one another. For example, a mother and son, or a father and

help. I feel so sorry for being so late in coming to her aid. Where were the defenders of your sacrosanctity when you became captive to *nāmahram* eyes?

Wow, what a divine *zīārat-nāmeh* this is that is pouring into my soul. I send salutations of peace and blessings for Khānūm Jān's ﷺ forbearance and longanimity, for her having been taken prisoner and made to march in the desert [from Karbalā to Damascus], and for her grieving heart. A lady to whom my family and I are devoted and would gladly offer ourselves up as ransom for the sake of the protection of her sanctity. I continue to recite the *zīārat-nāmeh* and keep on wailing, and make sacred vows and promises. I promise that I will not allow anything to have a greater appeal to me than the mission of defending the sanctity of her shrine and that I will not allow anything to prevent me from coming back in order to do so. I promise that I will remain in the ranks of the Defenders of her Shrine, even if this means my

---

daughter or daughter in law, or brothers and sisters. Because there is such a close familial bond between them that no sexual intercourse can ever take place between them, the females within the mahram circle are not obligated to veil their hair with a scarf when they are in the company of males (such as their father or brothers) within their mahram circle and not in public. *Mahram* is contrasted with *nāmahram*, which is a category of people who are strangers and whose gaze, therefore, is not licit according to the sacred law of God. Men must lower their gaze when in the company of *nāmahram* women.]

Threads of Compassion

continuing to serve her neighbors on the fringes of ISIS territory. I promise to cut off any ties that would keep me away from her House.

I am standing behind the arrivals gate at the airport, looking expectantly at the opening. An hour's delay has spent all my patience. I've been here for over two hours, and there is no sign of them. No sign of Somayyeh, or the kids, or of any of the other passenger from the Tehran flight that landed an hour ago by now. I am restless, pacing back and forth behind the metal railing of the waiting area. I go up to the entrance to the gate but don't see them. The officer respectfully turns me back over and over again.

Finally, passengers start arriving out of the gate, causing no end of pleasure for their loved ones who have been waiting patiently for their arrival on the other side of the metal railings. Everyone is looking for the other half of his *jihād*. If it wasn't for these halves, we wouldn't be here. In all probability, each of us would be in some corner of Iran, sitting behind an office desk and minding our own business and seeing to the demands of our own affairs. Somayyeh is holding Fātima in her arms. Fātima waves to me and melts my heart as if it were an ice cream. I am so full of joy I could burst. I can't wait for them to make their way to me; I fly towards them.

Threads of Compassion

Now it is just us and the open box of Arabic-style baklava. Its sweetness is nothing compared to the sweetness of our being together. Ours is the sweetest of nights. Our suite is now drowned in the silence of the kids having fallen asleep, leaving Somayyeh and I, our Bin Haseeb coffee, and the delicious baklava. Leaving Somayyeh and I and a whole world's worth of words. Leaving Somayyeh and I and the never-ending sound of the explosions in Ghouta. Leaving Somayyeh and I and a night that I wish would never end.

We have no more than three days' time for this unrepeatable trip. There are a lot of places for me to take my family in Damascus, but nothing comes close to Khānūm Jān's ﷺ shrine. We start every day by praying the morning prayers together in the sanctuary of her shrine. I can still taste the savour of those prayers in the depths of my soul. I recite elegies, and we shed tears. It has become a family ritual. We can never get enough of Khānūm Jān's ﷺ shrine, but we tear ourselves away from it so that we can make a pilgrimage to Lady Ruqayya's ﷺ shrine as well. We spend so much time between the two that we become saturated with the spiritual light of both shrines.

Our three-day allotment passes by like greased lightning. For me, these days were like living in a cloud or in a dream. Things went by so fast that we can't figure out when it started and how it came to an end so soon. Somayyeh is dejected. None of us want to go back. The sadness of the whole world has nestled in my soul, and the farewell pilgrimages have burned a gaping hole in my heart. We would spend the morning in the shrine of Khānūm Jān ﷺ, and the afternoon in the shrine of the three-year-old lady whom I can't stop adoring. I lean against the metal latticework that protects her small sepulcher and recite the following verse.

دلم تنگِ، دلم خونِ، دلم می‌خواد همه باهم، بریم خونه.

My heart is homesick,
My heart is bleeding,
I wish that we could all go home together.

My pent-up emotions burst out in a flood of tears. I feel that these four months have passed by even faster than the three days Somayyeh and the kids were with me. No pain is as painful as the pain of bidding goodbye to a loved one. I do not want to leave...

I wish life had a repeat button so that I could repeat these four months over and over again. My life has been divided into two major subdivisions: the part before these four months and these four months themselves. There is no such thing as "after these four months". The rest has to be more of these four months.

Sunday 1 April 2018

I have come back to that day again. The day that nestled a place for itself between Khānūm Jān ﷺ and I. Brick by brick, it grew taller and thicker and eventually became so tall that it left me behind its walls.

The road back always takes longer; but this time it's different. I sing and press my foot down on the gas pedal, excited about returning to Khānūm Jān's ﷺ shrine. Fourteen days have passed since we have returned to Iran; fourteen days of my being away from Khānūm Jān ﷺ.

When we returned to Iran with Somayyeh and the kids, we were always kept busy with visits to the rest of the family on the occasion of the new year, a trip to Mashhad, and people coming to visit the pilgrims who had just come back from Khānūm Jān's ﷺ shrine, which was us, of course. I go to various shrines and the cemetery of the martyrs, next to Javād and my other late friends so many times, begging for their intercession and help to ensure that I get recalled for another tour of duty. I continued to do this until one day, I got another call telling me that my name was on the flight list for the following week and to get myself to the airport to make the flight.

These fourteen days were longer and more difficult for me to endure than all of the days of the five years it took me to get to Syria. I am counting the minutes to get back to Khānūm Jān ﷺ. I'm wearing a black shirt in mourning for her grief and misfortunes.

Threads of Compassion

I wish that I was in Syria in the sanctuary of her shrine, so that I could sing a lament for its pilgrims, most of whom consist of the Defenders of her Shrine. The kids are asleep. I sing under my breath and quietly drum a beat on my thighs with my hands. Somayyeh has perked up her ears. She likes it when I sing laments like this under my breath. On the morning of the anniversary of Khānum Jān's ﷺ martyrdom, our lot is to be in the car and on the road, where the two of us delight in singing elegies in honour of Khānum Jān ﷺ.

We are approaching Dāmghān.[48] My eyelids feel heavy, so Somayyeh takes the wheel so I can nap for a while. I hug Fātima and kiss her black eyelashes. She is asleep. I lean my head back. I have so many thoughts and plans. For the hospital, for the nurses in training, and for the people of the region. Plans on how to deliver public and government aid to them; plans on how to improve people's health and livelihoods. Sleep takes a greater hold of me and blurs my thoughts. Karīm has come to our hospital. The sound of a newborn baby's crying echoes in the hospital corridors. Asīla brings the child to me, and I recite the *adhān* in his ear. Fātima's head turns in my hands in sync with the curvature of the road. My heart has a craving for a dinner party in which I can recite elegies and laments. I have sent Ahmad to the support services warehouse. Hāj Majīd shouts on the two-way radio

---

[48] [Dāmghān is an ancient town a third of the way on the road that leads from Tehran to Mashhad.]

that one of his soldiers has been shot. Dr. Mustafā quickly changes into his operating room clothing. The car plods along. My mouth has taken on the taste of sleep. My head tilts to one side, and I fall asleep.

The sound of tires screeching on the ground suddenly wakes me from my nap. I am jolted up from my chair and thrown back into it. I'm holding onto Fātima tightly. I can smell soil, gasoline, and engine oil. I'm dazed and confused. The car has nosedived into a gulley to the side of the road. I can't hear anyone making any sounds other than Somayyeh's wheezing. Her safety belt is entangled around her neck. My shin is folded under the car seat and stuck and I can't turn my body towards it completely. I grope to find the buckle of my seatbelt. The flask of water has fallen on it due to the impact, but I am able to unbuckle the belt eventually with some difficulty. Somayyeh exhales on the steering wheel, setting my mind at rest. Fātima's head is slack on her neck. Her consciousness is below 5%, which is why her neck muscles are relaxed. Damn this shin of mine that is stuck under the seat and prevents me from being able to move. I raise Fātima up with my forearms and open her eyes. They are dilated. I perform some chest compressions on her, to no avail. I increase their speed and vigor. Her complexion has darkened. I punch her chest. I have forgotten about my own pain. Her face is turning very dark and she is not breathing. I cry out desperately, calling for Lady Zainab ﷺ to come to my aid. Fātima suddenly lets out a cry. I hold her head tight to my chest and kiss her to reassure her.

Somayyeh is still unconscious. Hāniyeh is scared and is crying and moaning, and calling out to me. I wish that at least I had some light. I stretch my hand to the back seat to reach Hāniyeh. When I turn to see her, a bolt of pain shoots up my leg. Muhammad-Husain is lying unconscious and motionless against the door. I need him to get up and go and get help. I call out to him, but it does no good. I tell Hāniyeh to strike her brother hard, and harder still. She hits him so hard that he eventually opens his eyes. He is semi-conscious. I keep repeating *Ya Zainab* without end. Our survival depends on Muhammad-Husain being able to get out of the car and get help. He pulls himself out through the cracked and occluded glass. He has grown into a man during my absence. And thank God for that, for without him, I don't know what would have happened to us in the 8-meter-deep gulch we are stuck in. Muhammad-Hasan has lost consciousness in his sleep and has fallen on the floor of the car. He is so silent that I first thought that he had been thrown out and that I needed to go and find his bloodied body. I make a head count. Muhammad-Husain pulls the others out of the car. I don't let him pull me out. My leg is twisted and swollen and there's nothing that he can do about it. I tell him to go up to the side of the road and get help. Having done that, I finally allow myself to feel the pain I'm in. I'm sure my leg is broken. It's a double fracture. I am pinned down and cannot move.

Threads of Compassion

The police see Muhammad-Husain standing on the side of the road. A quarter of an hour later, help arrives. The red lights of the ambulance flash on the car from the side of the road. I allow myself to close my eyes, knowing that Khānūm Jān ﷺ saved us from this dark gulley.

I get confused when they place me in the ambulance. I have done well to last as long as I did. I try to stay awake until we get to the hospital, but can't. Pain twists and shouts in the labyrinth of my soul. My chest feels like it is about to burst. I'm breathing with difficulty. Something is stabbing and burning my lung. The image of Fātimah's bruised face and Somayyeh's motionless body, who had fainted at the very first moment of the accident, race before my eyes. My leg feels heavy. I can't move it. I struggle to say something, but only a moan makes its way out of my throat. I don't know yet that six of my bones are broken.

The light of the fluorescent lamps of the hospital corridor passes in front of my eyes like a continuous white stripe. The smell of Savlon and Deconex make me nauseous. I never got used to that aseptic smell, even though I'm a nurse.

Somayyeh is draped over the steering wheel and wheezing; she can't breathe properly. On the day of our marriage, her father insisted on sending something in trust to my house. I move my body on the chair to turn towards him. Death does not differentiate between trusts and trustees, and does not recognize such obligations. He goes around the car and waves to us.

A nurse cuts my clothes away. I smell blood under my nose. I wish Somayyeh and the kids were not in the car with me and that I had returned from Mashhad on my own. Muhammad-Husain does not regain consciousness. My name is on the flight list for next week. I mustn't be taken captive by this bed.

I call Muhammad-Husain's name, but he doesn't answer or move. I shout his name. He needs to get out and take his siblings out of the car. My scream reverberates in my head. Muhammad-Husain finally opens his eyes. Hāniyeh wiggles her way out of the window through the broken glass.

I feel the sting of the catheter under my skin. Morphine courses through my soul. I can't keep up the struggle anymore. My eyelids grow heavy. I want to ask how Somayyeh is doing, but can't. I wish I could prevent them from separating the kids from me. Fātima will undoubtedly be frightened in my absence. Am I going to miss my flight? I have to call Dr. Karīm. The morphine is convoluting my thoughts. I can hear Hāniyeh crying in the distance. I can't go to her. Dr. Karīm calls. I have to take delivery of the Al-Bukamal Hospital's weekly palate of drugs. I haven't signed the transport papers. The medical team arrives today. I have to remain in the hospital. I get myself to the Imām Airport. The morphine is stronger than the tenacity of my thoughts. I go back and forth between the hospital's corridors. The commotion has not let me sleep for two nights straight. I'm beat. There's an hour left before the flight. My brain is pounding. I'm floating in time.

I go back and forth between the hospital and Syria. I have to fight a hard battle in order to be able to leave this hospital bed and get to Syria. It is a battle of the mind and soul as well as that of the body. My body remains in bed while my soul flies to Al-Harī, leaving all my pains behind. The sweet dream of making it back to Syria has given my body a new life. If I didn't have my memories of Syria, I wouldn't have survived with all the pain I have had to endure. I struggle to reach Syria again and repeat the experiences I had over those four months. I want to be able to go back in order to be able to serve.

As soon as I open my eyes, I ask how Fātima is doing. I'm told she is OK. Somayyeh's nose is broken; Muhammad-Husain has stitches in the corner of his mouth; Hāniyeh's jaw is broken; and there is nothing wrong with Muhammad-Hasan. This means that over all, things are pretty good. Thank you, Lady Zainab ﷺ.

I was hospitalized for a month, and I have been bed-ridden at home for three months. Every morning I wake up in pain, and go to bed at night, also in pain. Pain circles my body like a flock of vultures. I have headaches, pain in my ribs and sides, all the way to the soles of my feet. I can't even roll over. If I do, a sharp pain will shoot up the side of my body. Fātima spreads her sketchbook next to me so that I don't get bored. I wish I could hug her, and have her get up on my

Threads of Compassion

shoulders and give her rides around the room; but alas, this can't be done.

My phone is ringing. Hāniyeh brings me the phone. It's Hāj Salmān, calling from Syria. Hearing his voice puts a lump in my throat. He takes my hand and takes me out to the hospital courtyard. I take in a deep breath. The Iranian flag is waving high on the hospital's roof. I like the smell of this city. Hāj Salmān says that the people of the region have vowed to sacrifice a sheep to help me recover my health. He tells me to get well and come over, so that they can sacrifice the sheep at my feet. My heart breaks open like a pomegranate and I begin to weep. Damn this body of mine that has kept me prisoner here.

It's evening and I'm restless. I force myself to the window using a cane. The scene below is full of the hustle and bustle of the city. No one knows what's going on in my heart, and the kinds of thoughts I had had for my next tour of duty; the promises I had made to myself; and all of the kinds of things and commitments that were supposed to stay here while I returned... but it didn't turn out that way. None of it happened. Three months have passed since the 9th of April and the flight I was supposed to take, and I'm still here. With all my promises and commitments. With all my longings. Tears fall from my cheeks. Why should I be a prisoner to this city? What has been written in the book of my destiny? Why didn't that accident take my life, so that I don't melt away bit by bit like this? I ask myself these questions a thousand times a day. My heart feels like it will burst from the pain of separation from Lady Zainab ﷻ, and from being locked within the walls of this city that I am a prisoner in. It feels like the sorrows of the whole world have made a nest in my heart. I sing under my breath, 'No matter how much I tell you about the pain that I have in my heart, I still wouldn't have told you enough.' These are pains that only Khānūm Jān ﷻ and I know about.

دلم تنگِ، دلم خونِ، دلم می‌خواد همه باهم، بریم خونه.

My heart is homesick,
My heart is bleeding,
I wish that we could all go home together.

I want to go home. My home is not in this city that is holding me prisoner. My home is two thousand kilometres away from here, somewhere among Khānūm Jān's ﷻ neighbours.

Threads of Compassion

Chapter Nine Photos

The last supper and kabba, Aleppo style. Asīla cooked this dinner on the last night I was in the hospital as a way of sending me off with her blessings.

Threads of Compassion

Hāj Salmān, the regional security officer, who was as kind as a father to me and cared about me and always had my back.

Threads of Compassion

Fātima in Lady Ruqqaya's shrine.

Threads of Compassion

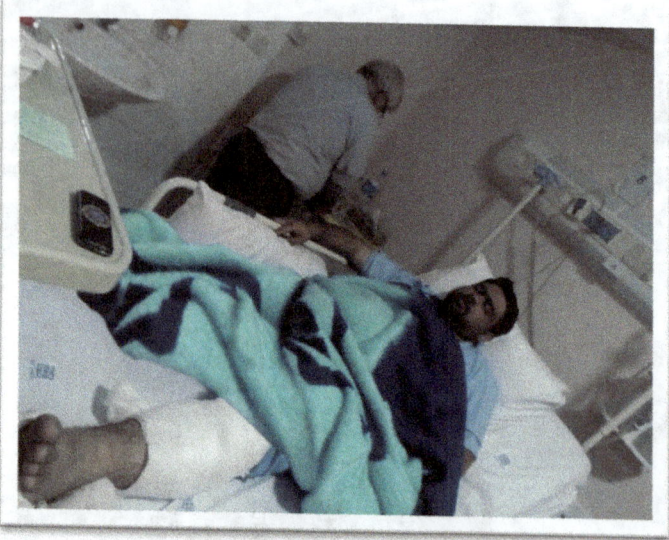

The first day after the accident, in Dāmghān Hospital. My leg is in a splint, and I am unconscious from the morphine and the intensity of the pain. My father was pinned to the bed and refused to leave me unattended.

Threads of Compassion

■ این نقشه‌ای‌است که داعش در روزهای نخست جنگ در سوریه منتشر کرد و در آن محدوده خلافت خود را ترسیم نمود. محدوده‌ای که شامل کشورهای زیادی از جمله عراق، سوریه، ترکیه، عربستان، یمن، لبنان، ایران، افغانستان، پاکستان، شمال آفریقا و اروپا می‌شد.

آنچه در عمل اتفاق افتاد نقشه زیر است که مناطق اشغال شده توسط گروه‌های تروریستی در عراق و سوریه که در آنها رسماً دولت خلافت اسلامی اعلام شد، نشان می‌دهد. تمام این مناطق توسط نیروهای مقاومت تحت فرماندهی سپهبد شهید حاج قاسم سلیمانی از چنگ گروه‌های تروریستی آزاد شد.

نکته قابل توجه اینکه به اذعان اندیشکده‌های وابسته به ارزش‌های کشورهای غربی، وسعت مناطق اشغال شده توسط داعش، به تنهایی از وسعت کل کشور سوریه بیشتر بود.

مناطق اشغال شده توسط جریان مسلح تکفیری در طول بحران
بیشترین اشغال: ۸۴ درصد

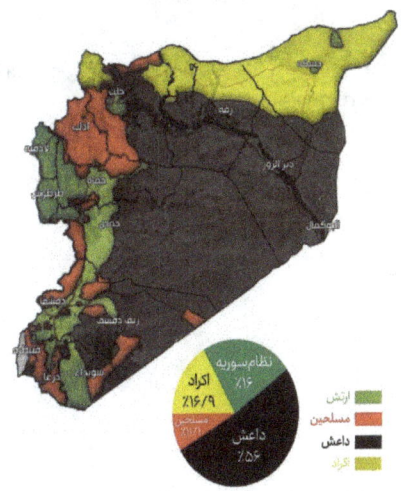

Threads of Compassion

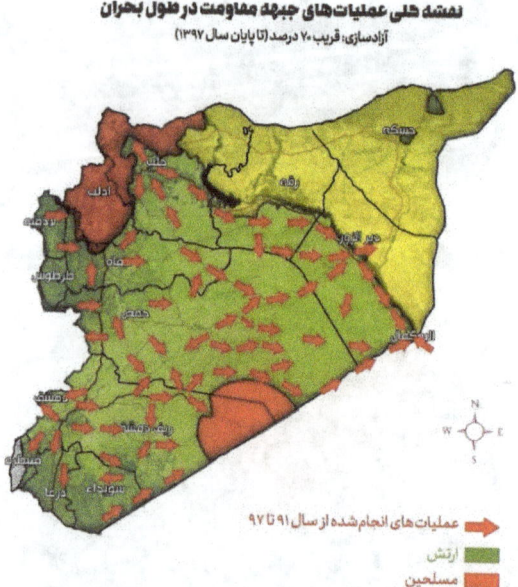

Territories taken over by ISIS before they were driven back underground, where they belong.

www.ingramcontent.com/pod-product-compliance
Lightning Source LLC
Chambersburg PA
CBHW052052110526
44591CB00013B/2179